COWLES COMMISSION
FOR RESEARCH IN ECONOMICS
Monograph No. 7

COWLES COMMISSION
FOR RESEARCH IN ECONOMICS

THE UNIVERSITY OF CHICAGO

COWLES COMMISSION MONOGRAPHS

No. 1. *Dynamic Economics*, by CHARLES F. ROOS. 1934. 275 pages. Price $3.50.

Mathematical analysis is here applied in the investigation of economic theory, especially by differentiating between theories of static and dynamic economics.

No. 2. *NRA Economic Planning*, by CHARLES F. ROOS. 1937. 596 pages. Price $5.00.

This book traces the historical background of the NIRA and its administration. The policies of the NRA are described and discussed. An endeavor is made to appraise constructively this great undertaking and to throw light on the important question: What can we expect from economic planning?

No. 3. *Common-Stock Indexes*, by ALFRED COWLES and ASSOCIATES. Second edition, 1939. 499 pages. Price $6.00.

New monthly indexes of (1) stock prices, (2) stock prices adjusted for the reinvestment of cash dividends, and (3) yield expectations; and annual indexes of (4) yields, (5) dividend payments, (6) earnings-price ratios, and (7) earnings; all for 69 industry groups or combinations of groups, and running from 1871 through 1938.

No. 4. *Silver Money*, by DICKSON H. LEAVENS. 1939. 439 pages. Price $4.00.

A sketch of the history of the monetary use of silver, followed by more detailed consideration of recent developments.

No. 5. *The Variate Difference Method*, by GERHARD TINTNER. 1940. 175 pages. Price $2.50.

A full account of the history and use of this method for the analysis of time series. Certain new devices of treatment are presented, and extensive tables are given to facilitate calculations which hitherto required a prohibitive amount of labor.

No. 6 *The Analysis of Economic Time Series*, by HAROLD T. DAVIS. 1941 620 pages. Price $5.00.

This work surveys the problem of analyzing economic time series beginning with historical origins and ending with a critical appraisal of what has been accomplished by modern statistical methods. Numerous examples illuminate the text. Many tables and 169 charts illustrate the contents of the book.

No. 7. *General-Equilibrium Theory in International Trade*, by JACOB L. MOSAK. 1944. 187 pages. Price $2.50.

This study applies the modern theory of economic equilibrium (as expounded by J. R. Hicks and others) to an important field.

No. 8. *Price Flexibility and Employment*, by OSCAR LANGE. 1944. About 110 pages. Price $2.00.

The author tries to clarify important concepts that have had much currency in the practical discussion of depressions and wars but have so far remained too vague to allow of useful treatment.

Orders should be sent to
THE PRINCIPIA PRESS, INC.
BLOOMINGTON, INDIANA

GENERAL-EQUILIBRIUM THEORY IN INTERNATIONAL TRADE

By
Jacob Louis Mosak

The Principia Press, Inc.
Bloomington, Indiana
1944

SET UP AND PRINTED IN THE UNITED STATES OF AMERICA
BY THE DENTAN PRINTING COMPANY
COLORADO SPRINGS, COLORADO

PREFACE

This book is an attempt to bridge the gap that has existed thus far between the general theory of value for a closed economy and the theory of international trade. It stems primarily from the work of the mathematical school of economists to which I was first introduced by the late Professor Henry Schultz. Although he died before I began this study, I am heavily indebted to him for instruction and inspiration. His friendship and warm personal interest in me will always be a treasured memory.

This study was presented as a doctoral dissertation at the University of Chicago in the summer of 1941. The members of my dissertation committee were Professor Jacob Viner, chairman, and Professors Oscar Lange and Theodore O. Yntema. I am indeed indebted to all three, not only for general intellectual stimulation, but also for their constant encouragement and friendly help. They each read the manuscript carefully and made many helpful suggestions. I need hardly add, however, that the responsibility for any errors is mine alone.

I also wish to express my sincere appreciation to Mr. Dickson H. Leavens, the editor of the Cowles Commission Monographs, for his invaluable aid in preparing the book for the printers.

JACOB L. MOSAK

Washington, D.C.
  July, 1944

TABLE OF CONTENTS

PART I

STATIC-EQUILIBRIUM THEORY IN INTERNATIONAL TRADE

CHAPTER I

TABLE OF CONTENTS

LIST OF FIGURES

PART I
STATIC-EQUILIBRIUM THEORY
IN INTERNATIONAL TRADE

CHAPTER I

The Equilibrium of Exchange for an Individual

The theory of value for a closed economy as developed in recent years has served particularly to clarify our thinking with respect to the perplexing problems of the interrelations between markets for different goods and services. With the new tools of analysis that have been shaped, it should now be possible to extend and generalize the traditional theory of international trade in which the interrelations between numerous markets are the essence of the subject matter. Such an extension should close the gap which has thus far separated the traditional theory of international value from the theory of value in a closed economy, and should pave the way for a unification of the two fields. That the two fields have thus far been approached essentially through different methods hardly requires any emphasis.[1] The theory of value for a closed economy of the neoclassical (Marshallian) writers is basically a partial-equilibrium theory, whereas their theory of international trade represents an approach to a general-equilibrium theory.[2] The former deals with the determination of the money price of a single commodity upon the assumption that all other prices remain unchanged. The latter, on the other hand, attempts to analyze the system of prices for the economy as a whole. Because of the complexity of the problems which are treated in this field, however, the classical theory was developed in terms of highly oversimplified assumptions which make it difficult to observe the full workings of the economic system. The analysis generally (although not exclusively) relates to the case of two countries trading in two commodities. The two countries are somehow assumed to be representative of all the individuals within them, so that utility and cost functions for the country as a whole can be employed. Likewise the two commodities are assumed to be representative of the entire range of the commodities which are produced and exchanged, so that the discussion is centered largely upon the determination of the "terms of trade" between

---

[1] A notable exception is to be found in the work of Bertil Ohlin. See his *Interregional and International Trade* (Cambridge: Harvard University Press, 1933).

[2] Cf. Jacob Viner, *Studies in the Theory of International Trade* (New York: Harper and Brothers, 1937), pp. 582–86; Gottfried Haberler, *The Theory of International Trade* (trans. from the original German ed., London, 1936), p. 154.

them. The extent of the vagueness of the whole approach was neatly summarized by Edgeworth in his statement:

> . . . a movement along a supply-and-demand curve of international trade should be considered as attended with rearrangements of internal trade; as the movement of the hand of a clock corresponds to considerable unseen movements of the machinery.[3]

The theory of value for a closed economy as developed by the mathematical school of economists is far more general than the classical theory of international trade. It deals with more meaningful economic units, the *individual* consumer, the individual firm, and the individual commodity, rather than with the *representative* consumer, the representative producer, and the representative commodity. It therefore permits us to obtain a much clearer picture of the full workings of the economic system. Until recently, however, this theory was too unwieldy to permit a very fruitful extension to the field of international trade.[4] The general-equilibrium analysis was extremely useful in describing the complex system of price interrelationships and in laying down the conditions which must be satisfied in equilibrium by this system of prices. But laws of change, which would permit us to analyze the effects of any given variation in the initial conditions upon the equilibrium situation, were not fully and systematically developed. Consequently, it was rather difficult to apply this theory to the field of international-trade theory which deals with such problems as the effects of loans, indemnities, duties, bounties, and the like. With the important advances made recently in the development of laws of change of equilibrium systems,[5] it now becomes possible to extend the general-equilibrium analysis in systematic fashion to the field of international trade.

This book stems from the work of the mathematical school of economists. Part I treats the equilibrium of a static economy along

[3] F. Y. Edgeworth, *Papers Relating to Political Economy* (London, 1925), Vol. II, p. 32.

[4] See the systems of equations for international trade as developed by Pareto and Ohlin: Vilfredo Pareto, *Cours d'économie politique* (Paris, 1896), Book I, chap. ii, pp. 180–82, and Book II, chap iii, pp. 208–40; Bertil Ohlin, *op. cit.*, Appendix I, pp. 553–62. The most fruitful mathematical development of the theory of international trade was given by T. O. Yntema in his book, *A Mathematical Reformulation of the General Theory of International Trade* (Chicago: University of Chicago Press, 1932).

[5] The basic work is due essentially to Hotelling and to Hicks: Harold Hotelling, "Edgeworth's Taxation Paradox and the Nature of Demand and Supply Functions," *Journal of Political Economy*, Vol. 40 (1932), pp. 577–616; J. R. Hicks, *Value and Capital* (Oxford, 1939). The theory was recently extended by Paul A. Samuelson in "The Stability of Equilibrium: Comparative Statics and Dynamics," *Econometrica*, Vol. 9 (April, 1941), pp. 97–120, and "The Stability of Equilibrium: Linear and Nonlinear Systems," *Econometrica*, Vol. 10, January, 1942, pp. 1–25.

the lines which are now standard in mathematical economics. The most comprehensive treatment of this subject to date is to be found in Hicks's *Value and Capital*. Part II is essentially a summary and development of Hicks's theory of intertemporal (dynamic) equilibrium, applied to international trade. The book is confined to a general-equilibrium analysis of an economy under pure competition. It thus fails to give a systematic treatment of two large portions of the present-day body of economic theory, imperfect competition on the one hand and sequence analysis on the other. These two fields cannot be adequately treated on the level of generalization employed in general-equilibrium analysis.

The following brief statement on the general-equilibrium analysis of a static economy is an outline of the essential framework of the theory of international trade which we shall present in Part I.

Static general-equilibrium analysis is traditionally divided into two fields: (1) *the theory of exchange* in which the total market supply of each commodity is assumed fixed, and (2) *the theory of production* in which the supply is assumed variable. Each field in turn consists of two parts: (a) the equilibrium of the economic unit, and (b) the equilibrium of the whole economy.

The equilibrium of the economic unit analyzes the behavior of the unit under a given set of conditions upon the assumption that it acts rationally. In the theory of exchange the only economic unit is the individual consumer. The given set of conditions consists of: (1) his preference or utility function, namely, his tastes; (2) his initial supply of goods and services; and (3) the set of market prices for each good and service. Conditions (2) and (3) together determine the value of his income. Rational behavior on the part of the individual is assumed to imply the maximization of utility. In the theory of production there are two sets of economic units, the individual consumer and the business firm. The given conditions for the firm are: (1) its production function or transformation function describing the technical conditions for transforming productive services into products, and (2) the set of prices for the products and productive services. Rational behavior for the firm is assumed to imply the maximization of its surplus, or the difference between its total receipts and its total costs. The given conditions for the consumer are essentially the same as in the theory of exchange, namely: given tastes, given initial supplies of goods, and given prices. They have to be modified only slightly to take into account the distribution of the firm's surpluses to the individuals. The problem of the equilibrium of the economic unit is to determine in each case what quantities of each of the goods and services the economic unit will demand and supply under different sets of prices. The problem of the equilibrium of the whole economy is then to analyze the conditions under which the equilibria of all units in the economy are mutually consistent.

I. THE CHARACTERISTICS OF THE EQUILIBRIUM POSITION

The problem at hand is to determine how an individual with given tastes and given supplies of goods and services determines his purchases and sales in a perfectly competitive market.

A. *The Scale of Preferences*

It is assumed that each individual is able to rank in order of preference different combinations of goods which he may have per unit of time, namely, it is assumed that he knows whether he prefers one combination to another or whether he is indifferent as between them. We can represent his set of preferences by means of a contour or "indifference map," consisting of a set of ordered "indifference curves." Any two combinations of goods between which the individual is indifferent are represented by points lying on the same indifference curve. If one combination is preferred to another, then the one that is preferred is represented by a point lying on a higher indifference curve. One and only one indifference curve passes through each point.[6] To each indifference curve we may assign some value indicating the level of utility represented by that curve. If there are n commodities it is assumed that each indifference curve may be characterized by an equation which states that the utility (u) derived from having the various combinations of goods which lie along that curve is a constant magnitude:

$$(1.1a) \qquad u(x_1, x_2, \cdots, x_n) = \text{a constant.}$$

Each time we vary the constant term on the right-hand side we obtain the equation to another indifference curve, a greater constant representing a higher indifference curve or a higher level of utility. Thus if we consider the right-hand side as constant only for a given indifference curve but as variable from one curve to another we may obtain a utility function:

$$(1.1b) \qquad u(x_1, x_2, \cdots, x_n) = \phi,$$

[6] The use of the term "indifference curve" is strictly valid only in the special case of two commodities. When there are more than two commodities the term "indifference surface" is required. Since a curve is easier to visualize than a surface we shall continue to use the term "curves" even in the general case of n commodities.

where ϕ represents the utility the individual derives from the combination of goods $x_1\, x_2\,, \cdots\,, x_n$. Instead of the symbol ϕ we may use any other symbol—in particular, u—to represent the level of utility corresponding to any given indifference curve. Thus, finally, we may write our utility function in the form:

$$(1.1c) \qquad\qquad u = u(x_1\,, x_2\,, \cdots\,, x_n).$$

Modern economic theory is not based upon the assumption of the measurability of utility.[7] This means that the indifference curves simply *indicate* levels of utility but do not *measure* them. Thus we can assign *any arbitrary* value to an indifference curve, provided that we assign a higher value to a higher indifference curve. This implies that, if u is some one index of utility corresponding to a combination $x_1\,, x_2\,, \cdots\,, x_n$, then any arbitrary function F of u is also a suitable index, provided that F increases when u increases and decreases when u decreases; namely, provided that $F' \equiv dF/du > 0$. Thus the function u is completely arbitrary except for the fact that a greater value of u denotes a higher indifference curve. This indeterminacy of the utility function, however, does not lead to any difficulties in the theory of value, since all of the objective economic behavior of the individual can be analyzed without the assumption of the measurability of utility.[8]

What are the basic properties of this arbitrary utility function?

[7] On the empirical meaning of the measurability of utility see Oscar Lange, "The Determinateness of the Utility Function," *The Review of Economic Studies*, Vol. 1, no. 3 (June, 1934), pp. 218–25; E. H. Phelps Brown, H. Bernardelli, and O. Lange, "Notes on the Determinateness of the Utility Function," *ibid.*, Vol. 2, no. 1 (October, 1934), pp. 66–77; R. G. D. Allen, "A Note on the Determinateness of the Utility Function," *ibid.*, Vol. 2, no. 2 (February, 1935), pp. 155–58; Paul A. Samuelson, "The Numerical Representation of Ordered Classifications and the Concept of Utility," *ibid.*, Vol. 6, no. 1 (October, 1938), pp. 65–70.

[8] Pareto first pointed out the indeterminacy of the utility function but his economic theory was largely based on the assumption of the measurability of utility. See his *Manuel d'économie politique*, especially chaps. iii and iv and the Appendix, and his article, "Economie mathématique" in the *Encyclopédie des sciences mathématiques*, Tome 1. Vol. IV, fasc. 4, 1911. The first mathematical development of a demand theory essentially free from the assumption of the measurability of utility was given by W. E. Johnson in his article, "The Pure Theory of Utility Curves," *Economic Journal*, 1913, pp. 483–513. A similar theory was developed by E. Slutsky in his article "Sulla teoria del bilancio del consumatore," *Giornale degli economisti*, Vol. 51 (1915), pp. 1–26. A summary of this paper appears in Henry Schultz, *The Theory and Measurement of Demand* (Chicago, 1938), chaps. i and xix, and in R. G. D. Allen's article, "Professor Slutsky's Theory of Consumers' Choice," *The Review of Economic Studies*, Vol. 3, no. 2 (February, 1936), pp. 120–29. In 1934 J. R. Hicks and R. G. D. Allen presented the modern version of the theory of consumer demand, entirely free from the assumption of measurability. This was built upon the work of W. E. Johnson but was arrived at independently of Slutsky's work which it resembles very closely. See their article, "A Reconsideration of the Theory of Value," *Economica*, New Series, Vol. 1 (February and May, 1934), pp. 52–76, 196–219.

It is assumed that the function u is continuous and has continuous partial derivatives of the first and second order:

$$u_s = \frac{\partial u}{\partial x_s} \text{ and } u_{st} = \frac{\partial^2 u}{\partial x_t \partial x_s} \qquad (s \text{ and } t = 1, 2, 3, \cdots, n).$$

We may call u_s the index of the marginal utility of x_s corresponding to the utility function u. The term u_{st} then represents the rate of change of the index u_s with respect to x_t.

The assumption that such a utility function exists implies that the preference ranking of any combination of goods depends only on the quantities of the goods in the combination and not upon the order in which they are arranged. This means that the rate of change of u_s with respect to x_t is equal to the rate of change of u_t with respect to x_s, namely,
$$u_{st} = u_{ts}.$$

If this were not true, then the individual's preferences could not be integrated into a complete system and they could not, therefore, be described by a utility function.[9]

Corresponding to each suitable utility function $F(u)$ there is an index of the marginal utility of x_s which we may denote by $F_s = F'u_s$. Since $F(u)$ is arbitrary except for the condition that $F'(u) > 0$, it follows that u_s is arbitrary in magnitude but uniquely determined in sign. We cannot therefore measure the marginal utility of any commodity; we can only determine its sign.

We shall confine ourselves to that region of the indifference map in which every u_s is greater than zero. This means that an increase in the quantity of any one commodity, the quantities of all other commodities remaining unchanged, involves a shift to a higher indifference curve. It also implies that the slope of an indifference curve is negative with respect to every axis, since if the quantity of one commodity increases while the quantities of all other commodities but one remain unchanged, the quantity of this last commodity must decrease if the new combination is to lie on the same indifference curve.

The rate of change of F_s with respect to x_t is given by $F_{st} = F'u_{st} + F''u_s u_t$. Since there are no restrictions on the sign of F'', it follows that the second-order partial derivatives of the utility function are arbitrary even as to sign.[10] The classical principle of diminishing mar-

[9] For a theory of consumer demand built on the assumption of nonintegrability see Hicks and Allen, "A Reconsideration of the Theory of Value," *op. cit.*; N. Georgescu-Roegen, "The Pure Theory of Consumer's Behavior," *Quarterly Journal of Economics*, Vol. 50, no. 4 (August, 1936), pp. 545–93; R. G. D. Allen, *Mathematical Analysis for Economists* (London, 1938), pp. 513–17.

[10] They become determinate in sign when u_s or $u_t = 0$, in which case $F_{st} = F''u_{st}$. The curve defined by the condition $u_s = 0$ is designated as the satiation curve for x_s.

ginal utility implies that F_{ss} shall be negative. Since the assumption of nonmeasurability of utility makes the sign of F_{ss} arbitrary, it necessitates discarding the traditional principle of diminishing marginal utility. The index of the marginal utility of any commodity may either rise or fall as x increases, the direction of change depending upon the arbitrary index of utility $F(u)$ which we happen to choose.

In modern economic theory the concept of the marginal rate of substitution replaces that of marginal utility.

The marginal rate of substitution of x_s for x_t is defined as the decrement in x_t which would just offset the additional utility resulting from the addition of a marginal unit of x_s when the quantities of all other commodities remain unchanged.[11] We designate this by the symbol

$$R_s^t = -\frac{\partial x_t}{\partial x_s}.$$

It follows from the definition that the marginal rate of substitution of x_s for x_t is equal to the ratio of u_s to u_t, or [12]

$$R_s^t = -\frac{\partial x_t}{\partial x_s} = \frac{u_s}{u_t}.$$

Since the marginal rate of substitution is defined in terms of the indifference curves it is obviously free from any assumption of measurability of utility. This may also be seen from the fact that the ratio u_s/u_t remains unchanged when we replace u by F:

$$\frac{F_s}{F_t} = \frac{F'u_s}{F'u_t} = \frac{u_s}{u_t}.$$

Instead of the traditional principle of diminishing marginal utility we have in modern theory the principle of diminishing marginal rate of substitution. This means that the marginal rate of substitution of x_s for x_t, or the decrement in x_t which would just offset an individual's gain of a marginal unit of x_s, diminishes as x_s is substituted for x_t along a given indifference curve. Geometrically this implies that the indifference curve must be convex to the origin; i.e., that the slope of the indifference curve must diminish numerically as we move

[11] Hicks, p. 20.

[12] The proof is simple. For any given indifference curve we have the implicit function in the variables x_1 to x_n:

$$u(x_1, x_2, \cdots, x_n) = \text{a constant.}$$

By the rule for the differentiation of an implicit function we have

$$-\frac{\partial x_t}{\partial x_s} = \frac{u_s}{u_t}.$$

down and to the right. Now the marginal rate of substitution is equal to the ratio of the index of the marginal utility of x_s to that of x_t. If the index of the marginal utility of x_s declined as x_s increased and that of x_t rose as x_t decreased, then the marginal rate of substitution of x_s for x_t would obviously decline for substitutions of x_s for x_t along an indifference curve. It might therefore be supposed that the principle of diminishing marginal rate of substitution implies that of diminishing marginal utility. This is false. For the index of the marginal utility of x_s is affected not only by the change in x_s but also by that in x_t. Even though the index should tend to rise as a result of the increase in x_s it might fall as a result of the decrease in x_t. Similarly even though the index of marginal utility of x_t should tend to fall as a result of the decrease in x_t it might tend to rise as a result of the increase in x_s. The ratio of the two indexes of marginal utility, or the marginal rate of substitution, can therefore diminish even though the principle of diminishing marginal utility is not valid.[13]

The generalization of the principle of diminishing marginal rate of substitution to n commodities is rather complicated. The full algebraic statement of this condition will be given later. The geometric statement of the condition, however, is simple. The indifference surface must be convex to the origin from every direction. This means that the marginal rate of substitution must diminish for substitutions in every direction along the indifference surface. The necessity for assuming this principle will appear later in the discussion of the stability conditions for equilibrium.

---

[13] The proof of this is simple. The principle of diminishing marginal rate of substitution requires that the following condition be satisfied for a substitution of x_s for x_t:

$$\frac{d}{dx_s}\left(\frac{u_s}{u_t}\right) \equiv \frac{u_t \dfrac{du_s}{dx_s} - u_s \dfrac{du_t}{dx_s}}{u_t^2} < 0.$$

But since we are considering variations in both x_s and x_t, we have

$$\frac{du_s}{dx_s} = \frac{\partial u_s}{\partial x_s} + \frac{\partial u_s}{\partial x_t}\frac{dx_t}{dx_s} = u_{ss} - u_{st}\frac{u_s}{u_t},$$

$$\frac{du_t}{dx_s} = \frac{\partial u_t}{\partial x_s} + \frac{\partial u_t}{\partial x_t}\frac{dx_t}{dx_s} = u_{ts} - u_{tt}\frac{u_s}{u_t}.$$

We have therefore

$$\frac{1}{u_t^3}\left(u_t^2 u_{ss} - 2 u_s u_t u_{st} + u_s^2 u_{tt}\right) < 0.$$

This could be negative even for $u_{ss} > 0$, $u_{tt} > 0$, provided that u_{st} were positive and sufficiently large.

B. *The Determination of the Equilibrium Position*

It is assumed that the individual has given quantities per unit of time of the n commodities, which he seeks to exchange at the prevailing ratios of exchange for the most preferred collection per unit of time which he can obtain. We denote the initial quantities in the individual's collection by the symbols $\bar{x}_1$, $\bar{x}_2$, $\cdots$, $\bar{x}_n$. They represent his *gross supply* of the commodities. We denote the quantities in the most preferred collection which he can obtain in trade by the symbols x_1, x_2, $\cdots$, x_n. These are his equilibrium quantities of the n commodities, given his tastes, his initial quantities, and the ratios of exchange between the commodities. These equilibrium quantities represent his *gross demand* for the commodities. The difference between his gross demand for and gross supply of any commodity $(x_s - \bar{x}_s)$ represents his purchase of the commodity if it is positive, and his sale if it is negative. The purchase of any commodity is the *net demand* and the sale of it is the *net supply*. Algebraically, net supply is the equivalent of a negative net demand.

In a system of n commodities there are $n(n-1)$ exchange ratios, but only $n-1$ of these are mathematically independent of one another. Let the nth commodity (chosen arbitrarily) serve as the *numéraire* or standard commodity in terms of which the $n-1$ independent exchange ratios are calculated. These exchange ratios are the prices of the $n-1$ commodities in terms of the nth commodity. We shall denote these ratios by the symbols y_1, y_2, $\cdots$, y_{n-1}. For the sake of symmetry we may also introduce the symbol y_n to define the price of the nth commodity in terms of itself. By definition $y_n = 1$. It is obvious that the equilibrium position of any individual with given tastes and given initial quantities of the n commodities depends only upon the $n-1$ ratios of exchange y_s.

In the literature on static theory the term "money" is frequently used to refer to the *numéraire* or standard commodity. It should be noted that when the term is so used, the "money" is assumed to be a commodity which has direct utility and which differs in no respect from any other commodity except that it also serves as a standard in terms of which the prices of all other commodities are expressed. The demand for this money will be a function of the same variables as the demand for every other commodity; and the initial supply of this money, like the initial supply of any other commodity, will affect the demand for every commodity.

It is quite common in static theory, however, to introduce an outside standard which serves as a unit of account and as a medium of exchange but which is not part of the equilibrium system at all. We may denote the prices of the n commodities in terms of this outside unit of account by the symbols $p_1, p_2, \cdots, p_n$. It follows immediately that $y_s = p_s/p_n$. This outside standard is assumed to have no direct utility at all, i.e., it does not enter into the utility function (1.1). The gross demand for it is assumed to be identical with the gross supply for each individual, so that there is no exchange of it in equilibrium. Furthermore, the initial supply of it has no effect upon the demand for any commodity in the equilibrium system. This money is not a commodity at all. It is a completely "neutral" object, whose only function is to serve as a unit of account and as a medium of exchange. It is simply a token money, serving exactly the same function as chips in a card game. The equilibrium position of every individual and therefore of the economy as a whole is completely unaffected by the existence of such money. Though we may express the prices of the n commodities in terms of the token money, the equilibrium position depends only upon the ratios of these prices (y_s) and not upon the prices themselves (p_s). This is the type of money which is implied in the classical statement that money is simply a "veil" which masks the true barter nature of the economy.[14]

Since the token money is assumed to have no effect upon any individual's demand for or supply of any commodity, it is obvious that we could ignore it entirely in our discussion of equilibrium. In view of the voluminous literature which deals with the equilibrium of "money prices," however, we shall adopt this approach here also and introduce a token money into our discussion. It will be obvious from the analysis, however, that the introduction of the token money is a purely artificial device and that the equilibrium position depends only on the ratios of exchange between the n commodities, and not on the money prices themselves.

It is assumed at this first stage of the analysis that no individual has any unilateral receipts or payments. (This assumption is later dropped.) Consequently the value of his gross supply of all commodities must be equal to that of his gross demand for them, when these values are expressed either in terms of the *numéraire* (arbitrarily chosen) or in terms of the token money. The amount of the token money the individual has is excluded from both sides of the equation since his gross supply of it is assumed to be identical with his gross demand for it. Let us call the money value of the individual's initial supply of commodities his money income and let us denote it by the

---

[14] See Oscar Lange, "Say's Law," *Studies in Mathematical Economics and Econometrics* (Chicago: The University of Chicago Press, 1942), pp. 49–68.

symbol r. Then we have the budgetary restriction to which the individual is subject in the carrying on of his trade:

(1.2) $p_1x_1 + p_2x_2 + \cdots + p_nx_n = p_1\overline{x_1} + p_2\overline{x_2} + \cdots + p_n\overline{x_n} \equiv r$.

This equation is expressed in money values. To express the condition on the value in terms of the *numéraire* we need simply divide both sides of (1.2) by p_n. Under perfect competition each individual behaves as if he had no effect upon the prices. The prices in equation (1.2) are therefore to be treated as constants. The equation may thus be represented as a straight line (in the case of two commodities) or as a hyperplane (in the case of n commodities) on the same diagram as the indifference curves. For this line (hyperplane) the (partial) slope $\partial x_t/\partial x_s$ equals the ratio $-p_s/p_t$.

It follows immediately from the preceding discussion that the individual will obtain the most preferred collection of goods only when the marginal rate of substitution for any pair of commodities is equal to the ratio of their prices. For if the marginal rate of substitution of x_1 for x_2 is greater (or less) than the ratio p_1/p_2, then the individual can obtain a more preferred collection by getting more (less) of x_1 and less (more) of x_2. Since the marginal rate of substitution is the slope of an indifference curve and the price ratio is the corresponding slope of the budget line, it follows that the individual is in equilibrium only at a point where the budget line is tangent to an indifference curve.

In order that the equilibrium position should be stable, it is necessary that the point represent a most preferred rather than a least preferred combination of goods. This means that any departure from the equilibrium point must lead to a less preferred position. In the case of two commodities only, this is true only if the marginal rate of substitution of x_s for x_t diminishes as the individual increases the quantity of x_s in his collection in exchange for x_t; namely, only if R_s^t diminishes for substitutions of x_s for x_t. In the general case of n commodities, however, the marginal rate of substitution must be diminishing not only between each pair of commodities but also for substitutions in every other direction. Geometrically this implies that the indifference surfaces must be convex to the origin in the neighborhood of equilibrium. We shall assume that every point is capable of being an equilibrium position, so that this condition is satisfied everywhere on the indifference curves.

Mathematically the individual's equilibrium position may be determined as follows: The individual chooses the amounts $x_1, x_2, \cdots, x_n$ in such a way as to maximize his utility function u subject to the budgetary restriction (1.2). It is obvious that the equilibrium position remains unchanged if we replace u by F, since both will have their maxima and minima at the same points. Introducing the Lagrange multiplier for the maximization of a function subject to a constraint, we have

$$(1.3) \qquad u - \lambda \left[\sum_{\lambda}^{n} p_s x_s - \sum_{1}^{n} p_s \bar{x}_s \right] = \max.$$

Differentiating and setting the first-order partial derivatives equal to zero, we derive the well-known equilibrium conditions for the individual:

$$(1.4a) \qquad\qquad u_s = \lambda p_s \qquad\qquad (s = 1, 2, \cdots, n),$$

where $\lambda = \dfrac{\sum u_s x_s}{\sum p_s x_s}$.

Eliminating λ, we have:

$$(1.4b) \qquad \frac{u_1}{u_n} = \frac{p_1}{p_n}, \frac{u_2}{u_n} = \frac{p_2}{p_n}, \cdots, \frac{u_{n-1}}{u_n} = \frac{p_{n-1}}{p_n}.$$

These equations state that in equilibrium the marginal rate of substitution between any two goods must equal the ratio of their money prices. Stated somewhat differently these equations mean that the marginal rate of substitution between any good and the *numéraire* must equal its price in terms of the *numéraire*. These $n-1$ equations together with equation (1.2) are sufficient to determine the n unknown quantities $x_1, x_2, \cdots, x_n$ in the individual's equilibrium collection of commodities.

Equations (1.4) are only the first-order conditions for a maximum. In order that u shall be a true maximum rather than a minimum or minimax we must also have the second-order or stability condition

$$(1.5) \qquad d^2 u = \sum_{1}^{n} \sum_{1}^{n} u_{st} \, dx_s \, dx_t < 0,$$

where the x's are constrained to lie along the budgetary equation (1.2). This is the mathematical statement of the condition that the marginal rate of substitution must be diminishing for substitution in every direction, or that the indifference curves must be convex to the origin.

Let

$$(1.6) \qquad U = \begin{vmatrix} 0 & u_1 & u_2 & \cdots & u_n \\ u_1 & u_{11} & u_{12} & \cdots & u_{1n} \\ u_2 & u_{21} & u_{22} & \cdots & u_{2n} \\ \cdot & \cdot & \cdot & \cdots & \cdot \\ u_n & u_{n1} & u_{n2} & \cdots & u_{nn} \end{vmatrix} .$$

Then the restriction (1.5) is equivalent to the condition that the determinants

$$\begin{vmatrix} 0 & u_1 & u_2 \\ u_1 & u_{11} & u_{12} \\ u_2 & u_{12} & u_{22} \end{vmatrix} , \qquad \begin{vmatrix} 0 & u_1 & u_2 & u_3 \\ u_1 & u_{11} & u_{12} & u_{13} \\ u_2 & u_{12} & u_{22} & u_{23} \\ u_3 & u_{13} & u_{23} & u_{33} \end{vmatrix} , \text{ et cetera,}$$

shall be alternately positive and negative.[15] In this series the last determinant is U, the next to last is the cofactor U_{nn} of u_{nn} in U, the one preceding that is the cofactor $U_{nn,(n-1)(n-1)}$ of $u_{(n-1)(n-1)}$ in U_{nn}, et cetera. Consequently the stability conditions state that

$$\frac{U_{nn}}{U} , \quad \frac{U_{nn,(n-1)(n-1)}}{U} , \quad \frac{U_{nn,(n-1)(n-1),(n-2)(n-2)}}{U} , \quad \cdots , \frac{U_{nn,(n-1)(n-1),\cdots,22}}{U}$$

are alternately negative and positive.[16] Since the order of numbering the commodities is arbitrary, these conditions are equivalent to the conditions that

$$\frac{U_{11}}{U} , \quad \frac{U_{11,22}}{U} , \quad \frac{U_{11,22,33}}{U} , \quad \cdots , \frac{U_{11,22,33,\cdots,(n-1)(n-1)}}{U}$$

shall be alternately negative and positive. We shall have occasion to employ this form of the stability conditions in subsequent discussion.

It can easily be shown [17] that this condition is invariant under a substitution of $F(u)$ for u. Since the first-order equilibrium conditions (1.4b) are also invariant under such a transformation, it is thus easy to see that the equilibrium position of the individual can be determined without reference to any measurable utility function.

[15] R. G. D. Allen, *Mathematical Analysis for Economists* (London, 1938), pp. 485–92, and Hicks, Appendix, pp. 303–06.

[16] The numerator of the last expression equals $\begin{vmatrix} 0 & u_1 \\ u_1 & u_{11} \end{vmatrix}$ which is negative and therefore of opposite sign to the determinant in the numerator of the preceding expression.

[17] Schultz, *op. cit.*, pp. 652–54; Hicks, pp. 306–07.

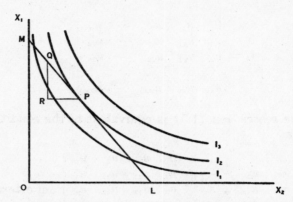

FIGURE 1.—DETERMINATION OF EQUILIBRIUM FOR THE INDIVIDUAL.

The determination of the equilibrium position of the individual for the case of two commodities is illustrated graphically in Figure 1. The curves I_1, I_2, and I_3 are three indifference curves representing ascending levels of utility. The line ML is the budgetary equation (1.2) to which the individual is restricted in his trading. The intercept OM (equals r/p_1) is the value of his income in terms of p_1 while the intercept OL (equals r/p_2) is its value in terms of x_2. The slope of the line equals the ratio $-p_2/p_1$. The individual comes to the market with a collection of goods represented by some point Q on the line ML, and seeks to trade it at the prevailing prices for a more preferred collection. It is clear from the convexity of the curves that the most preferred collection and, therefore, his equilibrium position is at the point P where ML is tangent to the indifference curve I_2. Thus he gives up QR of X_1 and obtains RP of X_2.

II.   THE LAWS OF CONSUMER DEMAND

It is clear from the derivation of the equilibrium conditions (1.2) and (1.4) that the equilibrium quantities x_1, x_2, $\cdots$, x_n demanded by an individual, as well as the equilibrium values of u and λ, depend upon three sets of factors:

(1) the individual's scale of preferences,

(2) the quantities of the various goods in his initial
collection, and

(3) the prices that prevail on the market.

Let the individual's scale of preferences be fixed and let us consider how his equilibrium position depends upon the other two factors. If the individual comes to the market with different initial quantities of the commodities or is confronted with different prices, he will choose different final combinations of goods. This means that the gross (and therefore the net) demand for each commodity is some function of the prices prevailing on the market and of the individual's initial quantities of the commodities:

$$x_s = x_s(p_1, p_2, \cdots, p_n, \bar{x}_1, \bar{x}_2, \cdots, \bar{x}_n).$$

It would be very awkward indeed, however, if we were compelled to solve anew the system of equations (1.2) and (1.4) in order to find the demand for each commodity corresponding to each set of his initial quantities and each set of prices. Moreover, such a procedure would not be very fruitful, since in general it is dangerous to establish any general laws or relationships between variables from results obtained in individual examples. What we need, therefore, is a method whereby we can determine general rules or relationships describing how the final equilibrium position changes when the prices or the initial quantities change.

To determine such relationships we need but return to the equations (1.2) and (1.4) which must be satisfied in equilibrium and reinterpret the prices p_s and initial quantities x_s as parameters subject to change rather than as fixed constants. We can then investigate the effects of changes in the prices and initial quantities by differentiating the equilibrium equations with respect to these parameters. If we are interested simply in the direction and not in the magnitude of the change in the equilibrium position, then it is sufficient to consider only the differentials of the first order. We then obtain a set of linear equations in the unknown rates of change of the equilibrium quantities with respect to each parameter. These equations, as we shall see, can readily be solved in terms of the determinant U and its cofactors. Geometrically this method involves shifting either the position or the slope of the budgetary line ML in Figure 1 and examining the resulting change in the equilibrium position.

The analysis will be carried on in terms of the money prices. As we have already seen, however, a difference in the money price of any commodity is important only insofar as it represents a difference in its exchange ratio with the other commodities. Thus if all the price ratios should be the same, the individual's equilibrium would also be the same even though the level of prices in terms of the token money were different. Thus the individual's demand is really a function of the $n-1$ price ratios y_s, rather than of the n prices p_s. It is, however, a simple matter to pass from the effect of a difference in the money price of a commodity to the effect of a difference in its prices in terms of the *numéraire*. Since $y_s = p_s/p_n$, the derivative with respect to y_s is simply p_n times the derivative with respect to p_s. Thus for any function f we have

$$\frac{\partial f}{\partial y_s} = \frac{\partial f}{\partial p_s} \frac{\partial p_s}{\partial y_s} = p_n \frac{\partial f}{\partial p_s}.$$

A.   *Effect of Variation in Income*

A change in the quantity of any one good in an individual's initial collection, all prices remaining unchanged, represents a change in the individual's money income. Let us therefore consider the effects of a change in income (prices being constant) upon the quantities demanded, $x_1, x_2, \cdots, x_n$.

Differentiating the equilibrium equations (1.2) and (1.4) with respect to money income r, we obtain:

$$p_1 \frac{\partial x_1}{\partial r} + p_2 \frac{\partial x_2}{\partial r} + \cdots + p_n \frac{\partial x_n}{\partial r} = 1,$$

$$-p_1 \frac{\partial \lambda}{\partial r} + u_{11} \frac{\partial x_1}{\partial r} + u_{12} \frac{\partial x_2}{\partial r} + \cdots + u_{1n} \frac{\partial x_n}{\partial r} = 0,$$

(2.1)

$$-p_2 \frac{\partial \lambda}{\partial r} + u_{21} \frac{\partial x_1}{\partial r} + u_{22} \frac{\partial x_2}{\partial r} + \cdots + u_{2n} \frac{\partial x_n}{\partial r} = 0,$$

$$\cdot \quad \cdot \quad \cdot \quad \cdot \quad \cdot \quad \cdot \quad \cdot \quad \cdot \quad \cdot \quad \cdot \quad \cdot$$

$$-p_n \frac{\partial \lambda}{\partial r} + u_{n1} \frac{\partial x_1}{\partial r} + u_{n2} \frac{\partial x_2}{\partial r} + \cdots + u_{nn} \frac{\partial x_n}{\partial r} = 0.$$

Since from equations (1.4) we have $p_s = u_s/\lambda$, the determinant of the coefficients in this system of equations is $-U/\lambda^2$, which by the stability conditions is different from zero. Let U_s be the cofactor of u_s and U_0 be the cofactor of zero in the determinant U. Then solving this system of equations we obtain for the rates of change of x_s and λ with respect to money income:

(2.2)
$$\frac{\partial x_s}{\partial r} = \frac{\lambda U_s}{U}, \quad \frac{\partial \lambda}{\partial r} = \frac{-\lambda^2 U_0}{U}.$$

Equations (2.2) give the rates of change with respect to the money value of an individual's initial supply of commodities. To determine the rates of change with respect to the value of the supply in terms of the *numéraire*, we need but multiply these equations by p_n.

1. *Effect on the quantities demanded in equilibrium*

The term $\lambda U_s/U$ can be shown to remain unchanged if we replace u by $F(u)$. Consequently $\partial x_s/\partial r$ is a determinate quantity.[18]

Since there are no restrictions on the sign of the ratio U_s/U, it follows that the quantity of x_s demanded in equilibrium may either increase or decrease with increases in income. A commodity for which the demand decreases as income increases is said to be an "inferior" good. Normally commodities are noninferior goods. It is evident that at least one commodity must be a noninferior good.

2. *Effect on the equilibrium level of utility*

Since the equilibrium quantities demanded are functions of income, the equilibrium level of utility must also be a function of income. Let us designate the equilibrium level of utility by the letter w. Differentiating the utility function (1.1) with respect to r, we obtain:

(2.3a)
$$\frac{\partial w}{\partial r} = u_1 \frac{\partial x_1}{\partial r} + u_2 \frac{\partial x_2}{\partial r} + \cdots + u_n \frac{\partial x_n}{\partial r}.$$

Here the u_i have equilibrium values and the $\partial x_i/\partial r$ satisfy equations (2.1). By substitution of the relationship (1.4) $u_s = \lambda p_s$ and by use of the first equation of (2.1), equation (2.3a) becomes

(2.3b)
$$\frac{\partial w}{\partial r} = \lambda.$$

Thus the Lagrange multiplier λ turns out to be the rate of change of the equilibrium value of the index of utility u with respect to money income. It is greater than zero, although it is completely arbitrary in magnitude, since it depends upon the particular utility function that is chosen. Thus if we replace u by $F(u)$ we shall have:

(2.4)
$$\frac{\partial F}{\partial r} = F' \frac{\partial w}{\partial r} = F' \lambda.$$

If utility could be assumed measurable, then λ could be interpreted as the marginal utility of money income. Equations (1.4a) would then be interpreted as stating that in equilibrium the marginal utility of any commodity must equal the marginal utility of money income multiplied by the price of the commodity. Since we have not assumed utility to be measurable, however, λ represents only an index of the marginal utility of money income, appropriate to the index of utility u. We may designate this as λ_u. To each index of utility $F(u)$ there

[18] Schultz, *op. cit.*, pp. 652–54.

will be an appropriate index of the marginal utility of money income $\lambda_F = F'\lambda_u$. The index is always positive, namely, an increase in money income, prices being constant, always leads to a higher indifference curve.

3.   Effect on the index of the marginal utility of money income, λ

The rate of change of λ with respect to r is arbitrary even in sign. Thus, if we replace u by $F(u)$, we obtain:

$$\frac{\partial \lambda_F}{\partial r} = F' \frac{\partial \lambda_u}{\partial r} + \lambda_u{}^2 F'' .$$

Since the sign of F'' is arbitrary, so is the sign of $\partial \lambda / \partial r$.

B.   Effect of a Variation in $\bar{x}_t$

A change in the initial quantity $\bar{x}_t$ of any one commodity, prices being constant, will change the money income by an amount equal to $p_t d\bar{x}_t$. The effect on the equilibrium position of such a change is therefore given by:

$$\frac{\partial x_s}{\partial \bar{x}_t} = \frac{\partial x_s}{\partial r} \frac{\partial r}{\partial \bar{x}_t} = p_t \frac{\partial x_s}{\partial r}$$

(2.5)
$$\frac{\partial w}{\partial \bar{x}_t} = p_t \frac{\partial w}{\partial r} ,$$

$$\frac{\partial \lambda}{\partial \bar{x}_t} = p_t \frac{\partial \lambda}{\partial r} .$$

C.   Effect of a Variation in Price

The effect on x_s of a change in the price p_t will differ according as the individual's money income r is or is not affected by the change in price. The latter will remain unchanged if the individual has no quantity $\bar{x}_t$ in his initial collection but will change if he has. Let us first consider the effect of a change in the price p_t, all other prices *and income* remaining constant. Differentiating the equilibrium equations (1.2) and (1.4) with respect to p_t, and putting $\bar{x}_t$ in (1.2) equal to zero,[19] we obtain:

[19] It should be recalled that the quantity of at least one commodity in the initial collection *must* be greater than zero, so that the first equation of (2.6) and therefore equations (2.7) will not hold for at least one price change. These equations could be applied to the case of $\bar{x}_t \neq 0$ only if it were assumed that a change in p_t were accompanied by such a change in x_t as to leave r unchanged.

$$p_1 \frac{\partial x_1}{\partial p_t} + p_2 \frac{\partial x_2}{\partial p_t} + \cdots + p_n \frac{\partial x_n}{\partial p_t} = -x_t,$$

$$-p_1 \frac{\partial \lambda}{\partial p_t} + u_{11} \frac{\partial x_1}{\partial p_t} + u_{12} \frac{\partial x_2}{\partial p_t} + \cdots + u_{1n} \frac{\partial x_n}{\partial p_t} = 0,$$

$$\cdots \cdots \cdots \cdots \cdots \cdots \cdots \cdots$$

(2.6)

$$-p_t \frac{\partial \lambda}{\partial p_t} + u_{t1} \frac{\partial x_1}{\partial p_t} + u_{t2} \frac{\partial x_2}{\partial p_t} + \cdots + u_{tn} \frac{\partial x_n}{\partial p_t} = \lambda,$$

$$\cdots \cdots \cdots \cdots \cdots \cdots \cdots \cdots$$

$$-p_n \frac{\partial \lambda}{\partial p_t} + u_{n1} \frac{\partial x_1}{\partial p_t} + u_{n2} \frac{\partial x_2}{\partial p_t} + \cdots + u_{nn} \frac{\partial x_n}{\partial p_t} = 0.$$

The determinant of the coefficients in this system of equations is the same as that for the set (2.1). If we let U_{st} be the cofactor of u_{st} in U, then we obtain for the solution of (2.6):

(2.7a)

$$\frac{\partial x_s}{\partial p_t} = \frac{\lambda(-x_t U_s + U_{st})}{U},$$

$$\frac{\partial \lambda}{\partial p_t} = \frac{-\lambda^2(x_t U_0 + U_t)}{U}.$$

The term $\lambda U_{st}/U$ can be shown to remain unchanged if we replace u by $F(u)$.[20] We may therefore replace it by the symbol x_{st} so as to show that it is not dependent upon any arbitrary utility function.[21]

If we now substitute from (2.2) into (2.7a) we obtain:

(2.7b)

$$\frac{\partial x_s}{\partial p_t} = -x_t \frac{\partial x_s}{\partial r} + x_{st},$$

$$\frac{\partial \lambda}{\partial p_t} = -x_t \frac{\partial \lambda}{\partial r} - \lambda \frac{\partial x_t}{\partial r}.$$

Equations (2.7) give the rates of change with respect to the money price of x_t. The rates of change with respect to the price of x_t in terms of the numéraire are given by multiplying the right-hand side of these equations by p_n. Thus, for $t \neq n$ we have

$$\frac{\partial x_s}{\partial y_t} = p_n \frac{\partial x_s}{\partial p_t} \quad \text{and} \quad \frac{\partial \lambda}{\partial y_t} = p_n \frac{\partial \lambda}{\partial p_t}.$$

[20] Schultz, op, cit., pp. 652–54.
[21] Hicks, p. 309.

1. *Effect on the quantities demanded in equilibrium*

The first equation in (2.7b) has been termed the fundamental equation of value theory. Its meaning may be made clear from the following considerations. Suppose that, when p_t changes, the individual's income is so adjusted as to permit him to consume exactly the same quantities of every commodity that he consumed before. Then in fact he will not consume the same quantities, but more (less) of the commodity whose price has fallen (risen), and less (more) of other goods. This substitution effect is measured by the term x_{st}. The amount by which r would have to change in order to keep the quantities $x_1, x_2, \cdots, x_n$ unchanged is obtained by differentiating r in (1.2) with respect to p_t keeping all x_i constant. It is

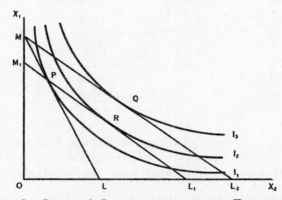

FIGURE 2.—SLUTSKY'S INTERPRETATION OF THE FUNDAMENTAL
EQUATION OF VALUE THEORY.

given by $\partial r / \partial p_t = x_t$. The change in x_s resulting from such a compensated change in price is therefore given by:

$$(2.8) \qquad \frac{dx_s}{dp_t} = \frac{\partial x_s}{\partial p_t} + \frac{\partial r}{\partial p_t} \frac{\partial x_s}{\partial r} = \frac{\partial x_s}{\partial p_t} + x_t \frac{\partial x_s}{\partial r}.$$

From equation (2.7b) this rate of change is equal to x_{st}.

Since x_{st} is the substitution effect which results from a change in price that is compensated for by a change in income, the term $-x_t \, \partial x_s/\partial_r$ in equation (2.7b) is the change in x_s resulting from the fact that income is not so adjusted. Thus we have:

$$(2.9) \qquad \frac{\partial x_s}{\partial p_t} - \frac{dx_s}{dp_t} = \frac{\partial x_s}{\partial p_t} - x_{st} = - x_t \frac{\partial x_s}{\partial r}.$$

The term $-x_t\, \partial x_s/\partial r$ therefore measures the income effect of the price change upon the demand for x_s. The fundamental equation of value theory thus states that the change in demand resulting from a change in price is made up of two parts: a substitution effect measured by x_{st} and an income effect measured by $-\,x_t\, \partial x_s/\partial r$.

The meaning of equation (2.7b) is illustrated graphically for the case of two commodities in Figure 2.

The initial budget line is ML and the initial equilibrium position is at P; when p_2 declines the budget line changes to ML_2 and the new equilibrium position is at Q. This change is divided into two parts: (1) the substitution effect from P to R which is obtained by shifting the budget line at the new price parallel to itself so as to pass through the initial equilibrium point P; and (2) the income effect from R to Q which is the result of the fact that income is not adjusted to compensate for the price change.[22]

2.   Effect on the equilibrium level of utility

Since the equilibrium quantities demanded are functions of the prices, it follows that the equilibrium level of utility w is also a function of the same prices. Thus, differentiating the utility function (1.1) with respect to p_t, we obtain:

$$(2.10a) \qquad \frac{\partial w}{\partial p_t} = u_1 \frac{\partial x_1}{\partial p_t} + u_2 \frac{\partial x_2}{\partial p_t} + \cdots + u_n \frac{\partial x_n}{\partial p_t}.$$

Substituting the relationship (1.4) $u_s = \lambda p_s$ and making use of the first equation of (2.4), we obtain:[23]

[22] This interpretation of the substitution and income effects is given by Slutsky, *op. cit.* (Fig. 2 is a modification of the chart which appears in Schultz, *op. cit.*, p. 44). It corresponds to that given by Hicks in the Appendix, p. 309, but is at variance with that given by him in the text, pp. 31–32. There Hicks interprets x_{st} as measuring the substitution effect that would result if money income were adjusted so as to permit the individual to buy such a combination of goods as would leave the level of utility unchanged. It can be shown that when differentials of a higher order are neglected both substitution effects may be measured by x_{st}. See my paper, "On the Interpretation of the Fundamental Equation of Value Theory," in *Studies in Mathematical Economics and Econometrics* (ed. O. Lange, T. O. Yntema, and F. McIntyre; Chicago: University of Chicago Press, 1942), pp. 69–74.

[23] This equation as well as (2.3) was first derived by R. G. D. Allen in his article, "On the Marginal Utility of Money and Its Application," *Economica*, Vol. 13, (1933), pp. 186–209. Note its bearing on the problem of the inverse utility function of the prices whose first partial derivatives are proportional to the quantities demanded. It is obvious that this inverse utility function is the negative of w. On this point see Hotelling, *op. cit.*, pp. 590–95; and L. M. Court, "A Theorem on Maxima and Minima with an Application to Differential Equations," *Journal of Mathematics and Physics*, Vol. 20, No. 1 (January, 1941), pp. 99–106.

(2.10b)
$$\frac{\partial w}{\partial p_t} = -\lambda\, x_t.$$

This term is negative but arbitrary in magnitude.

3.   Effect on the index λ

The second equation of (2.7b) relates to the effect of the variation in p_t upon λ. Like $\partial\lambda/\partial r$ the term $\partial\lambda/\partial p_t$ is arbitrary even in sign. Thus if we replace u by $F(u)$ we have:

(2.11)
$$\frac{\partial\lambda_F}{\partial p_t} = F'\frac{\partial\lambda_u}{\partial p_t} + \lambda_u F''\frac{\partial u}{\partial p_t} = F'\frac{\partial\lambda_u}{\partial p_t} - \lambda_u{}^2 F'' x_t.$$

One important conclusion, however, follows from the second equation of (2.7b). If corresponding to some index of utility $F(u)$ there is an index of marginal utility of money income λ_F such that it remains constant both with respect to income and with respect to p_t, we shall have:

$$\frac{\partial x_t}{\partial r} = 0.$$

Thus the constancy of the marginal utility of money income as here defined implies that the demand for x_t is not a function of income. Obviously the demand for at least one commodity must be a function of income.[24]

D.   Properties of the Substitution Term

The substitution term x_{st} provides us with the modern definition of complementarity between commodities.[25] If x_{st} is positive, then a compensated reduction in the price of x_t leads to a decrease in the demand for x_s, and the commodities are substitutes. If x_{st} is negative, a compensated reduction in the price of x_t leads to an increase in the demand for x_s and the commodities are complementary. If x_{st}

---

[24] See Paul A. Samuelson, "Constancy of the Marginal Utility of Income," in *Studies in Mathematical Economics and Econometrics* (ed. O. Lange, T. O. Yntema, and F. McIntyre; Chicago: University of Chicago Press, 1942), pp. 75–91.

This condition should not be confused with the one given by Hicks (p. 26) for a demand that is independent of income. Ours relates to the quantity demanded being independent of income ($\partial x_t/\partial r = 0$); Hicks's relates to the demand-price expressed in terms of the *numéraire* being independent of income ($\partial y_t/\partial r = 0$). The one does not necessarily imply the other when we are dealing with more than two commodities. As Hicks points out $\partial y_t/\partial r = 0$ when the marginal rate of substitution between x_t and the *numéraire* ($\equiv u_t/u_n = y_t$) is independent of money income.

[25] For a discussion of other definitions of complementarity which have been given in the economic literature see Schultz, *op. cit.*, Chap. XVIII.

is zero, then the commodities are independent.[26] It is obvious from the definition that two commodities may be substitutes at one set of prices and income level, and complementary to another. Likewise they may be substitutes for one individual, and complementary for another.

We may list several important properties of the substitution term:

    a.   Complementarity is a symmetric relationship; i.e.,

        Condition 1: $x_{st} = x_{ts}$.

    b.   Since $x_{ss} = \lambda U_{ss}/U$ it must be negative by the stability conditions; i.e.,

        Condition 2: $x_{ss} < 0$.

This means that a *compensated reduction* in the price of a commodity must lead to an increase in the quantity demanded of that commodity. If the commodity is not an inferior good (namely, if $\partial x_s/\partial r > 0$), then the income effect will work in the same direction as the substitution effect, and a reduction in price will lead to an increase in the quantity demanded. If, however, x_s is an inferior good then the income effect will work in the opposite direction from the substitution effect, and a reduction in price may lead to a decrease in the quantity demanded.

    c.   Another important property of the substitution term follows from the stability conditions. There is a well-known theorem in determinants which states that[27]

$$U_{1122\cdots kk} = U^{1-k} \begin{vmatrix} U_{11} & U_{12} & \cdots & U_{1k} \\ U_{21} & U_{22} & \cdots & U_{2k} \\ \cdot & \cdot & \cdot & \cdot \\ U_{k1} & U_{k2} & \cdots & U_{kk} \end{vmatrix}.$$

[26] This definition is that given by Hicks in his Appendix, p. 311, and is at variance with that given by him in the text, p. 44. There he takes the inverse demand functions with quantities as the independent and prices as the dependent variables, and defines complementarity in terms of the effect of a "compensated" reduction in the quantity of one commodity upon the price (in terms of the *numéraire*) of the other. For he writes, "X_s is a substitute for X_t if the marginal rate of substitution of X_s for money is diminished when X_t is substituted for money in such a way as to have the consumer no better off than before"; i.e., if

$$\frac{\partial(u_s/u_n)}{\partial x_t} = \frac{\partial y_s}{\partial x_t} < 0,$$

when the derivative is taken along the given indifference curve. Hicks, of course, uses money here in the sense of the *numéraire*. When there are more than two commodities, there is no reason why $\partial x_t/\partial y_s$ should be of opposite sign to $\partial y_s/\partial x_t$.

[27] Maxime Bôcher, *Introduction to Higher Algebra* (New York: Macmillan Company, 1938), pp. 31–33.

Substituting from this equation into the expressions given previously for the stability conditions, and recalling that $x_{st} = \lambda U_{st}/U$, we obtain the condition that the determinants involving the substitution terms,

$$
x_{11}, \quad \begin{vmatrix} x_{11} & x_{12} \\ x_{21} & x_{22} \end{vmatrix}, \quad \cdots, \quad \begin{vmatrix} x_{11} & x_{12} & \cdots & x_{1,n-1} \\ x_{21} & x_{22} & \cdots & x_{2,n-1} \\ \cdot & \cdot & \cdot & \cdot & \cdot & \cdot & \cdot \\ x_{n-1,1} & x_{n-1,2} & \cdots & x_{(n-1)(n-1)} \end{vmatrix},
$$

shall be alternately negative and positive. This is equivalent to the restriction that the quadratic form in x_{st} shall be negative definite;[28] i.e.,

$$
\text{Condition 3:} \quad \sum_1^{n-1} \sum_1^{n-1} p_s \, p_t \, x_{st} << 0.
$$

The meaning of this condition may be made clear from the following considerations: As we have already seen, the term x_{st} represents the increment in the demand for x_s associated with a compensated change in the price of x_t. The term $p_s x_{st}$ therefore represents the *value of the increment in the demand* for x_s associated with the compensated change in p_t, and the term $p_t p_s x_{st}$ represents the value of the increment in x_s resulting from a compensated *proportionate* change in p_t. If the prices of a group of commodities x_t all change by the same proportion and if the income is adjusted to compensate for these price changes, then the effect of this composite proportionate change on the value of the increment in x_s is given by summing the expression $p_t \, p_s \, x_{st}$ with respect to t, or by $\sum_t p_s \, p_t \, x_{st}$. The effect of this composite proportionate price change on the value of the increments in demand for an entire group of commodities x_s is then given by summing the last expression with respect to s, or by $\sum_s \sum_t p_s \, p_t \, x_{st}$. Thus the term $\sum_{s=1}^{n-1} \sum_{t=1}^{n-1} p_s \, p_t \, x_{st}$ represents the effect of a compensated proportionate change in the prices of $n-1$ commodities on the value of the increments in demand for the whole group taken together. Condition 3 is therefore analogous to Condi-

[28] Identical conditions on the terms $\partial x_s/\partial p_t$ for the case of a consumer (or a producer) who is not limited by any budgetary restrictions were first derived by Harold Hotelling in 1932, *op. cit.*, pp. 590–98. The substitution terms x_{st} have, of course, exactly the same properties as the terms $\partial x_s/\partial p_t$ in the case of an unlimited budget.

Hicks, pp. 310–11, gives the condition that the quadratic form $\sum \sum p_s \, p_t \, x_{st}$ must be negative definite. As we shall show later, however, his discussion of market stability indicates that he somehow overlooked the restrictions which this implies on the signs of the determinants of the substitution terms x_{st}, even though he explicitly stated the conditions on the signs of the corresponding determinants of the terms U_{st}.

tion 2. Just as the value of the increment in the demand for a single commodity associated with a compensated increase in the price for that commodity must be negative, so the values of the increments in the demand for the entire group of $n-1$ commodities associated with the compensated proportionate change in the prices of all of them must also be negative.[29]

d. The other conditions on the substitution terms are especially important in restricting the degree of complementarity which may exist between goods. If we multiply the cofactors of the terms in the sth row of the determinant U by the corresponding terms in the first row and add, we obtain the expression

$$0 \cdot U_s + u_1 U_{s1} + u_2 U_{s2} + \cdots + u_n U_{sn} .$$

This equals zero since it is the expansion of a determinant, two of whose rows are identical. Since $U_{st} = U x_{st}/\lambda$ and $u_s = \lambda p_s$, we have immediately

Condition 4. $\displaystyle\sum_{s=1}^{n} p_s x_{st} = 0.$

Condition 4 states that the value of the increments in demand for the entire group of n commodities associated with a compensated change in the price of one of them is equal to zero.

e. Since $x_{ss} < 0$, it follows further that

Condition 5: $\displaystyle\sum_{s \neq t} p_s x_{st} > 0.$

Condition 5 states that if there is a compensated change in the price of x_t, the value of the increments in the demand for all other commodities taken together must have the same sign as the compensated price change. This constitutes one restriction on the degree of complementarity which may exist between commodities. Even though some x_{st} may be negative, there must be sufficient substitutability in the system so as to satisfy Condition 5. This means, for instance, that

---

[29] It should be noted that the term $p_s x_{st}$ represents *the value of the increment* in x_s associated with the difference in the price of x_t. If $t \neq s$, then the *value of the increment* in x_s is the same as the *increment in the value* of x_s. It $t = s$, however, the two magnitudes are not equal. The difference between the two terms corresponds to the difference between

$$p_s \frac{\partial x_s}{\partial p_t} \quad \text{and} \quad \frac{\partial (p_s x_s)}{\partial p_t}.$$

For $t \neq s$ the two terms are equal. For $t = s$, however, we have

$$\frac{\partial (p_s x_s)}{\partial p_s} = p_s \frac{\partial x_s}{\partial p_s} + x_s.$$

in a two-commodity system the goods must be substitutes, while in a system consisting of three commodities only, at most one pair may be complementary. Indeed if we may anticipate the discussion in Section II, F, below and extend the concept of substitution to groups of commodities, we may then say that any one commodity must be a substitute of all other commodities taken together.

f.   From Conditions 3 and 4 together we obtain a further restriction on the degree of complementarity possible in a system of n commodities. It is:

$$\text{Condition 6:} \quad \sum_{s=1}^{m} \sum_{t=m+1}^{n} p_s\, p_t\, x_{st} > 0 \qquad (m < n).$$

Condition 6 states that when there is an equal proportionate change in the prices of a group of commodities x_1 to x_m that is compensated by a change in income, then the value of the increments in the demand for all other commodities taken together must have the same sign as the compensated price change. Again anticipating our discussion of Section II, F, below, we may say that if the n commodities are divided into any two groups whatsoever, the two groups must be substitutes of each other.

The Conditions 1, 2, and 4 were first given by Slutsky, Condition 3 was added by Hotelling, Condition 5 by Hicks and by Allen, and Condition 6 by Hicks.

E.   The Supply Side

In considering the effect of a variation in p_t we have thus far assumed that the initial quantity x_t of that commodity is zero. A change in p_t therefore leaves the individual's income r unchanged, so that in differentiating the equation (1.2) we put $\partial(\sum p_s\, x_s)/\partial p_t = 0$ [in equation (2.6)]. If, however, the individual comes to the market with a fixed quantity x_t different from zero, then a change in p_t will have an effect on the individual's initial money income. Thus we must no longer treat r as a constant with respect to p_t but as a variable. The only effect this will have upon our system (2.6) is to replace the term $-x_t$ in the first equation by $\overline{x}_t - x_t$. The solution of (2.6) will now be, instead of (2.7b):

$$\frac{\partial x_s}{\partial p_t} = (\overline{x}_t - x_t)\frac{\partial x_s}{\partial r} + x_{st},$$

(2.12)

$$\frac{\partial \lambda}{\partial p_t} = (\overline{x}_t - x_t)\frac{\partial \lambda}{\partial r} - \lambda\frac{\partial x_t}{\partial r}.$$

Similarly, instead of (2.10b) we shall have

(2.13)
$$\frac{\partial w}{\partial p_t} = \lambda \left(\bar{x}_t - x_t \right).$$

It may be well to clear up one point which might puzzle the reader at this stage. In our analysis we have assumed that the individual comes to the market only with a fixed initial collection of goods, $\bar{x}_1, \bar{x}_2, \cdots, \bar{x}_n$, the quantity of at least one of them being different from zero. Under this assumption the money value of the individual's income is dependent upon the prices of the commodities. In this case equations (2.12) and (2.13) are the appropriate ones.

Very frequently, however, economists have assumed that the individual comes to the market not with a fixed initial collection of goods but with a fixed initial money income. They have thus treated r as a constant with respect to every single price. In that case equations (2.7b) and (2.10b) are the appropriate ones. An assumption such as this implies, of course, that the individual obtains his initial income in a manner which is completely independent of the price system under consideration. It is therefore not an appropriate assumption to make, when we wish to study the entire price system including that part of it which determines his income.

The difference between the two approaches stands out very clearly when we consider the effects of a change in the entire price system. If we adopt the first approach then we have from (2.12) and (2.13):

(2.14a)
$$\sum_{t=1}^{n} p_t \frac{\partial x_s}{\partial p_t} = \sum_{t=1}^{n} p_t (\bar{x}_t - x_t) \frac{\partial x_s}{\partial r} + \sum_{t=1}^{n} p_t x_{st},$$

$$\sum_{t=1}^{n} p_t \frac{\partial \lambda}{\partial p_t} = \sum_{t=1}^{n} p_t (\bar{x}_t - x_t) \frac{\partial \lambda}{\partial r} - \lambda \sum_{t=1}^{n} p_t \frac{\partial x_t}{\partial r},$$

$$\sum_{t=1}^{n} p_t \frac{\partial w}{\partial p_t} = \lambda \sum_{t=1}^{n} p_t (\bar{x}_t - x_t).$$

From the budget equation (1.2) the first term on the right-hand side of each of these equations equals zero. From Condition (4) of the substitution terms x_{st}, the second term on the right-hand side of the first equation also equals zero. From the first equation of (2.1) the term $\sum p_t \, \partial x_t / \partial r = 1$. Consequently equations (2.14a) may be rewritten as:

(2.14b)
$$\sum_{t=1}^{n} p_t \frac{\partial x_s}{\partial p_t} = 0,$$

$$\sum_{t=1}^{n} p_t \frac{\partial \lambda}{\partial p_t} = -\lambda,$$

$$\sum_{t=1}^{n} p_t \frac{\partial w}{\partial p_t} = 0.$$

From these equations it follows that the demand for x_s is a homogeneous function of degree zero of all the prices $p_1, p_2, \cdots, p_n$. Likewise the equilibrium utility level w is a homogeneous function of degree zero of the same set of prices. This means that, if all money prices should change in the same proportion, then x_s and w would remain unchanged. This is simply a mathematical statement of the point previously noted that the equilibrium position of any individual is a function of the $n-1$ ratios of the money prices between the commodities and not of the n money prices themselves. The index of marginal utility of money income is, however, a homogeneous function of degree -1.[30] If all money prices should change in the same proportion k, then λ would become λ/k.[31] It should be noted that the second of equations (2.14b) implies that the index λ of marginal utility of money income must be a variable with respect to at least one price.

If we adopt the second approach and assume that the initial money income is fixed, then our budget equation becomes $\sum p_s x_s = r$ where r is a constant with respect to every price. Equations (2.7b) and (2.10b) should then be used. Multiplying by p_t and summing for all t we then have:

$$\sum_{t=1}^{n} p_t \frac{\partial x_s}{\partial p_t} = - \sum_{t=1}^{n} p_t x_t \frac{\partial x_s}{\partial r} + \sum_{t=1}^{n} p_t x_{st} = - r \frac{\partial x_s}{\partial r},$$

$$(2.15) \quad \sum_{t=1}^{n} p_t \frac{\partial \lambda}{\partial p_t} = - \sum_{t=1}^{n} p_t x_t \frac{\partial \lambda}{\partial r} - \lambda \sum_{t=1}^{n} p_t \frac{\partial x_t}{\partial r} = - r \frac{\partial \lambda}{\partial r} - \lambda,$$

$$\sum_{t=1}^{n} p_t \frac{\partial w}{\partial p_t} = - \lambda \sum_{t=1}^{n} p_t x_t = - \lambda r.$$

Here the equilibrium values of x_s and u are again homogeneous functions of degree zero and λ of degree -1, but now the independent variables are the set of prices $p_1, p_2, \cdots, p_n$ and the income r.

With this assumption it is quite possible for the index of marginal utility of money income to be a constant with respect to every price. Indeed in that case we shall have:

---

[30] If $y = f(z_1, z_2, \cdots, z_n)$ is a homogeneous function of degree m, then, for every k, $f(kz_1, kz_2, \cdots, kz_n) = k^m f(z_1, z_2, \cdots, z_n)$. It follows that $\sum_1^n z \, \partial f/\partial z = my$.

[31] This may also be seen by examining the equilibrium equations (1.2) and (1.4). If all prices change in the same proportion, (1.2) and (1.4a) remain unchanged, so that x_s and w are unchanged. Likewise u_s is unchanged, so that λ becomes λ/k.

$$\sum_{t=1}^{n} p_t \frac{\partial \lambda}{\partial p_t} = -r \frac{\partial \lambda}{\partial r} - \lambda = 0 ,$$

or

$$\frac{r}{\lambda} \frac{\partial \lambda}{\partial r} = -1 .$$

Substituting into equation (2.7b) we shall then have:

$$- x_t \frac{\partial \lambda}{\partial r} - \lambda \frac{\partial x_t}{\partial r} = 0 ,$$

and

$$\frac{\partial x_t}{\partial r} \frac{r}{x_t} = 1 .$$

Thus the assumption that money income remains constant when all prices change plus the assumption that marginal utility of money income is a constant with respect to all prices leads to the proposition that the income elasticity must be unity for every commodity.[32]

F.   Effect of a Proportional Variation in the Prices of Several Commodities

One of the most important propositions proved by Hicks is that "if the prices of a group of goods change in the same proportion that group behaves just as if it were a single commodity."[33] The proof is as follows:

The value of the increment in the demand for x_s associated with a proportionate change in p_t is given by:

$$(2.16) \quad p_t \frac{\partial (p_s x_s)}{\partial p_t} = p_t p_s \frac{\partial x_s}{\partial p_t} = - p_t (x_t - \bar{x}_t) \ p_s \frac{\partial x_s}{\partial r} + p_s p_t x_{st} .$$

The term $p_t (x_t - \bar{x}_t)$ is the expenditure on x_t and $p_s \partial x_s / \partial r$ is the increment in the expenditure on x_s associated with a change in income. If the prices of a group of goods $x_1 , x_2 , \cdots , x_m$ change in the same proportion, then the value of the increment in the demand for x_s is given by:

$$(2.17) \quad \sum_{t=1}^{m} p_t p_s \frac{\partial x_s}{\partial p_t} = - \sum_{t=1}^{m} p_t (x_t - \bar{x}_t) \ p_s \frac{\partial x_s}{\partial r} + \sum_{t=1}^{m} p_s p_t x_{st} .$$

The value of the increments in demand for the whole group of goods is then given by:

---

[32] Paul A. Samuelson, "Constancy of Marginal Utility of Income," cited above.
[33] Hicks, p. 312.

$$(2.18) \quad \sum_{t=1}^{m} \sum_{s=1}^{m} p_t p_s \frac{\partial x_s}{\partial p_t} = - \left(\sum_{1}^{m} p_t (x_t - \bar{x}_t) \right) \left(\sum_{1}^{m} p_s \frac{\partial x_s}{\partial r} \right) + \sum_{s=1}^{m} \sum_{t=1}^{m} p_s p_t x_{st}.$$

Equation (2.18) has exactly the same form as (2.16). The first factor in parentheses is the expenditure on the group of goods and the second factor is the increment in the expenditure on the group of goods associated with a change in income. The last term measures the substitution effect of the price change on the group of goods and is negative by the third property of the substitution terms.

It follows from this that a group of goods whose prices change proportionately behaves just as a single commodity. Indeed we may define a commodity as a class of goods whose prices change proportionately. It follows further that if the prices of a group of goods remain unchanged, the entire group may be treated as one commodity.[34]

G.   *The Individual Demand Functions*

Starting with equations (1.2) and (1.4) which determine the equilibrium position of an individual with a given initial collection of commodities $\bar{x}_1, \bar{x}_2, \cdots, \bar{x}_n$ under a given set of prices $p_1, p_2, \cdots, p_n$, we have shown how the equilibrium position varies with variations in each of the parameters. We have thus established the functional relationships between the equilibrium quantities demanded by the individual and the set of parameters. Thus we have derived the set of demand functions:

$$(2.19a) \qquad x_s = f_s (p_1, p_2, \cdots, p_n, \bar{x}_1, \bar{x}_2, \cdots, \bar{x}_n) \qquad (s = 1, 2, \cdots, n).$$

If we confine ourselves to the case where the initial quantities **are** fixed constants, then we may rewrite (2.19a) in the form:

$$(2.19b) \qquad x_s = g_s (p_1, p_2, \cdots, p_n) \qquad (s = 1, 2, \cdots, n).$$

Similarly the equilibrium value of the utility is also a function of these same prices. Designating this equilibrium level as w, we have:

$$(2.20) \qquad w = u [x_1 (p_1, p_2, \cdots, p_n), x_2 (p_1, p_2, \cdots, p_n),$$
$$\cdots, x_n (p_1, p_2, \cdots, p_n)]$$
$$= w (p_1, p_2, \cdots, p_n).$$

---

[34] In combining a group of goods into one commodity the weights to be used are proportional to the prices. Thus if we let x_c be the combined commodity we have:

$$p_c x_c = p_1 x_1 + p_2 x_2 + \cdots + p_m x_m.$$

Likewise the value of the index of the marginal utility λ is a function of the same set of prices:

$$(2.21) \qquad\qquad \lambda = \lambda(p_1, p_2, \cdots, p_n).$$

The partial derivatives of x_s and λ with respect to p_t are given by equations (2.12); the partial derivative of w with respect to p_t is given by (2.13).[35]

As we have already pointed out (II, E, above) the functions x_s and w are homogeneous of degree zero and λ of degree -1, so that they may in fact be written as follows:

$$x_s = x_s\left(\frac{p_1}{p_n}, \frac{p_2}{p_n}, \cdots, \frac{p_{n-1}}{p_n}\right),$$

$$(2.22) \qquad w = w\left(\frac{p_1}{p_n}, \frac{p_2}{p_n}, \cdots, \frac{p_{n-1}}{p_n}\right),$$

$$\lambda = \frac{1}{p_n}\lambda\left(\frac{p_1}{p_n}, \frac{p_2}{p_n}, \cdots, \frac{p_{n-1}}{p_n}\right).$$

It should be noted again that the demand functions (2.19) and (2.22) relate to the gross demand for x_s, namely, to the amount which the individual has in his equilibrim collection. The net demand is of course equal to his gross demand minus his initial supply $(x_s - \overline{x}_s)$ while his net supply equals his initial supply minus his gross demand $(\overline{x}_s - x_s)$. As we have already noted, an increase in the net demand is algebraically equivalent to a decrease in the net supply.

It should also be pointed out that of the n demand functions in (2.19) or (2.22) only $n-1$ are linearly independent. Given the $n-1$ independent demand functions, we immediately obtain from the budgetary restriction the demand function for the nth commodity:

$$x_n = \frac{p_1}{p_n}(\overline{x}_1 - x_1) + \frac{p_2}{p_n}(\overline{x}_2 - x_2) + \cdots + \frac{p_{n-1}}{p_n}(\overline{x}_{n-1} - x_{n-1}) + \overline{x}_n.$$

---

[35] We have assumed here that the individual comes to the market with a fixed initial collection of goods $\overline{x}_1, \overline{x}_2, \cdots, \overline{x}_n$, so that his money income r changes when the prices change. If, however, we had assumed that the individual comes to the market with an income that is unaffected by any price change, then the money income would be an additional independent variable in all our functions. Thus we should have:

$$x_s = x_s(p_1, p_2, \cdots, p_n, r),$$
$$w = w(p_1, p_2, \cdots, p_n, r),$$
$$\lambda = \lambda(p_1, p_2, \cdots, p_n, r).$$

See discussion under Part E of Section II, above.

H.   *The Aggregate Market Demand Functions*

To obtain the aggregate market demand functions we need but sum the demand functions (2.19b) or (2.22) for all individuals. We then obtain:

$$(2.23) \qquad \begin{aligned} X_s &= G_s(p_1, p_2, \cdots, p_n) \qquad\qquad (s=1, 2, \cdots, n) \\ &= X_s(y_1, y_2, \cdots, y_{n-1}), \end{aligned}$$

where $X_s = \sum x_s$ for all individuals, $y_s = p_s/p_n$, and

$$(2.24) \qquad \frac{\partial X_s}{\partial p_t} = \sum \frac{\partial x_s}{\partial p_t} = \sum \left((\bar{x}_t - x_t) \frac{\partial x_s}{\partial r} \right) + \sum x_{st}$$

from (2.12). As with the individual demand functions, only $n-1$ of the aggregate demand functions are linearly independent.

Since x_{st} has the same properties for every individual it follows that $\sum x_{st}$ also has the same properties. Let $X_{st} = \sum x_{st}$. Then we have from the conditions for the individual substitution terms:

Condition 1: $X_{st} = X_{ts}$,

Condition 2: $X_{ss} < 0$,

Condition 3: $\displaystyle\sum_{s=1}^{m} \sum_{t=1}^{m} p_s p_t X_{st} < 0$ $\qquad\qquad$ $(m < n)$,

Condition 4: $\displaystyle\sum_{s=1}^{n} p_s X_{st} = 0$,

Condition 5: $\displaystyle\sum_{s \neq t} p_s X_{st} > 0$,

Condition 6: $\displaystyle\sum_{s=1}^{m} \sum_{t=m+1}^{n} p_s p_t X_{st} > 0$ $\qquad\qquad$ $(m < n)$.

It should be noted that Condition 3 implies that the determinants

$$X_{11}, \quad \begin{vmatrix} X_{11} & X_{12} \\ X_{21} & X_{22} \end{vmatrix}, \cdots, \begin{vmatrix} X_{11} & X_{12} & \cdots & X_{1m} \\ X_{21} & X_{22} & \cdots & X_{2m} \\ \cdot & \cdot & & \cdot \\ X_{m1} & X_{m2} & \cdots & X_{mm} \end{vmatrix},$$

shall be alternately negative and positive. As will be seen later this means that, if we neglect income effects, the market stability conditions must be satisfied if the conditions for the maximization of every individual's utility subject to his budgetary restraint are satisfied. This point seems to have been overlooked by Hicks (Chapter V, especially page 71, and Appendix, pages 316–17).

Following up our definition of complementarity with respect to individuals we may say that two commodities are complements with respect to the market if $X_{st} < 0$ and substitutes if $X_{st} > 0$. This is the definition of true complementarity. We shall also have occasion, however, to make use of a concept of gross complementarity: We may say that X_t is a gross complement of X_s if the total effect $\partial x_s/\partial p_t$ is negative and is a gross substitute if $\partial X_s/\partial p_t$ is positive. It should be noted that this concept is not at all symmetric, since $\partial X_s/\partial p_t$ is not generally equal to $\partial X_t/\partial p_s$. Indeed the two terms may even have opposite signs.

APPENDIX TO CHAPTER I

A NOTE ON T. O. YNTEMA'S DEMAND FUNCTIONS

It may be well at this point to compare our demand functions with those employed by T. O. Yntema.[36]

Yntema writes the demand for each internationally traded commodity as a function of the money price of that commodity deflated by the level of domestic prices. If we assume that all domestic prices change in equal proportion, we may treat the whole group of domestic goods as a single commodity x_n with a price p_n. Then in terms of our formulae, Yntema's demand functions could be written as:

$$(2.25) \quad X_1 = X_1(\frac{p_1}{p_n}), \quad X_2 = X_2(\frac{p_2}{p_n}), \quad \cdots, \quad X_{n-1} = X_{n-1}(\frac{p_{n-1}}{p_n}).$$

This has the following two implications:

1. The quantity demanded of any internationally traded commodity does not change if there is a change in the price of any other internationally traded commodity relative to the domestic price level.[37]

2. The quantity demanded of any internationally traded commodity does not change if there is a change in income that is unaccompanied by any change in prices. Thus it is implied that the income effect $\partial X_s/\partial r$ is zero for every internationally traded commodity. This can be seen from the fact that when Yntema differentiates the net demand functions (equal to total quantity demanded minus total quan-

---

[36] T. O. Yntema, *A Mathematical Reformulation of the General Theory of International Trade* (Chicago: University of Chicago Press, 1932).

[37] In a later chapter Professor Yntema states that his system can be generalized so as to write the demand as a function of all prices, but he does not incorporate this generalization in discussing the laws of the working of his system.

tity supplied) with respect to a change in income (resulting from reparations payment) he writes[38]

$$(2.26) \qquad d(X_1 - \bar{X}_1) = \frac{d(X_1 - \bar{X}_1)}{d(p_1/p_n)} \, d(p_1/p_n) \, .$$

If the income effect is not zero then we should have:

$$(2.27) \qquad d(X_1 - \bar{X}_1) = \frac{\partial(X_1 - \bar{X}_1)}{\partial(p_1/p_n)} \, d(p_1/p_n)$$

$$+ \frac{\partial(X_1 - \bar{X}_1)}{\partial(r/p_n)} \, d(r/p_n) \, .$$

We should arrive at Yntema's system of equations as a special case of our own if we made the following two assumptions:

1.   The index of the marginal utility of money income remains constant with respect to income and with respect to the price of every internationally traded commodity. As we saw in Section II, C, 3, this implies that the income effect for each such commodity is zero.

2.   The utilities of the n goods are independent of one another, so that the utility function can be written in the form:

$$u(x_1, x_2, \cdots, x_n) = f_1(x_1) + f_2(x_2) + \cdots + f_n(x_n).$$

This implies that demand for any internationally traded commodity is a function only of its price in terms of the *numéraire,* and is independent of all other prices.[39]

In Section 4 of Chapter V, Yntema extends his technique of analysis by using a different deflator for each price. Thus he writes:

$$(2.28) \qquad X_1 = X_1 \left(\frac{p_1}{\theta_1} \right), \quad X_2 = X_2 \left(\frac{p_2}{\theta_2} \right), \cdots.$$

This is an attempt to take into account the fact that the demand for any one commodity depends upon other factors besides its own price and the level of domestic prices.

---

[38] See in particular his equation (95) which forms the basis of his equations (98) on page 66. I have taken the liberty of modifying the symbols to conform to mine. It should be noted that Yntema deals with a production rather than an exchange economy, so that the gross supplies are functions rather than constants. This is irrelevant for the point at hand.

[39] Compare Paul A. Samuelson, "Constancy of the Marginal Utility of Income," cited above.

It is well to keep in mind these differences between Yntema's approach and mine, since they account for most of the differences in our conclusions in the static analysis.[40]

[40] Two other differences in our approaches may be noted at this stage:
1.   Yntema begins with the assumption of aggregate demand and supply functions, instead of deriving them from individual utility functions and from transformation or production functions.
2.   Yntema's system of equations does not include the functions for domestic commodities or for productive services.

CHAPTER II

EQUILIBRIUM OF EXCHANGE IN A CLOSED ECONOMY

I. CHARACTERISTICS OF THE EQUILIBRIUM POSITION

A. *The First-Order Conditions*

The equilibrium of exchange for the whole economy requires that the prices shall be such as to equate the total quantity demanded of each commodity to the total quantity supplied. We thus have the n equations

$$(3.1) \qquad X_s = \bar{X}_s \qquad (s = 1, 2, \cdots, n),$$

where $X_s = \sum x_s$ is the total quantity demanded as defined by equation (2.23), and $\bar{X}_s = \sum \bar{x}_s$ is the total quantity supplied—a fixed constant.

Of these equations, however, one follows from the rest. For in determining X_s we have made use of the individual's budgetary equation

$$(1.2) \qquad \sum_1^n p_s x_s = \sum_1^n p_s \bar{x}_s,$$

which when summed for all individuals becomes

$$(3.2) \qquad \sum_1^n p_s X_s = \sum_1^n p_s \bar{X}_s.$$

Since (3.2) must hold regardless of whether (3.1) holds, it follows that if $n-1$ equations are satisfied, the nth must likewise be satisfied.

It would seem, therefore, that we have but $n-1$ independent equations to determine the n prices, $p_1, p_2, \cdots, p_n$. As we have already seen, however, the demand for each commodity is really a function of $n-1$ price ratios y_s, in terms of the *numéraire*:

$$(3.3) \qquad X_s = X_s(y_1, y_2, \cdots, y_{n-1}),$$

where

$$(3.4) \qquad \frac{\partial X_s}{\partial y_t} = p_n \frac{\partial X_s}{\partial p_t}.$$

Thus we have but $n-1$ unknowns—the price ratios y_s—to be determined by the $n-1$ independent equations of (3.1). Our equilibrium system (3.1) therefore reduces to the $(n-1)$-dimensional system

$$(3.5) \qquad X_s(y_1, y_2, \cdots, y_{n-1}) = \overline{X}_s \qquad (s = 1, 2, \cdots, n-1).$$

The equilibrium system then determines only the $n-1$ prices y_s in terms of the *numéraire*. It does not, however, determine the absolute level of the n prices p_s in terms of the token money because it does not determine the value of the *numéraire* in terms of the token money.

How is the value of the *numéraire* in terms of the token money determined? In the traditional theory of money this is determined by a supplementary equation, the so-called "equation of exchange." Assume that there is a fixed quantity of money—a fixed number of counters—in the economy and that each individual is given a sum of money in proportion to the value of his income. Given the quantity of money and the proportion in which money is held against income, it is easy to determine the level of prices in terms of this token money.

Let m be the sum of money held by an individual and K the proportion of m to his income r; and let $M = \sum m$ be the total fixed quantity of money and $R = \sum r$ be the total value of income in the economy. Then we have:

$$(3.6) \qquad m = Kr = K \sum_1^n p_s \overline{x}_s = p_n K \sum_1^n y_s \overline{x}_s \qquad (y_n \equiv 1),$$

and

$$(3.7) \qquad M = KR = K \sum_1^n p_s \overline{X}_s = p_n K \sum_1^n y_s \overline{X}_s.$$

Given M and K, the price p_n and therefore the general level of money prices are uniquely determined; namely

$$(3.8) \qquad p_n = \frac{M}{K \sum_1^n y_s X_s}.$$

The essential difference between the determination of the exchange ratios between the commodities and the determination of the money price of the *numéraire* must be noted at this point. Unlike the price ratios between the commodities, the money price of the *numéraire* is not a variable whose equilibrium level must be determined by the interplay of market forces. The money price of the *numéraire* does not equilibrate the demand and supply for any commodity, since these are equilibrated by the price ratios between the commodities. Nor does it equilibrate the demand and supply for money, since these are assumed to be identical. The money price of the *numéraire* is not a market-determined price at all, but is simply arrived at as a matter of definition of units. Given the quantity of money and the proportion in which money is held against income, the money price of the *numéraire* follows by definition.[1]

It is obvious that in terms of this token money, p_n or the general level of prices is directly proportional to the total quantity of money M, and inversely proportional to the fraction of income K which is held in the form of money. This is the rigorous interpretation of the so-called quantity theory of money. It should be noted that in this form all problems of index numbers are completely avoided.

It should be emphasized, however, that the level of money prices is directly proportional to the quantity of money, only when our money is simply a token with no direct utility of its own so that the quantity of it demanded is identically equal to the quantity supplied for each individual. Each individual spends all his money on commodities which have utility, but gets it back in exchange for the collection of goods which he brings to the market for trade. The existence of such a money can have no effect upon the equilibrium quantities bought and sold or on the price ratios y_s at which they are exchanged. Doubling such money will simply double all prices and leave the price ratios unaffected. If, however, we drop this token money and take as our money the Walrasian *numéraire*, a commodity which has direct utility just as every other commodity, it is clear from the equilibrium equations that the level of prices in terms of the *numéraire* will not be proportional to the quantity of the *numéraire*. In other words, if $\bar{X}_n$, the supply of the *numéraire*, were to double there is no reason why y_1, y_2, $\cdots$, y_{n-1} should necessarily double.

---

[1] This discussion should be compared with that of Oscar Lange in "Say's Law," *op. cit.*, especially p. 65. Lange writes that the equation of exchange is "an identity, which holds for *any* value of p_n and, therefore, cannot serve to determine p_n. But k cannot be constant and must be indeterminate to adjust itself to any value of p_n so that the identity be satisfied."

I agree, of course, that the equation of exchange is an identity, and that it could not determine the value of p_n if the money price had any "degree of freedom," i.e., if it were a variable whose value depended upon the market demand and supply conditions for any commodity or for money. My discussion differs from Lange's only in treating the equation of exchange as serving to *define* p_n. By definition then, p_n cannot take on any value except that which is assigned to it in the equation.

I admit, of course, that this is a purely artificial method of determining the money level of prices. This artificiality is inherent in the whole "neutral money" approach. I restate it here only to show to what extent the traditional theory of money can be made consistent with the general-equilibrium theory for the determination of relative prices.

B. *The Stability of the Equilibrium*

The system (3.5) provides us with a set of $n-1$ independent equations to determine the $n-1$ price ratios y_s under a given set of conditions. The given set of conditions includes:

(1)   the preference function for each individual, and

(2)   the initial collection of goods for each individual. A change in these givens will change the system (3.5) and give rise to a new set of equilibrium price ratios. What we need, therefore, is a technique whereby we may determine the nature of the changes in the price ratios resulting from a change in the given conditions.

It is impossible to deduce the direction of change of an equilibrium position without specifying the properties of any given equilibrium position under given conditions. We have already seen an example of this in deducing the laws of the individual consumer's demand from our knowledge of the properties of the individual's equilibrium position. We can deduce similar laws for the working of the market exchange equilibrium only by specifying the properties of any given equilibrium position. These properties are known as the stability conditions.

The importance of the stability conditions cannot be overemphasized. If we wish to examine the effects of a change in the given conditions upon the equilibrium position, it is obviously not enough simply to know that in both the old and the new positions the quantity demanded must equal the quantity supplied. We must know in addition what would happen to the quantity demanded and the quantity supplied should an accidental displacement from the equilibrium position occur. Once we know this, then we can investigate the laws of change.

The simplest illustration of this sort is to be found in the equilibrium analysis of a one-commodity market. The stability condition that is usually assumed for such a market is that a rise in price should decrease the quantity demanded and increase the quantity supplied. From this it follows that a change in the given conditions such as an increase in the demand function will lead to a rise in price. Our problem is to specify similar stability conditions in a general exchange economy.

Hotelling was, I believe, the first to specify the exact stability conditions for an economy in which income effects can be entirely neglected.[2] Hicks extended this work to include the field in which income effects must be taken into account.[3]

---

[2] Hotelling, *op. cit.*, pp. 590–98 and 600–601.

The stability conditions as postulated by Hicks are as follows:
Define the "excess demand" for any commodity as the difference between the total quantity demanded and the total quantity supplied. In equilibrium, then, the excess demand for each commodity must be equal to zero. In a one-commodity market, stability would require that a reduction in the price of that commodity should lead to an increase in the excess demand for that commodity. The rise in the excess demand would then tend to restore the price to its equilibrium level. In laying down stability conditions in a multiple-exchange market, however, we must take into account the repercussions that a fall in one price will have upon the excess demand and therefore upon the prices for the other commodities.

In our system (3.5) the unknowns to be determined in equilibrium are the $n-1$ price ratios. To determine the stability conditions we must therefore consider the effects of a change in a price ratio upon the system (3.5). The conditions of stability of a multiple-exchange equilibrium given by Hicks are these:

1.   A system will be said to be perfectly stable if a reduction in y leads to an increased excess demand for X under all of the following conditions:

(a)   when all other price ratios remain constant;

(b)   when only one other price ratio is adjusted so as to maintain equilibrium in the market for that commodity;

(c)   when only two other price ratios are so adjusted;
and so on, until we have adjusted all other price ratios.

2.   A system is said to be imperfectly stable if a reduction in y leads to an increased excess demand for X only when all other price ratios are adjusted so as to maintain equilibrium in those markets.

Without loss of generality, let us consider the stability conditions with respect to a change in y_1. The mathematical condition for imperfect stability is given by the system:

(4.1)
$$\frac{d(X_1 - \bar{X}_1)}{dy_1} = \frac{dX_1}{dy_1} = \sum_{t=1}^{n-1} \frac{\partial X_1}{\partial y_t} \frac{dy_t}{dy_1} < 0,$$

$$\frac{d(X_s - \bar{X}_s)}{dy_1} = \frac{dX_s}{dy_1} = \sum_{t=1}^{n-1} \frac{\partial X_s}{\partial y_t} \frac{dy_t}{dy_1} = 0$$

$$(s = 2, 3, \cdots, n-1).$$

---

[3] Hicks. *op. cit.*, Chap. V and Appendix, pp. 315 ff. The dynamic implications of the stability conditions have been developed by Paul A. Samuelson in "The Stability of Equilibrium: Comparative Statics and Dynamics," *Econometrica*, Vol. 9, April, 1941, pp. 97–120, and extended by Oscar Lange in a paper on "The Stability of Economic Equilibrium," read before the Econometric Society at its meeting in New York. December 28, 1941 (abstract in *Econometrica*, Vol. 10, April, 1942, pp. 176–177).

Let

(4.2)
$$a_{st} = \frac{\partial X_s}{\partial y_t} = p_n \frac{\partial X_s}{\partial p_t} \qquad (s, t = 1, 2, \cdots, n-1).$$

Further, let

(4.3)
$$J = \begin{vmatrix} a_{11} & a_{12} & \cdots & a_{1,\,n-1} \\ a_{21} & a_{22} & \cdots & a_{2,\,n-1} \\ \cdot & \cdot & \cdots & \cdot \\ a_{n-1,\,1} & a_{n-1,\,2} & \cdots & a_{n-1,\,n-1} \end{vmatrix},$$

and let J_{st} be the cofactor of a_{st} in J. Then from (4.1) it follows that

(4.4)
$$\frac{dX_1}{dp_1} = \frac{J}{J_{11}} < 0.$$

If the market is to be perfectly stable then dX_1/dy_1 must be negative regardless of whether the other price ratios remain constant or are adjusted so as to maintain equilibrium in those markets. For each additional price that is kept constant we have one less unknown and one less equation to set equal to zero in (4.1). Solving for every such system we obtain as the conditions of perfect stability that the determinants

(4.5)
$$a_{11}, \quad \begin{vmatrix} a_{11} & a_{12} \\ a_{21} & a_{22} \end{vmatrix}, \cdots, \quad \begin{vmatrix} a_{11} & a_{12} & \cdots & a_{1,\,n-1} \\ a_{21} & a_{22} & \cdots & a_{2,\,n-1} \\ \cdot & \cdot & \cdots & \cdot \\ a_{n-1,\,1} & a_{n-1,\,2} & \cdots & a_{n-1,\,n-1} \end{vmatrix}$$

shall be alternatively negative and positive. (Similar conditions must obviously hold with respect to accidental displacements in every other price ratio.)

Now a_{st} represents the total effect, or the sum of the income and the substitution effects of y_t upon X_s:

(4.6)
$$a_{st} = p_n \frac{\partial X_s}{\partial p_t} = p_n \sum \left[(\bar{x}_t - x_t) \frac{\partial x_s}{\partial r} \right] + p_n X_{st},$$

where the summation is taken with respect to all individuals. If the market income effects were all zero, then, except for a factor p_n, the determinants (4.5) would become

(4.7)
$$X_{11}, \quad \begin{vmatrix} X_{11} & X_{12} \\ X_{21} & X_{22} \end{vmatrix}, \cdots, \quad \begin{vmatrix} X_{11} & X_{12} & \cdots & X_{1,\,n-1} \\ X_{21} & X_{22} & \cdots & X_{2,\,n-1} \\ \cdot & \cdot & \cdots & \cdot \\ X_{n-1,\,1} & X_{n-1,\,2} & \cdots & X_{n-1,\,n-1} \end{vmatrix}.$$

These determinants, as we have already shown, are alternatively negative and positive by virtue of Condition (3) of the substitution terms. It follows, therefore, that if we neglect income effects, the multiple-exchange equilibrium must be perfectly stable. Stability can be destroyed only if the market income effects are sufficiently large to overcome the relationships which prevail between the substitution terms. It cannot be destroyed by any possible degree of complementarity. This point, as we have already indicated, was overlooked by Hicks who argued that the system might be rendered unstable by a sufficiently great degree of complementarity.[4]

The net income effect of y_t on X_s is given by $p_n \sum (\overline{x_t} - x_t) \partial x_s / \partial r$. If the rate of change of consumption with respect to income is the same for all individuals then this net income effect will be zero. In order that the net income effect should be at all large, $\partial x_s / \partial r$ must be considerably different for buyers of x_s from what it is for sellers. It is not too unreasonable to assume therefore that ordinarily the income effects will not be so large as to render the system unstable.

II. The Laws of the Working of the Equilibrium System

A. Effect of Change in Demand for One Commodity Only

From the stability conditions we can now proceed to deduce laws of change for the market-equilibrium system. In order to simplify the analysis let us assume that there is a change in the initially given conditions such as to increase the excess demand for only one commodity, the excess demand for every other commodity in the equilibrium system (3.5) remaining equal to zero. When once we have studied the effects of an increase in the demand for one commodity we may readily pass on to the case of a shift in the demands for several commodities. It is rather difficult to give a satisfactory example of such a change, since an alteration in the individual preference functions will in general lead to a change in the demand for every commodity in the system (3.5).

---

[4] See the following statements by Hicks:

"If income effects can be neglected, and if no complementarity is present, then the system of exchange equilibrium must be stable. In itself, this is not a very satisfactory result; for whatever may be the case with net income effects, complementarity, we know, does exist, and is likely to be present in any system of exchange with which we are likely to be concerned. It is therefore reassuring to observe that only very extreme degrees of complementarity are at all likely to produce instability." (P. 71.)

"It is evident that this condition [4.7] must be satisfied, even if all three pairs are substitutes; and it will still be satisfied, even if some complementarity is present, provided the amount of complementarity is not very great." (P. 317.)

We may suppose, however, as does Hicks,

. . . that a small number of the persons trading experience a certain change in their preferences. The most convenient change to take . . . is an increased desire for some particular commodity, which they are prepared to satisfy by increasing their [net] supply or diminishing their [net] demand for the standard commodity [*numéraire*], their demand and supplies for all other commodities being unaffected. (P. 73.)

Two points should be emphasized in the study of a case such as this. It is assumed that the demand function for only one commodity changes in terms of the *numéraire, the demand functions for all other commodities—complements and substitutes alike—remaining absolutely unchanged.*   Thus it is assumed, for instance, that *at given prices* the amount of tea demanded increases, but the amount of sugar and the amount of coffee demanded both remain unchanged. Secondly, it is assumed that the change in tastes is experienced by only a small group of persons trading, those of all other persons remaining unchanged. When this occurs, "the same relations of substitution and complementarity as before persist for all the rest of the market," and for practical purposes we may say that the same relations persist for the market as a whole. This point is of special importance, for, as Hicks points out:

It is the persistence of unchanged scales of preference for the rest of the market which enables us to deduce the economic laws from the properties—the unchanged properties—of these scales of preference.[5]

This is, of course, a very restrictive assumption, but it appears useful to consider the effects of a shift in only one of the functions in (3.5) before investigating the effects of a shift in several of them.

What changes in prices will result from such a change in demand? In the words of Hicks:

The change in prices must be such as to produce an excess supply, from other persons trading, sufficient to satisfy the increased demand from the first group. Now the stability conditions have already told us what changes in prices will lead to an excess supply in the market for X, while other markets remain, as they should, in equilibrium. The stability conditions thus enable us to say what will be the effect of such an increase in demand.

First of all, the price of X itself must be raised. This follows even if all secondary reactions through other markets are allowed for. The system can only be stable at all (even imperfectly stable) if a rise in the price of X (all secondary reactions considered) makes the supply of X greater than the demand. (P. 73.)

What about the effect on other prices? If the market for only one

[5] J. R. Hicks, "A Comment," *Review of Economic Studies*, Vol. 8, No. 1 (October, 1940), pp. 64–65. See also Oscar Lange, "Complementarity and Interrelations of Shifts in Demand," *ibid.*, pp. 58–63.

other commodity were affected we could easily determine the effect
on the price from the stability conditions. Thus suppose that there is
an increase in the demand for X_s (in terms of the *numéraire* X_n).
Then y_s must rise. If only one other price y_t were affected, we should
have from the stability conditions (4.1)

$$0 = \frac{\partial X_t}{\partial y_s} + \frac{\partial X_t}{\partial y_t} \frac{dy_t}{dy_s}$$

or

$$\frac{dy_t}{dy_s} = -\frac{\partial X_t}{\partial y_s} \bigg/ \frac{\partial X_t}{\partial y_t}.$$

Now $\partial X_t/\partial y_t$ is negative from the stability conditions and $\partial X_t/\partial y_s$
will, if we neglect income effects, be positive or negative according as
X_s and X_t are substitutes or complementary goods. Neglecting income effects, therefore, the price of X_t will rise if X_t and X_s are substitutes and will fall if they are complementary.

If more than one other price is affected then we have to take into
account the various indirect effects between the markets. If X_r and X_t
are substitutes for X_s their prices will both tend to rise, but if X_t is
complementary to X_r, the indirect effect of X_s on X_r through X_t will
be in the direction of a price fall. On the other hand, if X_r is complementary to X_s its price will tend to fall, but if it is a substitute for X_t
the indirect effect through X_t will be in the direction of a rise in price.
If both X_r and X_t are complementary to X_s their prices will tend to
fall, but if X_r is complementary to X_t the indirect effect will be a rise
in price. In the words of Hicks:

> Indirect effects through third markets thus obey the rule that an increased
> demand for X will raise the prices of those goods which are substitutes of sub-
> stitutes, or complements of complements, for X; it will lower the prices of those
> goods which are complements of substitutes, or substitutes of complements. (P.
> 74.)

Since the direct and indirect effects may work in opposite directions it follows that the total effect is not restricted with respect to
sign. A substitute for X which is a substitute only for its substitutes and a complement only to its complements will be affected in
the same direction as X. A complement of X which is a complement
only to its substitutes and a substitute only for its complements will
move in the opposite direction from X. If there were no complementarity at all throughout the entire system, then a rise in the demand for
X would increase not only the price of X but the prices of all other
commodities as well.

Income effects may, of course, complicate the matter, but we shall assume throughout that they are not sufficiently large to offset the relationships of substitution and complementarity. In other words, we shall assume that the total effect of a price change upon the demand for any commodity is in the same direction as the substitution effect; namely, that a_{st} has the same sign as X_{st}. This means that if two goods are true substitutes (as determined by the sign of X_{st}) they are also gross substitutes (as determined by the sign of a_{st}). It should be recalled, however, that while the true relationships of substitution and complementarity are symmetric ($X_{st} = X_{ts}$) the gross relationships are not ($a_{st} \neq a_{ts}$).

Hicks's treatment of the laws of the working of the equilibrium system may be considerably simplified by a mathematical restatement. Let α be the parameter with respect to which the demand for X_s increases. Then upon differentiating the equilibrium system (3.5) totally with respect to α and letting $\partial X_i / \partial y_j = a_{ij}$ (as before), we obtain

$$a_{11}\frac{dy_1}{d\alpha} + a_{12}\frac{dy_2}{d\alpha} + \cdots + a_{1,\,n-1}\frac{dy_{n-1}}{d\alpha} = 0,$$

$$\cdot \quad \cdot \quad \cdot \quad \cdot \quad \cdot \quad \cdot \quad \cdot \quad \cdot \quad \cdot \quad \cdot \quad \cdot \quad \cdot$$

$$(4.8) \qquad a_{s1}\frac{dy_1}{d\alpha} + a_{s2}\frac{dy_2}{d\alpha} + \cdots + a_{s,\,n-1}\frac{dy_{n-1}}{d\alpha} = -\frac{\partial X_s}{\partial \alpha},$$

$$\cdot \quad \cdot \quad \cdot \quad \cdot \quad \cdot \quad \cdot \quad \cdot \quad \cdot \quad \cdot \quad \cdot \quad \cdot \quad \cdot$$

$$a_{n-1,\,1}\frac{dy_1}{d\alpha} + a_{n-1,\,2}\frac{dy_2}{d\alpha} + \cdots + a_{n-1,\,n-1}\frac{dy_{n-1}}{d\alpha} = 0.$$

The determinant of this system is given by J in equation (4.3). In terms of this determinant and the cofactors J_{st} the solution of (4.8) is

$$(4.9) \qquad \frac{dy_t}{d\alpha} = -\frac{\partial X_s}{\partial \alpha}\frac{J_{st}}{J} \qquad\qquad (t = 1, 2, \cdots, n-1).$$

From the stability condition for market equilibrium J_{ss}/J is negative. Consequently y_s will increase if X_s increases. The changes in the other price ratios are not restricted in sign. If, however, all commodities are substitutes and the income effects are not sufficiently large to offset the substitution relationships, so that every a_{st} ($s \neq t$) is positive, then every J_{st}/J will be negative[6] and all price ratios will rise as a result of the increase in the demand for X_s.

The meaning of (4.9) may be made clear from the following considerations. We have written the $n-1$ independent demand functions in the form

[6] For proof see the Appendix to this chapter.

(3.3) $X_s = X_s(y_1, y_2, \cdots, y_{n-1})$ $(s = 1, 2, \cdots, n-1).$

These equations may be inverted and written in the form

(4.10) $y_s = y_s(X_1, X_2, \cdots, X_{n-1})$ $(s = 1, 2, \cdots, n-1),$

showing the $n-1$ price ratios as functions of the $(n-1)$ independent quantities demanded. For these equations it can easily be shown[7] that

(4.11) $$\frac{\partial y_t}{\partial X_s} = \frac{J_{st}}{J}.$$

Consequently we have

(4.12) $$\frac{dy_t}{d\alpha} = -\frac{\partial X_s}{\partial \alpha} \frac{\partial y_t}{\partial X_s}.$$

We have already defined gross complementarity between X_s and X_t in terms of the sign of $a_{st} = \partial X_s / \partial y_t$. Let us call that gross complementarity in the direct sense. We may similarly define the concept of gross complementarity in the inverse sense. We may say that X_s is a gross complement of X_t in the inverse sense if a rise in the quantity of X_s leads to an increase in the demand-price for X_t $(\partial y_t / \partial X_s > 0)$ and is a gross substitute in the inverse sense if it leads to a lower demand price for X_t $(\partial y_t / \partial X_s < 0)$. Then equation (4.12) tells us that an increase in the demand for X_s will lead to a rise or fall in y_t according as X_s is a gross substitute or gross complement of X_t in the inverse sense.

Two points need special emphasis. (1) The concept of gross com-

[7] The proof is simple. Differentiate the system (3.3) with respect to X_t. Letting $\partial X_s / \partial y_t = a_{st}$ as before, we have:

$$a_{11}\frac{\partial y_1}{\partial X_t} + \quad a_{12}\frac{\partial y_2}{\partial X_t} + \cdots + a_{1,n-1}\frac{\partial y_{n-1}}{\partial X_t} = 0,$$

$$a_{21}\frac{\partial y_1}{\partial X_t} + \quad a_{22}\frac{\partial y_2}{\partial X_t} + \cdots + a_{2,n-1}\frac{\partial y_{n-1}}{\partial X_t} = 0,$$

$$\cdots \cdots \cdots \cdots$$

$$a_{t1}\frac{\partial y_1}{\partial X_t} + \quad a_{t2}\frac{\partial y_2}{\partial X_t} + \cdots + a_{t,n-1}\frac{\partial y_{n-1}}{\partial X_t} = 1,$$

$$\cdots \cdots \cdots \cdots$$

$$a_{n-1,1}\frac{\partial y_1}{\partial X_t} + a_{n-1,2}\frac{\partial y_2}{\partial X_t} + \cdots + a_{n-1,n-1}\frac{\partial y_{n-1}}{\partial X_t} = 0.$$

The determinant of this system is given by J in equation (4.3). The solution is therefore

$$\frac{\partial y_s}{\partial X_t} = \frac{J_{ts}}{J}.$$

Note that since $a_{ts} \neq a_{st}$ we have $J_{ts} \neq J_{st}$.

plementarity in the inverse sense is not symmetric: $\partial y_t/\partial X_s \neq \partial y_s/\partial X_t$.
(2) Two goods may be substitutes in the inverse sense and comple-
ments in the direct sense, and conversely.[8]

B. Effect of Change in Demands for Several Commodities

The effect of a change in the demands for several commodities is
simply the combined effect of the change in demand for each commodity.

If the gross demands for two commodities X_s and X_t both rise
(namely, if the net demands increase, or the net supplies decrease)
then the direct effects of the change will be a rise in the prices of both
commodities. If the two commodities are gross substitutes (in the
inverse sense) then the indirect effect will work in the same direction
as the direct effect. If, however, the two commodities are gross complements (in the inverse sense) then the indirect effect will work in
the opposite direction from the direct effect. In that case it is possible
for one price, but not for both, to fall.

If the demand for X_s rises and that for X_t falls, then the direct
effect will be for y_s to rise and y_t to fall. If the two goods are gross
complements in the inverse sense then the indirect effect will work in
the same direction as the direct effect. If, however, the two goods are
gross substitutes in the inverse sense, then the indirect effect will
work in the opposite direction from the direct effect, and it will be
possible for both prices to rise or both to fall.[9]

[8] It is only in the case of a two-commodity system that complements (substitutes) in the direct sense are necessarily complements (substitutes) in the inverse sense.
[9] The proof of these statements is simple. If the demand for X_s and X_t
changes, then in the tth equation of (4.8) we shall have a term $-\partial X_t/\partial \alpha$ on the
right-hand side. The solution will then be given by

(1)
$$\frac{dy_s}{d\alpha} = -\frac{\partial X_s}{\partial \alpha}\frac{J_{ss}}{J} - \frac{\partial X_t}{\partial \alpha}\frac{J_{ts}}{J} = -\frac{\partial X_s}{\partial \alpha}\frac{\partial y_s}{\partial X_s} - \frac{\partial X_t}{\partial \alpha}\frac{\partial y_s}{\partial X_t},$$

$$\frac{dy_t}{d\alpha} = -\frac{\partial X_s}{\partial \alpha}\frac{J_{st}}{J} - \frac{\partial X_t}{\partial \alpha}\frac{J_{tt}}{J} = -\frac{\partial X_s}{\partial \alpha}\frac{\partial y_t}{\partial X_s} - \frac{\partial X_t}{\partial \alpha}\frac{\partial y_t}{\partial X_t}.$$

From the market stability conditions we have

(2)
$$\frac{J_{ss}}{J} = \frac{\partial y_s}{\partial X_s} < 0, \quad \frac{J_{tt}}{J} = \frac{\partial y_t}{\partial X_t} < 0,$$

(3)
$$\frac{J_{sstt}}{J} = \frac{J_{ss}J_{tt} - J_{st}J_{ts}}{J^2} = \frac{\partial y_s}{\partial X_s}\frac{\partial y_t}{\partial X_t} - \frac{\partial y_s}{\partial X_t}\frac{\partial y_t}{\partial X_s} > 0.$$

a. If the demands for both X_s and X_t rise, then $\partial X_s/\partial \alpha > 0$ and $\partial X_t/\partial \alpha > 0$.
We have then the following possibilities:

Using this approach we may obtain a very simple explanation of Edgeworth's Taxation Paradox. If a tax is levied on the sale of X_s the direct effect is to lower the net supply function for X_s and to increase the net supply function for a substitute X_t. The direct effect of this change is therefore to raise the price of X_s and to lower the price of X_t. The indirect effect, however, is to lower the price of X_s and to raise the price of X_t. It is therefore possible for both prices to fall.[10]

In the general case where the demands for all of the $n-1$ commodities change, the solution is given by

(4.13)
$$\frac{dy_t}{d\alpha} = -\frac{\partial X_1}{\partial \alpha}\frac{J_{1t}}{J} - \frac{\partial X_2}{\partial \alpha}\frac{J_{2t}}{J} - \cdots - \frac{\partial X_{n-1}}{\partial \alpha}\frac{J_{n-1,t}}{J}$$
$$= -\frac{\partial X_1}{\partial \alpha}\frac{\partial y_t}{\partial X_1} - \frac{\partial X_2}{\partial \alpha}\frac{\partial y_t}{\partial X_2} - \cdots - \frac{\partial X_{n-1}}{\partial \alpha}\frac{\partial y_t}{\partial X_{n-1}}.$$

[10] The proof that Edgeworth's Taxation Paradox was valid even for the case of pure competition was first given by Hotelling, *op. cit.*

---

(1) If the goods are gross substitutes in the inverse sense, then
$$\frac{\partial y_s}{\partial X_t} < 0, \quad \frac{\partial y_t}{\partial X_s} < 0; \quad \text{therefore } \frac{dy_s}{d\alpha} > 0 \text{ and } \frac{dy_t}{d\alpha} > 0.$$

(2) If the goods are gross complements in the inverse sense, then
$$\frac{\partial y_s}{\partial X_t} > 0, \quad \frac{\partial y_t}{\partial X_s} > 0;$$

and we have the following possibilities:

(a) In the normal case both
$$\frac{dy_s}{d\alpha} > 0 \text{ and } \frac{dy_t}{d\alpha} > 0.$$

We may have, however:

(b) $\dfrac{dy_s}{d\alpha} < 0$ and $\dfrac{dy_t}{d\alpha} > 0$ if $\dfrac{\partial X_t}{\partial \alpha}\dfrac{\partial y_s}{\partial X_t} > \left|\dfrac{\partial X_s}{\partial \alpha}\dfrac{\partial y_s}{\partial X_s}\right|$,

or

(c) $\dfrac{dy_t}{d\alpha} < 0$ and $\dfrac{dy_s}{d\alpha} > 0$ if $\left|\dfrac{\partial X_t}{\partial \alpha}\dfrac{\partial y_t}{\partial X_t}\right| < \dfrac{\partial X_s}{\partial \alpha}\dfrac{\partial y_t}{\partial X_s}$.

The case of both $dy_s/d\alpha < 0$ and $dy_t/d\alpha < 0$ is excluded by the stability conditions given above.

b. If the demand for X_s rises and that for X_t falls, then
$$\frac{\partial X_s}{\partial \alpha} > 0 \text{ and } \frac{\partial X_t}{\partial \alpha} < 0.$$

We then have the following possibilities:

The effects of an alteration in the total quantities of the initial supplies of the various commodities or in their distribution may easily be investigated by means of the same technique. For if the initial supplies $\bar{X}_s$ change, this means that there will be some change in the aggregate market demand functions of the system (3.5). The changes in the price ratios must then be such as to equate the quantity demanded and the quantity supplied for each commodity. We shall study such a problem in detail in the next chapter.

APPENDIX TO CHAPTER II

A THEOREM IN DETERMINANTS

In the text we showed that if all commodities are gross substitutes for one another, then all prices will rise whenever the demand for one of them rises. Since the price change resulting from the change in demand is given by

$$\frac{dy_t}{d\alpha} = -\frac{\partial X_s}{\partial \alpha} \frac{J_{st}}{J},$$

every J_{st}/J must be negative if every a_{st} is positive for $s \neq t$. (By assumption every a_{tt} is negative.)

(1) If the goods are gross complements in the inverse sense, then
$$\frac{\partial y_s}{\partial X_t} > 0, \quad \frac{\partial y_t}{\partial X_s} > 0; \quad \text{therefore } \frac{dy_s}{d\alpha} > 0 \text{ and } \frac{dy_t}{d\alpha} < 0.$$

(2) If the goods are gross substitutes in the inverse sense, then
$$\frac{\partial y_s}{\partial X_t} < 0, \quad \frac{\partial y_t}{\partial X_s} < 0;$$

and we have the following possibilities:

In the normal case

(a) $\dfrac{dy_s}{d\alpha} > 0$ and $\dfrac{dy_t}{d\alpha} < 0.$

We may have, however,

(b) $\dfrac{dy_s}{d\alpha} > 0$ and $\dfrac{dy_t}{d\alpha} > 0$ if $\left| \dfrac{\partial X_s}{\partial \alpha} \dfrac{\partial y_t}{\partial X_s} \right| > \left| \dfrac{\partial X_t}{\partial \alpha} \dfrac{\partial y_t}{\partial X_t} \right|$,

or

(c) $\dfrac{dy_s}{d\alpha} < 0$ and $\dfrac{dy_t}{d\alpha} < 0$ if $\left| \dfrac{\partial X_s}{\partial \alpha} \dfrac{\partial y_s}{\partial X_s} \right| < \left| \dfrac{\partial X_t}{\partial \alpha} \dfrac{\partial y_s}{\partial X_t} \right|$.

The case $dy_s/d\alpha < 0$ and $dy_t/d\alpha > 0$ is excluded by the stability conditions given above.

It should again be pointed out that in a two-commodity system gross complements (or substitutes) in the inverse sense are also gross complements (or substitutes) in the direct sense.

The mathematical proof may be obtained by induction. We first show that if the theorem holds for a determinant of rank $n-1$ it will hold for one of rank n. We then show that the theorem holds for a determinant of the lowest rank possible and the proof is complete.

Let

$$
J = \begin{vmatrix}
a_{11} & a_{12} & \cdots & a_{1i} & \cdots & a_{1j} & \cdots & a_{1n} \\
a_{21} & a_{22} & \cdots & a_{2i} & \cdots & a_{2j} & \cdots & a_{2n} \\
\cdot & \cdot & \cdot & \cdot & \cdot & \cdot & \cdot & \cdot \\
a_{i1} & a_{i2} & \cdots & a_{ii} & \cdots & a_{ij} & \cdots & a_{in} \\
\cdot & \cdot & \cdot & \cdot & \cdot & \cdot & \cdot & \cdot \\
a_{j1} & a_{j2} & \cdots & a_{ji} & \cdots & a_{jj} & \cdots & a_{jn} \\
\cdot & \cdot & \cdot & \cdot & \cdot & \cdot & \cdot & \cdot \\
a_{n1} & a_{n2} & \cdots & a_{ni} & \cdots & a_{nj} & \cdots & a_{nn}
\end{vmatrix}.
$$

Let J_{ss} be the cofactor of a_{ss} in J and let J_{sskt} be the cofactor of a_{kt} in J_{ss}. Then by assumption we have:

(1) $a_{ss} < 0$ $(s = 1, 2, \cdots, n)$,

(2) $a_{st} > 0$ $(s \neq t)$,

(3) $\dfrac{J_{ss}}{J} < 0.$

Suppose now that our theorem holds for a system in which the sth commodity is omitted, so that

(4) $\dfrac{J_{sskt}}{J_{ss}} < 0$ $(k \text{ and } t \neq s).$

From (3) and (4) it would then follow that

(5) $J_{sskt}/J > 0.$

Now expand the cofactor J_{st} of the term a_{st} in terms of the elements of the sth column, and divide through by J. Then we have:

(6) $\dfrac{J_{st}}{J} = a_{1s} \dfrac{J_{st,1s}}{J} + a_{2s} \dfrac{J_{st,2s}}{J} + \cdots + a_{s-1,s} \dfrac{J_{st,(s-1)s}}{J}$

$$
+ a_{s+1,s} \dfrac{J_{st,(s+1)s}}{J} + \cdots + a_{ns} \dfrac{J_{st,ns}}{J}.
$$

Now we know that[11]

---

[11] Maxime Bôcher, *Introduction to Higher Algebra* (New York, 1938), p. 33

(7) $J_{st,ks} = \dfrac{J_{st} J_{ks} - J_{ss} J_{kt}}{J} = - J_{ss,kt}.$

Substituting into (6) and making use of conditions (2) and (5), we find that

(8) $\dfrac{J_{st}}{J} < 0.$

Thus, if the theorem holds for a system containing only $n-1$ commodities, it holds also for one with n commodities.

It is sufficient now to show that condition (4) holds for a determinant J of the lowest rank.

For $n = 3$ we have:

$$J = \begin{vmatrix} a_{ss} & a_{st} & a_{sk} \\ a_{ts} & a_{tt} & a_{tk} \\ a_{ks} & a_{kt} & a_{kk} \end{vmatrix} < 0,$$

$$J_{ss} = \begin{vmatrix} a_{tt} & a_{tk} \\ a_{kt} & a_{kk} \end{vmatrix} > 0,$$

$$J_{ss,kt} = - a_{tk} \qquad < 0,$$

Consequently $J_{ss,kt} / J_{ss} < 0$ and the proof is complete.

CHAPTER III

EQUILIBRIUM OF EXCHANGE IN AN INTERNATIONAL ECONOMY

In the preceding chapter we presented the basic properties of a general-equilibrium system for a closed exchange economy. It should now be a relatively simple matter to extend this theory of exchange to the case of trade between several countries. The analysis in this chapter will proceed in several stages. In the first section we shall deal with the problem of international exchange upon the assumption that there are no unilateral payments such as indemnities, gifts, et cetera, and that there are no cost barriers to international trade such as transportation costs, tariffs, and the like. In the succeeding sections we shall modify our system to take into account unilateral payments and to show the effects of changes in such payments. In a final section we shall consider the effects of "impediments" to international trade.

I. INTERNATIONAL EXCHANGE IN THE ABSENCE OF UNILATERAL PAYMENTS

A. *Under Assumption that All Commodities Are Traded Internationally*

The theory of exchange given in the previous chapter is directly applicable to the field of international trade under the simplified assumptions of this section. Each country may have its own unit of account and consequently the absolute level of money prices in terms of the token or counter money may be different in each country. But under pure competition the price ratios between internationally traded commodities must be the same for all countries in the absence of transportation costs. Since our equilibrium system of exchange (3.5) determines only the price ratios y_s (prices in terms of some standard commodity or *numéraire*) and not the absolute level of prices p_s in terms of a token money, a strictly analogous system may be used to determine the price ratios in an international economy.

Let the number of commodities in all countries taken together be n. In each country there exist demand functions for each of the n commodities of the type (3.3). Equilibrium requires that the $n-1$ price ratios shall be such as to equate the demand and supply of all countries taken together for each commodity. Let the superscripts

(1), (2), $\cdots$, (v) refer to the respective countries. Then we shall have in equilibrium:

(5.1a) $\qquad X_s^{(1)} + X_s^{(2)} + \cdots + X_s^{(v)} = \bar{X}_s^{(1)} + \bar{X}_s^{(2)} + \cdots + \bar{X}_s^{(v)}$

$$(s = 1, 2, \cdots, n-1).$$

If we define $I_s = X_s - \bar{X}_s$ as the import demand (if positive) or the export supply (if negative), then equation (5.1a) may be rewritten in the form

(5.1b) $\qquad I_s^{(1)} + I_s^{(2)} + \cdots + I_s^{(v)} = 0 \qquad (s = 1, 2, \cdots, n-1),$

which states that for each commodity the net import for all countries taken together must equal zero. These $n-1$ equations are sufficient to determine the $n-1$ equilibrium price ratios.

Superficially it might appear that we have an additional equation for the nth commodity, namely, $I_n^{(1)} + I_n^{(2)} + \cdots + I_n^{(v)} = 0$. In determining I_s for each country, however, we have already made use of equation (3.2), which, restated in the more familiar form,

$$\sum_1^n p_s(X_s - \bar{X}_s) = \sum_1^n p_s I_s = 0,$$

simply means that for each country the total value of its imports must equal the total value of its exports. Since this equation must hold for each country regardless of whether (5.1) is satisfied, it follows that if (5.1) holds we also have $I_n^{(1)} + I_n^{(2)} + \cdots + I_n^{(v)} = 0$.

The conditions of stability for the equilibrium of international exchange are likewise strictly analogous to those given for a closed economy. Perfect stability of the international economy requires that an increase in the price ratio of any one commodity shall lead to a reduction in the world excess demand for that commodity in all of the following cases:

(a) when all other price ratios remain constant,

(b) when only one other price ratio is adjusted so as to maintain equilibrium in the world market for that commodity,

(c) when only two other price ratios are so adjusted, and so on until all other price ratios are adjusted.

Imperfect stability requires only that there shall be a reduction in the world excess demand when all other price ratios are adjusted. Thus we have the conditions that

(5.2a) $\qquad \dfrac{d(I_1^{(1)} + I_1^{(2)} + \cdots + I_1^{(v)})}{dy_1} < 0,$

$$(5.2b) \qquad \frac{d\left(I^{(1)}_{s} + I^{(2)}_{s} + \cdots + I^{(v)}_{s}\right)}{dy_1} = 0 \qquad (s = 2, 3, \cdots, n-1).$$

Let us extend the definition of a_{st} to an international economy:

$$(5.3) \; a_{st} = \frac{\partial\left(I^{(1)}_{s} + I^{(2)}_{s} + \cdots + I^{(v)}_{s}\right)}{\partial y_t} = \frac{\partial\left(X^{(1)}_{s} + X^{(2)}_{s} + \cdots + X^{(v)}_{s}\right)}{\partial y_t}$$

$$\text{(since } \overline{X}_s = \text{a constant)}.$$

Then the principal minors (4.5) of successive orders of the determinant (4.3) $J = |a_{st}|$ must again be alternatively negative and positive.[1] As in a closed economy the system must be perfectly stable so far as the substitution effect is concerned by virtue of the properties of the individual demand functions. We shall assume, as before, that the income effects are not sufficiently large to render the system unstable.

The only new problem introduced by the theory of international exchange is the determination of the absolute level of money prices in each country in terms of its own token money. Let e_{1i} be the number of units of the token money of country (i) obtainable for one unit of the token money of country (1). Since the money prices of internationally traded commodities must be the same in all countries when allowance is made for the exchange rate, we have:

$$(5.4) \qquad e_{1i} \, p^{(1)}_{s} = p^{(i)}_{s}, \qquad (i = 1, 2, 3, \cdots, v; \; e_{11} \equiv 1).$$

Let K be the proportion of one's income held in the form of money by individuals of country (i), and let $M^{(i)}$ be the number of units of the token money in country (i). Then by the reasoning given above in connection with equations (3.6) and (3.7) we have for each country:

$$(5.5a) \qquad M^{(i)} = p^{(i)}_{n} K \sum_{1}^{n} y_s \overline{X}^{(i)}_{s};$$

or, when we convert all currencies into that of the first:

$$(5.5b) \qquad \frac{M^{(i)}}{e_{1i}} = p^{(1)}_{n} K^{(i)} \sum_{s=1}^{n} y_s \overline{X}^{(i)}_{s}.$$

Summing for all countries we have:

$$(5.6) \qquad \sum_{1}^{v} \frac{M^{(i)}}{e_{1i}} = p^{(1)}_{n} \sum_{1}^{v} \left(K^{(i)} \sum_{1}^{n} y_s \overline{X}^{(i)}_{s}\right).$$

[1] Yntema postulates a different set of stability conditions for his system of equations. See his book, *A Mathematical Reformulation of the Theory of International Trade*, (Chicago: University of Chicago Press, 1932).

If the exchange rates e_{1i} are fixed then $p_n^{(1)}$ is determined from equation (5.6) when the total sum of money for all countries expressed in units of the first is given. The level of money prices in the other countries $p_n^{(i)}$ is then given by equations (5.4) and the distribution of the total quantity of money amongst the countries by equations (5.5). On the other hand, if each country determines for itself the quantity of money which it wants to hold, then the level of money prices is determined in each country by equations (5.5a). The exchange rates rather than the distribution of the total quantity of money are then the unknowns and these are determined by equations (5.4).

The purchasing-power-parity theory may be restated in such a way as to give it the same limited validity as may be accorded to the quantity theory of money. *Assume that the factors which determine the equilibrium price ratios are given.* Then by equations (5.5a) the ratio of the price levels for any two countries is directly proportional to the ratio between their quantities of money (for given $K^{(i)}$ and $K^{(j)}$), while by (5.4) the exchange rates between their currencies is inversely proportional to the ratio between their quantities of money.

B.   Under Assumption that Domestic Commodities Exist

Domestic commodities may be introduced into our equilibrium system (5.1) without any difficulty. A commodity is defined as domestic to a given country if the quantities demanded and supplied of that commodity in every other country are *identically* zero. Commodities in different countries must be treated as different when they are not transportable, even though they may be physically identical. We may therefore define a domestic commodity as one whose transportation costs to every other country are infinite.

For the individuals in each country the utility functions and budget equations (1.1) and (1.2) must obviously exclude the domestic commodities of other countries. If we again let one of the *internationally traded commodities* serve as the *numéraire* X_n and express the prices of all commodities in terms of X_n, then we can again write the demand functions for each commodity in every country as in (3.3). The equations of equilibrium are again given by (3.5), with the only proviso that if X_t is a domestic commodity for country (j), the demand for and supply of (and therefore the import demand or export supply of) X_t in every other country is *identically* equal to zero. The equilibrium equation for that commodity therefore reduces to the condition that the demand for X_t shall equal the supply in country (j):

$$X^{(j)}_t = \overline{X}^{(j)}_t \text{ or } I^{(j)}_t = 0.$$

Except for these modifications the entire preceding analysis of the equilibrium of international trade remains intact.[2]

II. INTERNATIONAL EXCHANGE UNDER UNILATERAL PAYMENTS

Only minor modifications in our equilibrium system are required to take into account the existence of unilateral payments. We distinguish between two cases in our analysis, one where the value of payments in terms of a standard commodity or *numéraire* is a fixed constant and the other where it is a variable.

A. *Value of Payments Assumed Constant*

1. *Determination of the equilibrium price ratios*

Assume that country (i) receives ($+$) or pays ($-$) a sum equal to $Z^{(i)}$ when expressed in terms of the *numéraire* X_n. The sum of $Z^{(i)}$ for all countries is, of course, zero. Assume further that of this amount, each individual in the country receives ($+$) or pays ($-$) an amount z which depends in a known way upon the magnitude of $Z^{(i)}$.

$$(6.1) \qquad\qquad z = z(Z^{(i)}).$$

Then the individual's demand function for every commodity will depend not only upon the price ratios and the initial supplies of every commodity but also on the amount of his unilateral payments or receipts. Indeed his budget equation expressed in terms of the *numéraire* will be:

$$(6.2) \qquad\qquad \sum_{s=1}^{n} y_s\, x_s = \sum_{s=1}^{n} y_s\, \overline{x}_s + z\,;$$

and his demand function will therefore be

$$(6.3a) \qquad x_s = g_s(y_1, y_2, \cdots, y_{n-1}, \overline{x}_1, \overline{x}_2, \cdots, \overline{x}_n, z).$$

If the initial supplies of all commodities are constants, then the demand function becomes

$$(6.3b) \qquad x_s = x_s(y_1, y_2, \cdots, y_{n-1}, z).$$

---

[2] Yntema omits the equations for domestic commodities from his equilibrium system. He therefore has to introduce the balance-of-payments equation explicitly as an independent equation in his final system. We retain the equations for the domestic commodities, so that the balance-of-payments equation follows automatically from our equilibrium system.

In this equation $\partial x_s/\partial y_t = p_n\,\partial x_s/\partial p_t$ may again be obtained from equation (2.12):

$$(6.4) \qquad \frac{\partial x_s}{\partial y_t} = p_n \frac{\partial x_s}{\partial p_t} = p_n(\bar{x}_t - x_t)\frac{\partial x_s}{\partial r} + p_n\,x_{st}.$$

A change in the individual's payments or receipts represents an equal change in the value of his income expressed in terms of the *numéraire*. We have therefore:

$$(6.5) \qquad \frac{\partial x_s}{\partial z} = \frac{\partial x_s}{\partial (r/p_n)} = p_n \frac{\partial x_s}{\partial r}.$$

Since the individual's payment or receipt is a function of the total amount of the country's payments or receipts, we may replace z in the demand function (6.3b) by $Z^{(i)}$:

$$(6.3\text{c}) \qquad x_s = x_s(y_1, y_2, \cdots, y_{n-1}, Z^{(i)}).$$

The effect of a change in $Z^{(i)}$ upon the individual's demand is then given by:

$$(6.6) \qquad \frac{\partial x_s}{\partial Z^{(i)}} = \frac{\partial x_s}{\partial z}\frac{dz}{dZ^{(i)}}.$$

Summing (6.3c) for all individuals in the ith country we have for the aggregate market demand functions $X_s^{(i)}$:

$$(6.7) \qquad X_s^{(i)} = X_s^{(i)}(y_1, y_2, \cdots, y_{n-1}, Z^{(i)}) \qquad (s = 1, 2, \cdots, n).$$

For this equation we have:

$$(6.8) \qquad \begin{aligned} \frac{\partial X_s^{(i)}}{\partial y_t} &= \Sigma\,\frac{\partial x_s}{\partial y_t} \quad \text{for all individuals in country } (i), \\[2ex] \frac{\partial X_s^{(i)}}{\partial Z^{(i)}} &= \Sigma\left(\frac{\partial x_s^{(i)}}{\partial z}\frac{dz}{dZ^{(i)}}\right) \text{for all individuals in country } (i). \end{aligned}$$

It is clear that $\partial X_s^{(i)}/\partial\Sigma^{(i)}$ will depend upon the way in which the total payments are distributed among the individuals in the country.

As before, equilibrium requires that the total quantity demanded of each commodity by all countries shall be equal to the total quantity supplied, or that the net import demand for all countries shall be zero for each commodity.

We therefore have

(6.9a) $X^{(1)}_s + X^{(2)}_s + \cdots + X^{(v)}_s = \overline{X}^{(1)}_s + \overline{X}^{(2)}_s + \cdots + \overline{X}^{(v)}_s$

$$(s = 1, 2, \cdots, n-1),$$

or

(6.9b) $I^{(1)}_s + I^{(2)}_s + \cdots + I^{(v)}_s = 0$ $(s = 1, 2, \cdots, n-1)$.

Given the value of each country's payments or receipts in terms of the nth commodity, these $n-1$ equations are sufficient to determine the $n-1$ price ratios. Again we have but $n-1$ independent equations rather than n because in determining the individual's demand function we have made use of the budgetary equation (6.2). For the country as a whole this implies:

(6.10a) $$\sum_1^n y_s I^{(i)}_s = Z^{(i)},$$

and for all countries taken together

(6.10b) $$\sum_{i=1}^{(v)} \sum_{s=1}^n y_s I^{(i)}_s = \sum_{i=1}^v Z^{(i)} = 0.$$

Since (6.10b) must hold whether or not equilibrium exists it follows from (6.9b) that $I^{(1)}_n + I^{(2)}_n + \cdots + I^{(v)}_n = 0$.

The conditions of stability of the equilibrium remain unchanged, since the only new terms which we have introduced into our demand functions (6.7) (the unilateral payments) remain unaffected by a change in any price ratio.

2. *Determination of the absolute level of money prices*

We may make two alternative assumptions concerning the determination of money prices when unilateral payments take place. We may assume, as does Robertson, that the quantity of money held in each country is proportional to the income excluding reparations receipts and including reparations payments. In this case the level of money prices and the distribution of the total quantity of money amongst the countries (or, alternatively, the exchange rates) can be determined just as before by means of equations (5.4), (5.5), and (5.6). On the other hand, we may assume, as does Viner, that the quantity of money held in each country is proportional to income including reparations receipts and excluding reparations payments.[3] In

[3] See D. H. Robertson, "The Transfer Problem," in A. C. Pigou and D. H. Robertson, *Economic Essays and Addresses* (London, 1931), pp. 170–81; J. Viner, *Studies in the Theory of International Trade* (New York, 1937), pp. 365–74; D. H. Robertson, "Indemnity Payments and Gold Movements," *Quarterly Journal of Economics*, Vol. 53, No. 2, February, 1939, pp. 312–14; J. Viner, "A Reply," *ibid.*, pp. 314–17; D. H. Robertson, "Rejoinder," *ibid.*, p. 317.

that case equations (5.4) to (5.6) must be replaced by the following three equations:

(6.11a)
$$M^{(i)} = p_n^{(i)} K^{(i)} \left(\sum_{s=1}^{n} y_s \bar{X}_s^{(i)} + Z^{(i)} \right),$$

(6.11b)
$$\frac{M^{(i)}}{e_{1i}} = p_n^{(1)} K^{(i)} \left(\sum_{s=1}^{n} y_s \bar{X}_s^{(i)} + Z^{(i)} \right),$$

and

(6.12)
$$\sum_{i=1}^{v} \frac{M^{(i)}}{e_{1i}} = p_n^{(1)} \sum_{i=1}^{v} K^{(i)} \left(\sum_{s=1}^{n} y_s \bar{X}_s^{(i)} + Z^{(i)} \right).$$

Note that, since $\sum Z^{(i)} = 0$, (6.12) reduces to (5.6) if
$$K^{(1)} = K^{(2)} = \cdots = K^{(v)}.$$

B. *Value of Payments Assumed Variable*

In the general case the unilateral receipts or payments $Z^{(i)}$ of any country will be a function of all of the economic variables in the system. Here we shall assume that the receipts or payments are a function of the value of the country's initial supply (exclusive of unilateral receipts and inclusive of unilateral payments) of every commodity. We shall further assume that all scales of preferences as well as all initial supplies of all commodities are given. Then $Z^{(i)}$ becomes a function only of the $n - 1$ price ratios. Let us include in our function a parameter α with respect to which Z may shift. Then we have the known function:

(6.13)
$$Z^{(i)} = Z^{(i)} (y_1, y_2, \cdots, y_{n-1}, \alpha).$$

Similarly we may assume that the distribution of the total payments or receipts amongst the individuals in the country is also a known function of the price ratios and of Z:

(6.14)
$$z = z(y_1, y_2, \cdots, y_{n-1}, Z^{(i)}).$$

The individual's budgetary equation (6.2) remains unchanged and we may again write his demand functions in the form:

(6.15)
$$x_s = x_s(y_1, y_2, \cdots, y_{n-1}, z).$$

In this equation, however, z is no longer a constant with respect to the price ratios but is instead a function of them. Consequently equation (6.4) must be replaced by:

$$(6.16) \qquad \frac{\partial x_s}{\partial y_t} = p_n \frac{\partial x_s}{\partial p_t} = p_n \left(\bar{x}_t - x_t + \frac{\partial z}{\partial y_t} \right) \frac{\partial x_s}{\partial r} + p_n \, x_{st}.$$

Equation (6.5) for $\partial x_s / \partial z$ remains unchanged. Given the $n-1$ price ratios, the individual payment or receipt is a function of Z which in turn is then a function of the parameter of shift α. Thus we may replace z in the individual's demand function (6.15) by α:

$$(6.17) \qquad\qquad x_s = x_s (y_1, y_2, \cdots, y_{n-1}, \alpha).$$

The effect of a change in α upon the individual's demand is then given by:

$$(6.18) \qquad\qquad \frac{\partial x_s}{\partial \alpha} = \frac{\partial x_s}{\partial z} \frac{\partial z}{\partial Z^{(i)}} \frac{\partial Z^{(i)}}{\partial \alpha}.$$

Summing (6.17) for all individuals in the ith country, we have for the aggregate market demand functions $X_s^{(i)}$:

$$(6.19) \qquad\qquad X_s^{(i)} = X_s^{(i)} (y_1, y_2, \cdots, y_{n-1}, \alpha).$$

The rest of the analysis remains unchanged. Equilibrium is given by equations (6.9), except that $X_s^{(i)}$ is now defined by (6.19) instead of (6.7). Similarly the stability conditions remain unchanged except for the fact that $\partial X_s / \partial y_t$ refers to the partial derivatives of (6.19) rather than (6.7).

III. EFFECTS OF CHANGES IN UNILATERAL PAYMENTS

A. On the Equilibrium Price Ratios

The preceding section dealt with the determination of the international equilibrium when unilateral payments take place. If the total payments of a country are constant with respect to the price ratios, then the equilibrium position depends upon the value of the constant Z. If the total payments are a function of the price ratios, then the equilibrium position depends upon the value of the function, which is assumed to change as the parameter of shift α changes. In the first case we may study the effects upon equilibrium of a change in Z; in the second the effects of a change in α. In both cases we may make use of the same technique which we previously adopted in studying the laws of the working of the general equilibrium for a single country. For the change in Z or in α involves a change in the world distribution of incomes and therefore leads to a general shift in the demands for all commodities. We have already seen how to determine the effects of such changes.

It is conceivable though highly improbable that any increase in the demand for each commodity on the part of the receivers of payments should be exactly offset by an equivalent decrease in the demand on the part of the payers. In that case there would be no change in any price ratio whatsoever.[4] Suppose, however, that there is a net increase in the demand of the world as a whole for only one commodity X_s, which is offset by a net decrease in the world demand for the *numéraire* X_n. In other words, suppose that the change is such that, at the old price more of X_s is wanted and more of X_n is offered, the demands for all other commodities remaining unchanged. Then the price of X_s in terms of X_n must rise, since equilibrium can be maintained only if an excess supply is induced from those who possess X_s, sufficient to satisfy the increased demand. The price ratios of substitutes for X_s in whatever country they may be will also tend to rise unless they are also substitutes of complements of X_s, in which case they may fall. The price ratios of complements of X_s will tend to fall unless they are also complements of complements of X_s, in which case they may tend to rise. If we make use of the inverse demand functions, writing the price ratios as functions of the quantities, then we may say, as before, that the price ratio of X_t will rise or fall according as it is a substitute or a complement of X_s in the inverse sense.

If the net world demands for two commodities rise, the direct effect will be for both price ratios to rise. If the two commodities are substitutes in the inverse sense, the indirect effect will work in the same direction as the direct effect; if they are complements, it will work in the opposite direction. The total effect may then be that the price ratio for one commodity may fall.

If the world demand in terms of the *numéraire* changes for every commodity, then the results may be obtained by combining the effects of the individual changes. If there is no complementarity present throughout the system and if the total world demand for each commodity in terms of the *numéraire* changes in the same direction, then all price ratios will move in that direction in all countries.

Mathematically, the general solution is obtained by differentiating the equilibrium system (6.9) totally with respect to changes in reparations. If Z is a constant with respect to the price ratios, then the demand functions $X_s^{(i)}$ are defined by equation (6.7). The differentiation of the equilibrium system (6.9) is then with respect to Z. If Z is a function of the price ratios, then the demand functions $X_s^{(i)}$

---

[4] Such a result is, of course, impossible if there are domestic commodities for which the income elasticity is different from zero, since a change in the demand for the domestic commodity in any country cannot be offset by opposite changes in other countries.

are defined by (6.19) and the differentiation of the equilibrium system (6.9) is with respect to α. The same set of equations may be used to determine the changes in the equilibrium position resulting from changes in Z or in α, provided that we interpret the formulae appropriately.

Let

$$(7.1) \qquad a_{st} = \sum_{i=1}^{v} \frac{\partial I_s^{(i)}}{\partial y_t} = \sum_{i=1}^{v} \frac{\partial X_s^{(i)}}{\partial y_t}$$

be the partial derivative of $\sum_{i=1}^{v} I_s^{(i)}$ with respect to y_t. The value of this derivative will, of course, be different according as we are dealing with the demand functions (6.7) or (6.19). Further, let

$$(7.2) \qquad b_s = \sum_{i=1}^{v} \frac{\partial I_s^{(i)}}{\partial Z^{(i)}} dZ^{(i)} = \sum_{i=1}^{v} \frac{\partial X_s^{(i)}}{\partial Z^{(i)}} dZ^{(i)}$$

when we are referring to (6.7) ; and let

$$(7.3) \qquad b_s = \sum_{i=1}^{v} \frac{\partial I_s^{(i)}}{\partial \alpha} d\alpha = \sum_{i=1}^{v} \frac{\partial X_s^{(i)}}{\partial \alpha} d\alpha$$

when we refer to (6.19). Then upon differentiating the equilibrium system (6.9) we obtain:

$$(7.4) \qquad \begin{aligned} a_{11}\,dy_1 + \quad a_{12}\,dy_2 + \cdots + \quad a_{1,n-1}\,dy_{n-1} &= -b_1\,, \\ a_{21}\,dy_1 + \quad a_{22}\,dy_2 + \cdots + \quad a_{2,n-1}\,dy_{n-1} &= -b_2\,, \\ \cdots \qquad\qquad\qquad\qquad\qquad\qquad\qquad & \\ a_{n-1,1}\,dy_1 + a_{n-1,2}\,dy_2 + \cdots + a_{n-1,n-1}\,dy_{n-1} &= -b_{n-1}\,. \end{aligned}$$

The determinant of the coefficients in this system is given by

$$(7.5) \qquad\qquad\qquad J = |a_{st}|$$

and the solution is given by

$$(7.6) \qquad dy_s = -\frac{b_1 J_{1s} + b_2 J_{2s} + \cdots + b_{n-1} J_{n-1,s}}{J}.$$

Again making use of the inverse demand functions in which the prices are the dependent variables, we have:

$$(7.7) \qquad\qquad \frac{\partial y_s}{\partial \left(\sum_{i=1}^{v} X_t^{(i)} \right)} = \frac{J_{ts}}{J}.$$

Substituting into (7.6), we have:

$$
(7.8) \quad dy_s = - \left(b_1 \frac{\partial y_s}{\partial \left(\sum\limits_{i=1}^{v} X_1^{(i)} \right)} + b_2 \frac{\partial y_s}{\partial \left(\sum\limits_{i=1}^{v} X_2^{(i)} \right)} + \cdots + b_{n-1} \frac{\partial y_s}{\partial \left(\sum\limits_{i=1}^{v} X_{n-1}^{(i)} \right)} \right).
$$

In the general case dy_s may be positive, zero, or negative. If for each commodity the rate of change of demand with respect to income were the same for all individuals in the world, then all b's would equal zero and there would be no price change whatsoever. On the other hand, if every b were of the same sign and there were no complementarity in the system, then dy_s for every s would have the same sign as the b's.[5]

B. On the Absolute Level of Money Prices

The change in the absolute level of prices in terms of the token money in each country depends upon the type of monetary standard which prevails.

1. If the exchange rates between the currencies are constant, then $p_n^{(1)}$ is determined either by equation (5.6) or by equation (6.12) according as we adopt Robertson's or Viner's assumption. For the former we have:

$$
(7.9a) \quad \frac{dp_n^{(1)}}{p_n^{(1)}} = - \frac{\sum\limits_{i=1}^{v} K^{(i)} \, d \left(\sum\limits_{s=1}^{n} y_s \, \overline{X}_s^{(i)} \right)}{\sum\limits_{i=1}^{v} K^{(i)} \sum\limits_{s=1}^{n} y_s \, \overline{X}_s^{(i)}};
$$

for the latter we have:

$$
(7.9b) \quad \frac{dp_n^{(1)}}{p_n^{(1)}} = - \frac{\sum\limits_{i=1}^{v} K^{(i)} \, d \left(\sum\limits_{s=1}^{n} y_s \, \overline{X}_s^{(i)} + Z^{(i)} \right)}{\sum\limits_{i=1}^{v} K^{(i)} \left(\sum\limits_{s=1}^{n} y_s \, \overline{X}_s^{(i)} + Z^{(i)} \right)}.
$$

The proportional change in the absolute level of prices in each of the other countries is of course the same as for the first country:

$$
\frac{dp_n^{(i)}}{p_n^{(i)}} = \frac{dp_n^{(1)}}{p_n^{(1)}}.
$$

The change in the quantity of money held in any one country is then obtained either from (5.5) under Robertson's assumption or from (6.11) under Viner's assumption; for the former we have:

[5] See the Appendix to Chapter II.

$$(7.10a) \qquad \frac{dM^{(i)}}{M^{(i)}} = \frac{dp_n^{(i)}}{p_n^{(i)}} + \frac{d \sum_{s=1}^{n} y_s \bar{X}_s^{(i)}}{\sum_{s=1}^{n} y_s \bar{X}_s^{(i)}};$$

for the latter we have:

$$(7.10b) \qquad \frac{dM^{(i)}}{M^{(i)}} = \frac{dp_n^{(i)}}{p_n^{(i)}} + \frac{d \left(\sum_{s=1}^{n} y_s \bar{X}_s^{(i)} + Z^{(i)} \right)}{\sum_{s=1}^{n} y_s \bar{X}_s^{(i)} + Z^{(i)}}.$$

2.   If, on the other hand, the countries are on independent currencies, each one fixing $M^{(i)}$ for itself, then $p_n^{(i)}$ is determined from (5.5) according to Robertson or from (6.11) according to Viner. In that case $dp_n^{(i)}/p_n^{(i)}$ is obtained by differentiating these equations as in (7.10) and setting $dM^{(i)} = 0$. Thus we have:

$$(7.11a) \qquad \frac{dp_n^{(i)}}{p_n^{(i)}} = - \frac{d \sum_{s=1}^{n} y_s \bar{X}_s^{(i)}}{\sum_{s=1}^{n} y_s \bar{X}_s^{(i)}} \qquad \text{according to Robertson;}$$

or

$$(7.11b) \qquad \frac{dp_n^{(i)}}{p_n^{(i)}} = - \frac{d \left(\sum_{s=1}^{n} y_s \bar{X}_s^{(i)} + Z^{(i)} \right)}{\sum_{s=1}^{n} y_s \bar{X}_s^{(i)} + Z^{(i)}} \qquad \text{according to Viner.}$$

The effect on the exchange rates is then determined from (5.4):

$$(7.12) \qquad \frac{de_{1i}}{e_{1i}} = \frac{dp_n^{(i)}}{p_n^{(i)}} - \frac{dp_n^{(1)}}{p_n^{(1)}}.$$

IV. EFFECTS OF "IMPEDIMENTS" TO TRADE

The classical literature on the theory of international trade—particularly the theory of Marshall and Edgeworth—deals at great length with the problems of "impediments" to international trade. The impediments generally considered are taxes on imports or exports and transportation costs. The essence of such impediments is that they create divergences between the prices paid by the importers and those received by the exporters. While such divergences complicate our general-equilibrium analysis, they do not alter it fundamentally. The demand and supply functions give for each commodity the quantities demanded and supplied at any given set of prices. A tax on the purchase of a given commodity simply represents an addition to the purchase price, while a tax on the sale of a commodity represents a subtraction from the sales price. If we know the demand functions for the buyers and sellers on whom the tax is imposed and if we also know the demand functions for the recipients of the proceeds of the tax, then we can readily determine the effects of the tax.[6]

The analysis will proceed by stages as follows: We shall first assume that the government spends the proceeds of the tax on the *numéraire* only. We shall next assume that the government spends *the proceeds on the taxed* commodity only. Third, we shall assume that the government has known demand functions for each of the commodities in the system. Finally we shall assume that the government redistributes the tax proceeds amongst the individuals in the economy. If it gives the proceeds to a foreign government then we have the case of reparation payments which are not constants but functions of the sales or purchases of specified commodities.

A. Under the Assumption that the Government Spends the Tax Proceeds on the Numéraire Only

It is assumed that the government spends the proceeds of the tax on the *numéraire* only, its demand and supply for the other $n-1$ commodities being identically zero. Under this assumption only the private demand and supply functions for the $n-1$ commodities need be considered in examining the equilibrium under the tax. It is further assumed that the private demand and supply functions are totally unaffected by the government "consumption" of the *numéraire*. It is therefore readily possible to determine the effects of the tax on the private demand and supply functions.

1. Import taxes

Let $\tau_s^{(i)}$ measured in terms of the *numéraire* be the duty levied on the imports of X_s by country (i). Let y_s be the price in terms of the *numéraire* received by the foreign exporter of X_s. It is assumed that $\tau_s^{(i)}$ is some known function of y_s. The two special cases of this function which have received attention in the literature are (1) the case in which $\tau_s^{(i)}$ is a constant, and (2) that in which it is proportional to y_s. The former is designated as a specific tax, and the latter as an *ad valorem tax*. The total price for X_s in the importing country is $y_s + \tau_s^{(i)}$ in terms of the *numéraire*. Thus for every unit of X_s bought,

[6] Our entire analysis will run in terms of taxes, but it is equally applicab'e to transportation costs.

the importer must pay over the equivalent of y_s units of the *numéraire* X_n to the exporter and the equivalent of $\tau_s^{(i)}$ units of X_n to the Government. Domestic sellers in the importing country receive, of course, the full amount of the price including tax, or $y_s + \tau_s^{(i)}$. If we assume that the government spends the total proceeds of the tax on the *numéraire* X_n, and that its use of the *numéraire* does not in any way affect the civilian demand for any commodity, then a very simple relationship exists between the civilian demands for any commodity before and after the tax. At the price ratio (to the exporter, i.e., less tax) y_s, the quantity demanded of any commodity by the importing country (given all other prices and the distribution of income) would now be the same as it had been before the tax at a price of $y_s + \tau_s^{(i)}$. Unless X_s were a markedly inferior good in the importing country for which the income effect were greater than the substitution effect,[7] the import tax would thus lead to a decline in the total demand for X_s. If we assume that there are no effects on and through other markets it would then follow from the stability conditions, that, except in the abnormal case just noted, y_s—i.e., the net price less the tax—must fall. The extent of the price decline would depend upon the net export supply curve for the rest of the world taken together. If, as is normally true, the net export supply is such that less would be exported at lower prices, then y_s would fall by less than the tax. If, on the other hand, the net export supply were such that more would be exported at lower prices, then the price (less tax) would fall by more than the tax.[8]

That this case is not inconsistent with our stability conditions has already been shown above. For stability we require that the sum

$$\frac{\partial I_s^{(1)}}{\partial y_s} + \frac{\partial I_s^{(2)}}{\partial y_s} + \cdots + \frac{\partial I_s^{(v)}}{\partial y_s}$$

for all countries taken together shall be negative, and not that each one shall be negative. The classical stability conditions for international trade, however, are different from ours and explicitly rule out such cases. See Alfred Marshall, *Money, Credit, and Commerce* (London: 1923) Appendix J.

[8] This corresponds to the classical distinction between elastic and inelastic reciprocal-demand curves. In our notation let $I_1^{(1)}$ be the quantity of X_1 imported by country (1) and $I_1^{(2)}$ the quantity of X_1 exported by country (2). The price y_1 represents the terms of trade or the exchange ratio between the internationally traded commodities X_1 and X_2. It is assumed that there are only two commodities in the system. Then for the country which imports X_1, the reciprocal-demand curve is defined as elastic or inelastic according as the elasticity of the import demand $I_1^{(1)}$ with respect to y_1 is numerically greater than or less than unity. If it is greater than unity an increase in the value of its imports in terms of its exports will give rise to a proportionately greater decline in its quantity of imports demanded, so that the quantity of its exports will de-

As soon as we take even one other commodity into account we must modify our conclusions.[9] If X_t is complementary with X_s, then the tax on X_s will not only decrease the import demand for X_s but will also decrease the import demand or increase the export supply for X_t in country (i). The direct effect will therefore be to reduce both y_s and y_t. But the indirect effect of the decline in demand for X_t is to increase y_s, while the indirect effect of the decline in demand for X_s is to increase y_t.[10] It is therefore possible that both y_s and y_t will fall, or that *either* (*not both*) will rise. On the other hand, if X_t is a

[9] See Chapter II, Sec. II B.
[10] In the traditional discussion of the effects of tariffs only the direct effect on the imports and exports of other goods is considered while the indirect substitution effects are ignored. Hotelling, however, does take these substitution effects into account. See his "Edgeworth's Taxation Paradox," *loc. cit.*

---

cline. If it is less than unity, the converse will be true. (It may be noted that the definition of elasticity for the reciprocal-demand curve is analogous to the definition of price elasticity for domestic demand curves, the export commodity serving as the *numéraire* or as "money.")

For the country which exports X_1, the reciprocal-demand curve $I_1^{(2)}$ is defined as elastic or inelastic according as the slope of $I_1^{(2)}$ with respect to y_1 is negative or positive. Thus if it is elastic, an increase in the value of its exports in terms of its imports leads to an algebraically smaller value of $I_1^{(2)}$ or to a numerical increase in the quantity of its exports. If it is inelastic the converse is true.

In the special case in which there are only two countries and two commodities, if country (1) has an import tax of τ_1 on X_1, its import demand $I_1^{(1)}$ will be a function of the price including tax, $y_1 + \tau_1$. The export supply curve of country (2), $I_1^{(2)}$, however, remains a function of the price less tax, y_1. Equilibrium requires that the import demand plus the export supply (negative) shall be zero: $I_1^{(1)}(y_1 + \tau) + I_1^{(2)} = 0$. To determine the effects of a change in the tax we have:

$$\frac{d(I_1^{(1)} + I_1^{(2)})}{d\tau} = \frac{\partial(I_1^{(1)} + I_1^{(2)})}{\partial y_1} \frac{dy_1}{d\tau} + \frac{\partial I_1^{(1)}}{\partial y_1} = 0,$$

or

$$\frac{dy_1}{d\tau} = - \frac{\dfrac{\partial I_1^{(1)}}{\partial y_1}}{\dfrac{\partial I_1^{(1)}}{\partial y_1} + \dfrac{\partial I_1^{(2)}}{\partial y_1}}.$$

From the stability conditions the denominator is negative. Consequently $dy_1/d\tau$ will be negative except in the unlikely case (completely ruled out in the classical stability conditions) when the import demand curve in country (1) is positively sloping.

If the reciprocal-demand is elastic in country (2), then

$$\frac{\partial I_1^{(2)}}{\partial y_1} < 0 \quad \text{and} \quad \frac{dy_1}{d\tau} > -1,$$

so that the price will fall by less than the tax. If it is inelastic then the signs are reversed, and the price will fall by more than the tax.

substitute for X_s, the tax on X_s will decrease the demand for X_s but will increase the import demand for, or decrease the export supply of X_t. The direct effect of the tax will therefore be to reduce y_s and to increase y_t. But the indirect effect of X_s on X_t will be to reduce y_t while the indirect effect of X_t on X_s will be to increase y_s. It is therefore possible that both y_s and y_t should fall or that both should rise, or that y_s should fall and y_t should rise. (It should be understood that y_s refers to the price *less* tax).

2. *Export taxes*

Similar statements can be made with respect to a per-unit tax on exports. Let $\tau_r^{(i)}$ be the tax levied per unit of exports of X_r by country (i), and let y_r be the price in terms of the *numéraire* paid by foreign importers of X_r. Then the net price received by the exporters of X_r is $y_r^{(i)} - \tau_r^{(i)}$. If the proceeds of the tax are spent by the government on the *numéraire* only, and if the government's use of the *numéraire* does not affect the civilian demand for any commodity, then at the market price y_r (including the tax) the quantity demanded and supplied of any commodity by the exporting country (given all other prices and income) would now be the same as it had been at a price of $y_r - \tau_r^{(i)}$ before the tax.

If, as is normally true, the supply function is such that less would be supplied at a lower price than at a higher price, then the levy of the export tax is equivalent to a fall in the supply of X_r. From the stability conditions it would then follow that the price of X_r (including the tax) must rise. Unless the net import demand for X_r in the rest of the world were so abnormal that more would be imported at higher prices than at lower prices, the price would not, however, rise by the full amount of the tax. This latter possibility is ruled out by the classical stability conditions but not by ours.

If, however, the income effect of the price change is so great that more is supplied at a lower than at a higher price, then the levy of the export tax is equivalent to an increase in the supply of X_r and its price including the tax will actually fall.[11] This is possible even under the classical stability conditions.

---

[11] The distinction made here again corresponds to the classical distinction between elastic and inelastic reciprocal-demand curves. Let $I_1^{(1)}$ be the quantity of X_1 exported by country (1) and $I_1^{(2)}$ the quantity of X_1 imported by country (2). If there is an export tax of $\tau_1^{(1)}$ then the export supply will be a function of the price less tax $y_1 - \tau_1^{(1)}$. The foreign import demand will, however, be a function of the price including the tax, y_1. Equilibrium requires that

$$I_1^{(1)} (y_1 - \tau_1^{(1)}) + I_1^{(2)} (y_1) = 0.$$

Differentiating with respect to $\tau_1^{(1)}$ we have:

When we take a second commodity into account parallel modifications are required. If X_t is complementary with X_r the tax on X_r will not only decrease the export supply of X_r (in the normal case) but will also decrease the export supply or increase the import demand for X_t. The direct effect of the tax will therefore be to raise the price (including the tax) of both X_r and X_t. But the indirect effect of each on the other will be to lower the price. Both prices may therefore rise or one may rise and the other may fall. But both cannot possibly fall. If, however, X_t is a substitute of X_r then the tax on X_r will decrease the supply of X_r and increase the export supply or decrease the import demand for X_t. The direct effect of the tax will therefore be to raise the price of X_r and to reduce the price of X_t. But the indirect effect of X_r on its substitute X_t will be to raise its price, while the indirect effect of X_t on X_r will be to reduce its price. The price of X_r (including the tax) may therefore rise and the price of X_t fall, or both may rise in price, or both may fall.

B. Under the Assumption that the Government Spends the Tax Proceeds on the Taxed Commodity Only

The civilian demand and supply functions change exactly as described in the previous section. However, since it is now assumed that the government also demands the taxed commodity, it is no longer possible to determine the new equilibrium by means of the civilian demand and supply functions alone. Instead, we must add the government demand to the private demand functions in order to determine the new equilibrium.

1. Import taxes

We assume as in Section A that country (i) levies a duty amount-

---

$$\frac{dy_1}{d\tau} = \frac{\dfrac{\partial I_1{}^{(1)}}{\partial (y_1 - \tau)}}{\dfrac{\partial I_1{}^{(1)}}{\partial (y_1 - \tau)} + \dfrac{\partial I_1{}^{(2)}}{\partial y_1}}.$$

The denominator is negative from the stability conditions. The possibilities are now as follows:

(a)   If the reciprocal-demand curve for the exporting country is elastic the exports increase with increases in price. The numerator is therefore negative and $dy_1/d\tau$ is positive. It is less than 1, however, so that the market price (including the tax) rises by less than the tax except in the unlikely case ruled out by the classical conditions when $\partial I_1{}^{(2)}/\partial y_1 > 0$.

(b)   If, however, the reciprocal-demand curve is inelastic, then the numerator is positive and $dy_1/d\tau < 0$ or the market price (including the tax) will actually fall.

ing to $\tau_s^{(i)}$ on its imports of X_s, and that y_s is the price of X_s received by the exporters and $y_s + \tau_s^{(i)}$ is the price paid by the importers. The quantity of X_s demanded by the civilians of country (i) at a price of y_s is therefore the same as it had been before the tax at a price of $y_s + \tau_s^{(i)}$. To the exporters the civilians pay an amount equal to y_s times the quantity they import and to the government they pay the amount $\tau_s^{(i)}$ times the quantity they import; so that the total amount they now pay out at the price y_s is equal to the amount they would previously have paid at the price $y_s + \tau_s^{(i)}$. By assumption the government spends the full tax proceeds on the taxed commodity. Consequently, taking the government and civilians together, the amount spent on the import commodity at each price y_s will be the same as the amount that would previously have been spent at a price $y_s + \tau_s^{(i)}$. The new import demand curve for the government and civilians combined may therefore be obtained by shifting the old curve so that at each price y_s the import quantity demanded will be equal to the quotient of (1) the amount previously spent at a price of $y_s + \tau_s^{(i)}$ divided by (2) the price y_s.

In contrast to the discussion in Section A in which it was assumed that the government spent the tax proceeds on the *numéraire* rather than on the taxed commodity, it is now possible even under classical conditions for the import demand curve to rise. If the civilian import demand curve is inelastic (in the case of two commodities if the reciprocal-demand is inelastic) then civilians would spend a larger amount on imports at a higher import price than at a lower one. Consequently, since the quantity demanded by the government and civilians combined at each price y_s is equal to the amount previously spent by civilians at a price of $y_s + \tau_s^{(i)}$, divided by y_s, it follows that if the civilian import demand is inelastic, more imports will now be demanded than previously at each price y_s. The import demand curve would, therefore, rise as a result of the tax and the import price (less tax) would be higher in the new equilibrium.

Thus the tax on imports turns out to be analogous in its effect to a tax on exports when the tax proceeds in both cases are spent on the import commodity.

2. *Export taxes*

We now assume as in Section A that country (i) levies a duty of $\tau_r^{(i)}$ on its exports of X_r, and that y_r is the price of X_r paid by the importers and $y_r - \tau_r^{(i)}$ is the net price received by the exporters. The quantity of the export commodity supplied by the civilians of country (i) at a price of y_r is, therefore, the same as it had been before the tax at a price of $y_r - \tau_r^{(i)}$. From the importers the civilians receive an amount equal to y_r times the quantity they export. Of this they turn over to the government an amount equal to $\tau_r^{(i)}$ times the quantity exported. In this case, however, the government spends the entire tax proceeds on the taxed export commodity. It is convenient to assume that the suppliers are taxed on sales to the government as well as on their exports. Under this assumption the price to the government will be the same as the price to the foreign countries.

Let the quantity previously supplied at a price of y_r be q_1 and the quantity previously supplied at the price $y_r - \tau_r^{(i)}$ (and now supplied at a price of y_r) be q_2. The government receives in tax an amount $\tau_r q_2$ which it spends on the export commodity. The amount exported at the price y_r, therefore, will be the amount supplied at y_r less the amount taken by the government,[12] or $q_2 - \tau_r q_2/y_r$. This amount is less than that previously exported at y_r under the classical stability conditions (although not necessarily under ours). For under the classical conditions the *value* of the amount supplied at a lower price must be less than that of the amount supplied at a higher price. (This is simply the reverse of the condition that the quantity demanded at a higher price must be less than that demanded at a lower price). This means that

$$(y_r - \tau_r) q_2 < y_r q_1,$$

or

$$q_2 - \frac{\tau_r q_2}{y_r} < q_1.$$

It follows, therefore, that when the government spends the entire tax proceeds on the taxed export commodity, the export supply function will (except in the most extreme instance) fall. The price of the export commodity in terms of the *numéraire* will, therefore, rise. In a two-commodity system the terms of trade would change in favor of the tax-levying country.

Thus a tax on exports is analogous to a tax on imports when the proceeds in both cases are spent on the export commodity.

C. *Under the Assumption that the Government Spends the Tax Proceeds on All Commodities*

The excess-demand functions of the civilians will again shift in the manner indicated in the two preceding sections. Adding the gov-

---

[12] For the sake of convenience it is assumed here that the government is the only domestic consumer of the export commodity. This assumption may readily be dropped.

ernment demands to the civilian demand functions, we readily obtain
the country's import demand (and export supply) functions after the
imposition of the tax. This may readily be shown in mathematical
form. The analysis will be carried through for the case of an import
tax, but it is applicable with only slight modifications to export taxes.

In the case of an import tax on X_1, the individual civilian budget equations become

$$(y_1 + \tau_1) x_1 + y_2 x_2 + \cdots + x_n = (y_1 + \tau) \overline{x}_1 + y_2 \overline{x}_2 + \cdots + \overline{x}_n .$$

The civilian demand functions then take the form:

$$x_s = x_s (y_1 + \tau_1 , y_2 , \cdots , y_{n-1}) .$$

Summing for all civilians and subtracting the supply from the demand, we obtain the civilian import demand (and export supply)
functions:

$$I^{(c)}_s = I^{(c)}_s (y_1 + \tau_1 , y_2 , \cdots , y_{n-1}) ,$$

the superscript (c) denoting that the equation refers only to civilians.
The government receives in import taxes an amount equal to $\tau_1 I^{(c)}_1$,
which it spends according to given demand functions on the n commodities. Its budget equation is thus

$$y_1 x^{(g)}_1 + y_2 x^{(g)}_2 + \cdots + x^{(g)}_n = \tau_1 I^{(c)}_1$$

and its demand functions are then given by:

$$x^{(g)}_s = x^{(g)}_s (y_1 , y_2 , \cdots , y_{n-1} , \tau_1 I^{(c)}_1) .$$

It is assumed that the government demand functions have all of the
basic properties of the individual demand functions. Summing the
government and the civilian demand functions we obtain the total
import demand (and export supply) functions for every commodity
for country (i). As before equilibrium requires that the total world
demand for each commodity shall be equal to the total world supply.
Letting country (1) be the tax-levying country, we have as our equilibrium equations:

$$I^{(c)}_s + x^{(g)}_s + \sum_{i=2}^{v} I^{(i)}_s = 0 \qquad\qquad (s = 1, 2, \cdots, n-1) .$$

$[I^{(c)}_s$ is the civilian import demand in country (1), and $x^{(g)}_s$ is the government demand in that country.] The imposition of an import tax
$\tau^{(1)}_1$ will shift both the civilian and the government demand functions
in country (1). The resulting price changes will have to be such as
to equilibrate the total world demand for each commodity with the
total world supply. Let

$$a_{st} = \frac{\partial I_s^{(c)}}{\partial y_t} + \frac{\partial x_s^{(g)}}{\partial y_t} + \tau \frac{\partial x_s^{(g)}}{\partial (\tau I_1^{(c)})} \frac{\partial I_1^{(c)}}{\partial y_t} + \sum_{i=2}^{v} \frac{\partial I_s^{(i)}}{\partial y_t},$$

$$b_s = \left[\frac{\partial I_s^{(c)}}{\partial (y_1 + \tau)} + \frac{\partial x_s^{(g)}}{\partial (\tau I_1^{(c)})} I_1^{(c)} + \tau \frac{\partial x_s^{(g)}}{\partial (\tau I_1^{(c)})} \frac{\partial I_1^{(c)}}{\partial (y_1 + \tau)} \right] d\tau.$$

Then, differentiating the equilibrium equations above with respect to τ, we obtain a system of equations formally identical with the system (7.4) which we developed and solved in dealing with the effects of reparations payments.

The basic difference between the two systems is that whereas in the case of reparations the "disturbance" is one of a redistribution of income between countries, in the present case the disturbance consists of (1) the change in the price to the civilians of the importing country resulting from the imposition of the tax and (2) the acquisition of additional income by the government. Since the demand and supply functions tells us how each of the affected consuming units reacts to each such change, it is readily possible to determine the combined effect on the equilibrium system.

D. Under the Assumption that the Government Redistributes the Proceeds of the Tax

1. Amongst its own residents only

In this case if an import tax is levied on X_1, the individual civilian budget equation becomes

$$(y_1 + \tau_1) x_1 + y_2 x_2 + \cdots + x_n = (y_1 + \tau) \overline{x_1} + y_2 \overline{x_2} + \cdots + \overline{x_n} + z$$

where z represents the amount of the tax proceeds received by the individual. It is clear that the individual's reaction to a change in the tax will depend upon the relationship between the tax he pays and the amount of the proceeds he receives from the government.

If the individual knows that the government will redistribute to him the full amount of any excise tax he may pay, then the tax will obviously have no effect upon his demand or supply for any commodity.[13] We shall, therefore, assume that each individual treats his portion of the redistributed tax funds as a fixed constant, completely

---

[13] This can easily be seen by writing $z = \tau_1 (x_1 - \overline{x_1})$ in the individual's budget equation. All the tax terms will then cancel out and we shall have:

$$\Sigma y_i x_i = \Sigma y_i \overline{x_i},$$

or the same budget equation as exists under a completely tax-free system.

independent of the amount of excise taxes he pays. Under these conditions the individual is subject to two types of changes: (1) a price change represented by the excise tax, and (2) an income change represented by the receipt of a portion of the redistributed funds. The problem in this section is, therefore, analogous to that of the preceding section with the sole difference that the income change is experienced by the same people who pay the excise tax rather than by an outsider—i. e., the government. But if we know how each individual reacts to a change in income and also how he reacts to a change in price, there is no special difficulty in determining the effects of the imposition of a tax whose proceeds are redistributed.

2.   *Amongst the residents of a foreign country*
     This is an extension of the problem of reparations to the case in which the payments are a function of the country's imports or exports, the level of the function depending upon the rate of excise taxes imposed. In view of the analysis of the preceding cases the solution of this problem is readily apparent. The taxes represent a change in price which in turn affects the quantities demanded and supplied. The proceeds of the tax are distributed abroad to the reparations-receiving country where they affect the demand and supply functions through the change in income. The new equilibrium is the resultant of these changes taken together. If we let superscript (R) denote the receiving country and write:

$$a_{st} = \sum_{i=1}^{v} \frac{\partial I_s^{(i)}}{\partial y_t} + \tau \frac{\partial I_1^{(1)}}{\partial y_t} \frac{\partial I_s^{(R)}}{\partial (\tau I_1^{(1)})},$$

$$b_s = \frac{\partial I_s^{(1)}}{\partial y_1} d\tau + \frac{\partial I_s^{(R)}}{\partial (\tau I_1^{(1)})} I_1^{(1)} d\tau,$$

then the solution is again given by the system (7.4).

The analysis may readily be extended to the case in which the government of the receiving country reduces or abolishes an excise tax as a result of its reparations receipts. It may also be extended to the case of a bounty by treating the latter as a negative tax.

CHAPTER IV

THE SPECIAL CASE OF TWO COMMODITIES AND TWO COUNTRIES

I. THE "TERMS OF TRADE"

It will be instructive to apply our analysis to the special case generally considered in the literature in which there are only two countries and only two commodities and in which transportation costs are zero. Let there be two countries, (1) and (2), and two commodities X_1 and X_2, the second commodity serving as *numéraire*. Let country (1) import X_1 and export X_2 and let country (2) export X_1 and import X_2. Let y_1 be the "terms of trade," defined as the value of a unit of X_1 in terms of the *numéraire* X_2, and let Z be the value in terms of the *numéraire* of the reparations paid by country (2) to country (1). We shall assume, for the sake of simplicity, that the amount Z is fixed regardless of the value of y_1. Then we have for country (1) the budget equation

$$(8.1) \qquad y_1 I_1^{(1)} + I_2^{(1)} = Z,$$

where $I_1^{(1)}$ is the volume of its imports ($+$) of X_1, and $I_2^{(1)}$ is the volume of its exports ($-$) of X_2. Similarly for country (2) we have the budget equation

$$(8.2) \qquad y_1 I_1^{(2)} + I_2^{(2)} = -Z,$$

where $I_1^{(2)}$ is the volume of its exports ($-$) of X_1, and $I_2^{(2)}$ of its imports ($+$) of X_2. Imports and exports of X_1 (and therefore of X_2) are functions of y_1 and Z.

In equilibrium the import demand for X_1 must equal its export supply, or

$$(8.3) \qquad I_1^{(1)} + I_1^{(2)} = 0.$$

From (8.1) and (8.2) which must be true regardless of whether equilibrium prevails it then follows that $I_2^{(1)} + I_2^{(2)} = 0$.

If there is a change in the reparations then we have

$$(8.4) \qquad \frac{dI_1^{(1)}}{dZ} + \frac{dI_1^{(2)}}{dZ} = 0,$$

or

$$(8.5) \qquad \frac{\partial I_{1}^{(1)}}{\partial y_1} \frac{dy_1}{dZ} + \frac{\partial I_{1}^{(1)}}{\partial Z} + \frac{\partial I_{1}^{(2)}}{\partial y_1} \frac{dy_1}{dZ} + \frac{\partial I_{1}^{(2)}}{\partial Z} = 0.$$

Solving we obtain

$$(8.6) \qquad \frac{dy_1}{dZ} = - \frac{\dfrac{\partial I_{1}^{(1)}}{\partial Z} + \dfrac{\partial I_{1}^{(2)}}{\partial Z}}{\dfrac{\partial I_{1}^{(1)}}{\partial y_1} + \dfrac{\partial I_{1}^{(2)}}{\partial y_1}}.$$

Since the denominator is negative from the stability conditions, it follows that the change in the terms of trade y_1 will be of the same sign as the sum in the numerator. In the normal case if X_1 is not an inferior good in either country, the import demand for X_1 in the reparations-receiving country will increase while the export supply in the reparations-paying country will increase. Consequently the first term in the numerator will be positive while the second will be negative. The terms of trade will therefore change in favor of the paying country, remain unchanged, or change in favor of the receiving country according as the first term in the numerator is greater, equal to, or less than the absolute magnitude of the second term. Exactly the reverse is true if X_1 is an inferior good in both countries. If, however, X_1 is an inferior good in only one country then the terms of trade will definitely change in its favor.

The solution may easily be demonstrated graphically either on Viner's "terms of trade" charts (which correspond to ordinary demand and supply diagrams) or by the use of the Marshallian reciprocal-demand curves.

In Figure 3, let $I_{1}^{(1)}$ be the import demand for X_1 of country (1) and let $-I_{1}^{(2)}$ be the export supply of X_1 of country (2), drawn with its sign reversed so as to make it positive. The intersection of the two curves represents the equilibrium point, with a price (in terms of the *numéraire*) of Ob and a volume of imports of Oa. The normal position of the two curves is that shown in Figure 3, where the import-demand curve $I_{1}^{(1)}$ is negatively sloped and the export-supply curve $-I_{1}^{(2)}$ is positively sloped. It is possible, however, for $-I_{1}^{(2)}$ to be negatively sloped, or even for $I_{1}^{(1)}$ to be positively sloped, provided that the slope of $I_{1}^{(1)}$ with respect to the price axis is algebraically smaller than that of $-I_{1}^{(2)}$. The stability conditions exclude the possibility of a positively sloping demand curve alongside a negatively sloping supply curve.

Let country (2) pay reparations to country (1). If X_1 is not an inferior commodity in either country, then the receiving country's

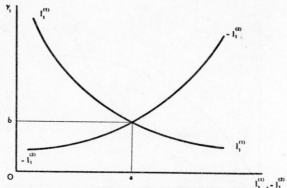

FIGURE 3.—DETERMINATION OF EQUILIBRIUM BY MEANS OF
"TERMS OF TRADE" CURVES.

demand for X_1 will increase while the paying country's demand will decrease or its export supply increase. Consequently both curves will shift to the right. The imports of X_1 will definitely increase, but the direction of change in y_1 will depend upon the relative shifts in the two curves. If X_1 is an inferior good in both countries then both curves will shift to the left, the imports of X_1 will decline and the direction of change in y_1 will again depend upon the relative shifts in the two curves. If, however, X_1 is an inferior good in only one country, then the curve for that country will shift to the left and the terms of trade will change in its favor.

From equations (8.1) and (8.2) it follows that once we are given the import demand and export supply for X_1 in the two countries we immediately have the export supply and import demand for X_2 in the two countries. These are, respectively,

$$(8.7) \qquad\qquad I_2^{(1)} = Z - y_1 I_1^{(1)},$$

and

$$(8.8) \qquad\qquad I_2^{(2)} = - Z - y_1 I_1^{(2)}.$$

Instead of the curves for $I_1^{(1)}$ and $-I_1^{(2)}$ we could therefore have drawn the curves $-I_2^{(1)}$ and $I_2^{(2)}$ which can be derived directly from the former two and we should have obtained identical results.

Instead of the terms-of-trade diagrams we might make use of the Marshallian reciprocal-demand curves. In Figure 4 let the horizontal axis represent $I_1^{(1)}$ imports into country (1) of X_1 and $-I_1^{(2)}$ exports of X_1 from country (2), and let the vertical axis represent $-I_2^{(1)}$ exports of X_2 from country (1) and $I_2^{(2)}$ imports of X_2 into country (2). At each given price y_1, country (1) is willing to import a quantity $I_1^{(1)}$ as

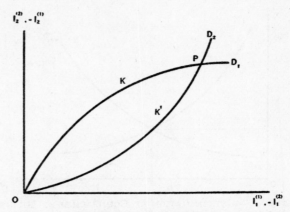

FIGURE 4.—DETERMINATION OF EQUILIBRIUM BY MEANS OF
RECIPROCAL-DEMAND CURVES.

seen in Figure 3 and must therefore export an amount $-I_{2}^{(1)}$ as determined by equation (8.7). For this country we can therefore draw up a
reciprocal-demand curve OD_1, showing the volume of its exports of X_2
(by the ordinate of each point) which it will be willing to supply for a
given volume of imports of X_1 (the abscissa of each point). A similar
curve OD_2 can be drawn up for country (2) showing the volume of its
exports of X_1 (the abscissa) which it will be willing to supply for
each given volume of imports of X_2 (the ordinate). The point P of
intersection of these curves, where the quantity of imports of either
commodity is equal to the exports, is the point of equilibrium. If Z
is equal to zero, namely, if there are no reparations, then y_1 corresponding to any point K on D_1 or K' on D_2 is given by the slope of the
vector through O to that point. If, however, Z is different from zero,
then y_1 corresponding to K or K' is the slope of the vector through O
to a point Z units vertically above K or K' respectively; i.e.,

$$y_1 = \frac{-I_{2}^{(1)} + Z}{I_{1}^{(1)}} = \frac{I_{2}^{(2)} + Z}{-I_{1}^{(2)}}.$$

In Taussig's terminology y_1 represents the net barter terms of trade,
while the slope of the vector to the point on the reciprocal-demand
curve itself represents the gross barter terms of trade.

The reciprocal-demand curve of country (1) is elastic, has unit
elasticity, or is inelastic according as the slope of OD_1 with respect to
the horizontal axis is positive, zero, or negative. Similarly the reciprocal-demand curve of country (2) is elastic, has unit elasticity, or is inelastic according as the slope of OD_2 with respect to the *vertical* axis

is positive, zero, or negative. It is even possible by our stability conditions for OD_1 to bend around backwards so that a vertical line would cut it twice, or for OD_2 to bend backwards so that a horizontal line would cut it twice.[1] This would mean that more would be imported at a higher import price than at a lower one; i.e., it would correspond to a positively sloping import-demand curve in Figure 3, a possibility which must be included if the import good is an inferior commodity in the importing country and the income effect of the price change is large. From the stability conditions, however, it follows that if either curve has this shape in the neighborhood of the equilibrium point, then the other curve *must* be elastic.

For the sake of convenience let us assume that Figure 4 is drawn for a case in which there are no reparations, so that $Z = 0$. Now let country (2) pay to country (1) a sum in reparations equal to Z when measured in terms of the *numéraire* X_2. Then OD_2 must shift in such a way that at any given price in terms of the *numéraire* X_2, imports of X_1 are equal to the exports of X_2 (with sign reversed) minus the reparations, both expressed in terms of the *numéraire*. But there is an infinite variety of such shifts, depending upon the magnitude of $\partial I_1^{(2)}/\partial Z$ or the propensity to consume X_1. [Given $\partial I_1^{(2)}/\partial Z$ the term $\partial I_2^{(2)}/\partial Z$ is uniquely determined from (8.8).]

Graphically we may illustrate this shift as follows: In Figure 5 let OD_2 be the reciprocal-demand curve for country (2) drawn for $Z = 0$, namely, before reparations. The price ratio y_1, corresponding to any point P along OD_2 is given by the slope of the vector OP or Oa/Ob. Now if country (2) pays a sum of reparations Z to country (1), the price ratio Oa/Ob will correspond to some point on a line parallel to OP but Z units below it, namely, on the line QT, where $PR = Z$. In other words, after reparations, the exports of X_1 and the corresponding imports of X_2 at a price of Oa/Ob will be represented by the co-ordinates of a point lying somewhere along QT. Just where it lies along QT depends upon the rate of change in the export supply of X_1 with respect to a change in income, or upon $\partial I_1^{(2)}/\partial Z$.

a.   If, at the given price ratio, country (2) is willing to consume the same amount of X_1 after the reparations payments as before, then $\partial I_1^{(2)}/\partial Z = 0$ and the export supply will remain unchanged. (This means, of course, that the rate of change in the import demand for X_2 with respect to income is unity.) The new point corresponding to the price ratio Oa/Ob will therefore be at R, or Z units directly below P.

---

[1] Marshall's stability conditions which differ from ours exclude this possibility. Alfred Marshall, *Money, Credit, and Commerce* (London, 1923), Appendix J.

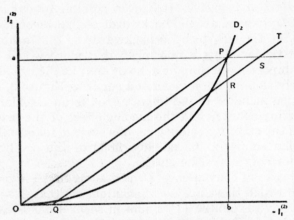

FIGURE 5.—EFFECT OF UNILATERAL PAYMENTS UPON THE
RECIPROCAL-DEMAND CURVE.

b.   If, on the other hand, X_1 is a superior good, then when the income of country (2) declines by Z units it will demand less of X_1 or it will be willing to export more of it. (This means, of course, that $\partial I_2^{(2)}/\partial Z < 1$.) The new point corresponding to the price ratio Oa/Ob will therefore be to the right of R. How far up along QT it will be depends upon $\partial I_2^{(2)}/\partial Z$. If X_2 is not an inferior good, then the point will lie between R and S (where PS is horizontal). If X_2 is an inferior good, however, then it may lie even to the right of S, for country (2) will now demand more of X_2 than it did formerly at any given price ratio.

c.   If X_1 is an inferior good, country (2) will demand more of it after the reparations payments. Less of X_1 will, therefore, be exported at the price Oa/Ob than before, and the new point corresponding to this price will be to the left of R.

Parallel statements hold for the receiving country. In Figure 6, let the curve OK be the reciprocal-demand curve for country (1) before reparations, the point K showing that when $y_1 = Oc/Od$, country (1) will be willing to import Od units of X_1 and to export Oc units of X_2. Now if country (1) receives a sum Z in reparations then the point corresponding to the price ratio Oc/Od will lie on a line parallel to the vector OK but Z units below it, namely, on the line QT. If, at the given price Oc/Od, country (1) is willing to consume just as much of X_1 after the reparations receipts as before, then $\partial I_1^{(1)}/\partial Z = 0$, and the new point corresponding to the price ratio Oc/Od will be at R which is Z units vertically below K. If X_1 is a superior good, the new point wil l lie to the right of R but below S (where KS is horizontal) unless X_2 is

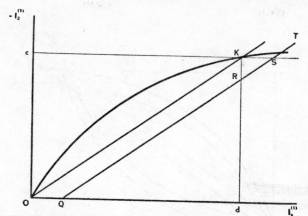

FIGURE 6.—EFFECT OF UNILATERAL RECEIPTS UPON THE
RECIPROCAL-DEMAND CURVE.

an inferior good, in which case the new point may even lie above the
curve OK. Conversely, if X_1 is an inferior good then the new point
will lie to the left of R.

We may now briefly summarize the effects of reparations upon
the terms of trade. In Figure 7, let OD_1 and OD_2 be the reciprocal-demand curves for countries (1) and (2) respectively before reparations.
The point P is the equilibrium point with a price ratio equal to Oa/Ob
and with imports of X_1 equal to Ob and of X_2 equal to Oa. If in each
country the income elasticity of demand for X_1 is zero, namely, if
$\partial I_1^{(1)}/\partial Z = \partial(-I_1^{(2)})/\partial Z = 0$, then after reparations the curves OD_1
and OD_2 will both shift vertically downwards by Z units, as in Figure
7. The new point of intersection will be directly below the old, the
terms of trade will remain unchanged, the exports of X_1 will remain
unchanged, but country (2) will now import Z units less of X_2.

If, however, $\partial I_1^{(1)}/\partial Z$ and $\partial(-I_1^{(2)})/\partial Z$ are both different from
zero, then OD_1 will shift in such a way that the point P (on OD_1)
will fall somewhere on RT, say, at $S^{(1)}$, and OD_2 will likewise shift
so that the point P (on OD_2) will fall somewhere on RT, say at $S^{(2)}$.
If $\partial I_1^{(1)}/\partial Z = \partial(-I_1^{(2)})/\partial Z$ then $S^{(1)}$ and $S^{(2)}$ coincide, the new curves
intersect along RT, and the terms of trade remain unchanged. If
X_1 is a superior good in both countries then the new point of intersection will lie to the right of R, so that the paying country will not
only import less of X_2 but also export more of X_1. If on the other
hand X_1 is an inferior good in both countries, then the paying country
will, in fact, export less of X_1 than it did prior to the reparations,
but this decline will be offset by a greater drop in the imports of X_2
than in the previous case.

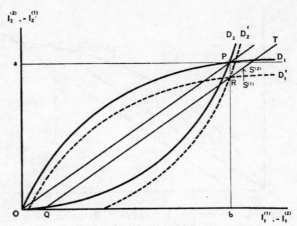

FIGURE 7.—EFFECT OF UNILATERAL PAYMENTS UPON THE EQUILIBRIUM POSITION.

If $\partial I_1^{(1)}/\partial Z$ is different from $\partial(-I_1^{(2)})/\partial Z$ then the terms of trade will change in favor of that country for which the rate of change is algebraically smallest. Thus if $S^{(1)}$ is to the left of $S^{(2)}$ the new reciprocal-demand curves will intersect below the line RT and the terms of trade will change in favor of the receiving country. Conversely, if $S^{(1)}$ is to the right of $S^{(2)}$ the new curves will intersect above the line RT and the terms of trade will change in favor of the paying country. This is valid regardless of whether X_1 is a superior or inferior good. It follows, therefore, that, if X_1 is an inferior good in one country only, the terms of trade will necessarily change in favor of that country.[2]

We may now analyze the factors determining the magnitude of the change in terms of trade for a given net change in the demand for X_1; namely, for a given magnitude of the sum in the numerator of (8.6). Suppose that the numerator is negative, so that y_1 declines. Then it can easily be seen that for a given magnitude of the numerator the extent of the fall will depend upon the terms in the denominator of (8.6). Given the value of $\partial I_1^{(2)}/\partial y_1$, then dy_1 will be smaller numerically, the smaller is $\partial I_1^{(1)}/\partial y_1$ algebraically. In other words, the greater the elasticity of reciprocal demand in country (1), the smaller numerically will be the favorable change in her terms of trade y_1. Given the value of $\partial I_1^{(1)}/\partial y_1$, then dy_1 will be the smaller numerically, the smaller is $\partial I_1^{(2)}/\partial y_1$ algebraically. This means that the greater the

[2] Marshall's error in the analysis of the effects of unilateral payments was twofold: 1. He shifted only the reciprocal-demand curve of the paying country but not that of the receiving country. 2. He implicitly assumed a zero income elasticity in the paying country for the receiving country's commodity. Marshall, *op. cit.*, Appendix J.

elasticity of reciprocal demand in country (2), the smaller numerically will be the unfavorable change in her terms of trade. Analogous statements can be made for a rise in y_1.

Thus far we have investigated the effects of a change in **reparations** upon the equilibrium by examining the effects on the demand functions

(8.9)
$$I_1^{(1)} = G_1^{(1)}(y_1, Z),$$
$$I_1^{(2)} = G_1^{(2)}(y_1, Z).$$

We might just as well have written these demand functions in the inverse form, treating y_1 as the dependent variable:

(8.10)
$$y_1 = H_1^{(1)}(I_1^{(1)}, Z),$$
$$y_1 = H_1^{(2)}(I_1^{(2)}, Z).$$

In equilibrium the import demand price must equal the export supply price, or

(8.11)
$$H_1^{(1)} = H_1^{(2)}.$$

The effect of a change in reparations is then obtained by differentiating (8.11) totally with respect to Z:

(8.12)
$$\frac{\partial H_1^{(1)}}{\partial I_1^{(1)}}\frac{dI_1^{(1)}}{dZ} + \frac{\partial H_1^{(1)}}{\partial Z} = \frac{\partial H_1^{(2)}}{\partial I_1^{(2)}}\frac{dI_1^{(2)}}{dZ} + \frac{\partial H_1^{(2)}}{\partial Z}.$$

But since $I_1^{(1)} = -I_1^{(2)}$ it follows that $dI_1^{(1)}/dZ = -dI_1^{(2)}/dZ$ and therefore

(8.13)
$$\frac{dI_1^{(1)}}{dZ} = \frac{\dfrac{\partial H_1^{(2)}}{\partial Z} - \dfrac{\partial H_1^{(1)}}{\partial Z}}{\dfrac{\partial H_1^{(2)}}{\partial I_1^{(2)}} + \dfrac{\partial H_1^{(1)}}{\partial I_1^{(1)}}}.$$

Again the denominator must be negative from the stability conditions, so that $dI_1^{(1)}/dZ$ will vary in the opposite direction from the numerator. If X_1 is a superior good in both countries then

$$\frac{\partial H_1^{(2)}}{\partial Z} < 0 \text{ and } \frac{\partial H_1^{(1)}}{\partial Z} > 0, \text{ so that } \frac{dI_1^{(1)}}{dZ} > 0.$$

In other words, if X_1 is a superior good, country (1) will increase its imports of X_1 after reparations. If it is an inferior good in both countries all of the signs in the expressions above will be reversed and the imports of X_1 will decline. If it is neither an inferior nor a superior good in either country, then the terms in the numerator of (8.13) are zero, and there is no change in the imports of X_1. This confirms our previous findings in connection with equation (8.6).

The change in the terms of trade is given by either side of equation (8.12). We may now ask the question: For given shifts in the reciprocal-demand curves, namely, for given $\partial H_1^{(2)}/\partial Z$ and $\partial H_1^{(1)}/\partial Z$, what are the factors determining the magnitude of the change in the terms of trade? It should be noted that this question is not the same as the one we asked in the preceding discussion of equation (8.6). There it was assumed that there were given changes in the *quantity demanded and offered at each given price*. Here it is assumed that there are given changes in the *price at which each given quantity is demanded and offered*. This difference may easily be illustrated by means of Figure 3. The first question relates to a given *horizontal* shift while the second question relates to a given *vertical* shift in the two curves.

Making use of equations (8.12) and (8.13) we have for the change in the terms of trade:

$$(8.14) \qquad \frac{dy_1}{dZ} = \frac{\dfrac{\partial H_1^{(1)}}{\partial I_1^{(1)}} \dfrac{\partial H_1^{(2)}}{\partial Z} + \dfrac{\partial H_1^{(2)}}{\partial I_1^{(2)}} \dfrac{\partial H_1^{(1)}}{\partial Z}}{\dfrac{\partial H_1^{(1)}}{\partial I_1^{(1)}} + \dfrac{\partial H_1^{(2)}}{\partial I_1^{(2)}}}.$$

Again we confine ourselves to the case where $dy_1/dZ < 0$. To determine how dy_1/dZ varies with each of the terms in the denominator for given $\partial H_1^{(2)}/\partial Z$ and $\partial H_1^{(1)}/\partial Z$, we need but differentiate this equation partially with respect to each of these terms. Let us rewrite equation (8.14) in the form

$$(8.15) \qquad w = \frac{ab + cd}{a + c}.$$

Then we have

$$(8.16) \qquad \frac{\partial w}{\partial a} = \frac{c(b - d)}{(a + c)^2}$$

and

$$(8.17) \qquad \frac{\partial w}{\partial c} = \frac{-a(b - d)}{(a + c)^2}$$

If X_1 is a superior good in both countries and if the reciprocal demand of the paying country is elastic, then both factors in the numerator of (8.16) are negative and $\partial w/\partial a$ is positive. This means that the larger $\partial H_1^{(1)}/\partial I_1^{(1)}$ is algebraically, the larger will dy_1/dZ be algebraically. Stated in terms of elasticities, the more elastic the reciprocal demand of country (1), the smaller is the fall in y_1; i.e., the less does y_1 change in its favor.

If, on the other hand, X_1 is an inferior good in both countries, *or* the reciprocal demand of the paying country is inelastic, then $\partial w/\partial a$ is negative.[3] This means that the more elastic the reciprocal demand of country (1), the smaller is the fall in y_1.

Equation (8.17) may be interpreted in a parallel manner. If X_1 is a superior good in both countries then $(b-d)$ is negative and $\partial w/\partial c$ is negative. The latter will also be true if X_1 is an inferior good in both countries and the import demand of country (1) for X_1 is positively sloped. This means that the larger $\partial H_1^{(2)}/\partial I_1^{(2)}$ is algebraically, the smaller is dy_1/dZ algebraically. Stated in terms of elasticities, the more elastic the reciprocal demand of country (2), the greater is the fall in y_1; namely, the less favorable does y_1 become for country (2). If on the other hand, X_1 is an inferior good in both countries and the import demand of country (1) for X_1 is negatively sloped, then $\partial w/\partial c$ is positive. This means that the more elastic the reciprocal demand of country (2), the smaller is the fall in y_1. Analogous statements can be made with respect to a rise in y_1.

If we take the "normal" case in which X_1 is a superior good in both countries and consider a shift in the two reciprocal-demand curves leading to a fall in y_1, then the results we have obtained may be summarized as follows:

For a given decline in the *quantity* of X_1 demanded at a given price by both countries taken together, the fall in y_1 will be smaller, the *greater* is the elasticity in the importing country and the *greater* is the elasticity in the exporting country. For a given decline in the *price* at which a given quantity of X_1 will be demanded by both countries taken together, the fall in y_1 will be smaller, the *greater* is the elasticity in the importing country and the *smaller* is the elasticity in the exporting country. The lack of symmetry with respect to the elasticity of the exporting country should be emphasized. It is the source of the difference between Viner's and Marshall's results in their analysis of the effects of differing elasticities on the magnitude of the change in E's demand for G-goods. Viner confined himself to a shift

[3] It is impossible for X_1 to be an inferior good and for the exporting country's reciprocal-demand curve to be inelastic at the same time.

of the first type, whereas Marshall's analysis relates to a shift of the second type.[4]

II. MONETARY ASPECTS

Having determined the effects of changes in unilateral payments upon the terms of trade y_1 and upon the imports and exports of X_1 and X_2, we may now proceed to the monetary aspects. These will depend upon whether we adopt Viner's assumption that the quantity of token money held is proportional to income including unilateral receipts and excluding payments, or Robertson's assumption that it is proportional to income excluding receipts and including payments.

A. Under Viner's Assumption

Let P equal the total value (in terms of the *numéraire*) of the income of a country, including its unilateral receipts and excluding its payments:

$$(8.18) \qquad P^{(1)} = \bar{X}_1^{(1)} y_1 + \bar{X}_2^{(1)} + Z$$

and

$$(8.19) \qquad P^{(2)} = \bar{X}_1^{(2)} y_1 + \bar{X}_2^{(2)} - Z,$$

where the barred X's relate to the initial supplies of these commodities before trade. Consequently the change in P is given by:

$$(8.20) \qquad dP^{(1)} = \bar{X}_1^{(1)} dy_1 + dZ$$

and

$$(8.21) \qquad dP^{(2)} = \bar{X}_1^{(2)} dy_1 - dZ.$$

If the exchange rate is assumed fixed, then the relative change in money prices [see (7.8)] will be given by:

$$(8.22) \qquad \begin{aligned} \frac{dp_2}{p_2} &= \frac{-K^{(1)} dP^{(1)} - K^{(2)} dP^{(2)}}{K^{(1)} P^{(1)} + K^{(2)} P^{(2)}} \\ &= -\frac{K^{(1)} (\bar{X}_1^{(1)} dy_1 + dZ) + K^{(2)} (\bar{X}_1^{(2)} dy_1 - dZ)}{K^{(1)} (\bar{X}_1^{(1)} y_1 + \bar{X}_2^{(1)} + Z) + K^{(2)} (\bar{X}_1^{(2)} y_1 + \bar{X}_2^{(2)} - Z)}. \end{aligned}$$

[4] Viner, *op. cit.*, pp. 542–46; Marshall, *op. cit.* This point was made by D. H. Robertson, in "Changes in International Demand and the Terms of Trade," *Quarterly Journal of Economics*, Vol. 52, (May, 1938), pp. 539–40.

If there is no change in the terms of trade and if the K's (the reciprocals of the "velocities") are the same for both countries, then there will be no change in monetary prices at all. If the K's are different (but the terms of trade remain unchanged), then money prices will rise or fall according as K for the paying country is greater or smaller than that for the receiving country; namely, according as the "velocity" in the paying country is smaller or greater than in the receiving country.[5] If the K's are the same but the terms of trade (y_1) do change, then the money prices must change in the opposite direction from the change in the terms of trade. This will generally be true even where the K's are different, unless the K of the country which is favored by the change in the terms of trade is extremely large in comparison with that of the other country.

The relative change in money prices will of course be the same in both countries. The absolute change in the money prices in country (2) will be equal to e_{12} times the absolute change in the money prices in country (1). [See equation (7.9).]

From equation (7.10) we have for the change in the quantity of money held in the two countries:

$$(8.23) \quad \begin{aligned} \frac{dM^{(1)}}{M^{(1)}} &= \frac{K^{(2)}(P^{(2)}\,dP^{(1)} - P^{(1)}\,dP^{(2)})}{P^{(1)}(K^{(1)}\,P^{(1)} + K^{(2)}\,P^{(2)})}, \\[2ex] \frac{dM^{(2)}}{M^{(2)}} &= \frac{-K^{(1)}(P^{(2)}\,dP^{(1)} - P^{(1)}\,dP^{(2)})}{P^{(2)}(K^{(1)}\,P^{(1)} + K^{(2)}\,P^{(2)})}. \end{aligned}$$

If the terms of trade remain unchanged then the numerators of (8.23) reduce to $K^{(2)}dZ(P^{(1)} + P^{(2)})$ and $-K^{(1)}dZ(P^{(1)} + P^{(2)})$. This means that the receiving country will gain money from the paying country.[6]

To obtain the absolute change in the quantity of money in country (1) resulting from the reparations we simply multiply both sides of the first equation of (8.23) by $M^{(1)} = K^{(1)}p^{(1)}_{2}P^{(1)}$ and simplify. We then obtain

---

[5] These conclusions confirm Viner's analysis in his *Studies*, pp. 371–74.

[6] This result is based on Viner's assumption that the quantity of money held in each country is proportional to the value of the income including reparations receipts and excluding reparations payments. If we adopt Robertson's assumption that the quantity of money is proportional to income excluding receipts and including payments, then there will be no transfer of money at all when the terms of trade remain unchanged. Robertson, "The Transfer Problem," *op. cit.*, p. 172; Viner, *Studies*, pp. 366–74; Robertson, "Indemnity Payments and Gold Movements," Viner, "A Reply," and Robertson, "Rejoinder," *op. cit.*

$$(8.24) \qquad dM^{(1)} = \frac{p^{(1)}_2 dZ}{\dfrac{P^{(2)}}{K^{(1)}(P^{(1)} + P^{(2)})} + \dfrac{P^{(1)}}{K^{(2)}(P^{(1)} + P^{(2)})}}.$$

Let $f^{(1)}$ be the fraction of its income (expressed in terms of the *numéraire*) which country (1) devotes to imports of X_1 and let $f^{(2)}$ be the fraction of its income which country (2) devotes to imports of X_2. (In the general case $f^{(1)}$ and $f^{(2)}$ will vary with variations in y and Z.) Then we have

$$(8.25) \qquad \begin{aligned} y_1 I^{(1)}_1 &= f^{(1)} P^{(1)}, \\ I^{(2)}_2 &= f^{(2)} P^{(2)}. \end{aligned}$$

Making use of (8.25) we obtain for the value of $P^{(2)}/(P^{(1)} + P^{(2)})$:

$$(8.26a) \qquad \frac{P^{(2)}}{P^{(1)} + P^{(2)}} = \frac{\dfrac{I^{(2)}_2}{f^{(2)}}}{\dfrac{y_1 I^{(1)}_1}{f^{(1)}} + \dfrac{I^{(2)}_2}{f^{(2)}}} = \frac{f^{(1)} I^{(2)}_2}{f^{(2)} y_1 I^{(1)}_1 + f^{(1)} I^{(2)}_2}.$$

Prior to the reparations we have in equilibrium $y_1 I^{(1)}_1 = I^{(2)}_2$, so that (8.26a) reduces to:

$$(8.26b) \qquad \frac{P^{(2)}}{P^{(1)} + P^{(2)}} = \frac{f^{(1)}}{f^{(1)} + f^{(2)}}.$$

Similarly:

$$(8.27) \qquad \frac{P^{(1)}}{P^{(1)} + P^{(2)}} = \frac{f^{(2)}}{f^{(1)} + f^{(2)}}.$$

Substituting from (8.26b) and (8.27) into (8.24) and letting $V = 1/K$, we obtain:

$$(8.28) \qquad dM^{(1)} = \frac{p^{(1)}_2 dZ (f^{(1)} + f^{(2)})}{f^{(1)} V^{(1)} + f^{(2)} V^{(2)}}.$$

In this equation $p^{(1)}_2 dZ$ equals the volume of the change in reparations expressed in terms of the money in country (1), the V's are the "velocities" of circulation of money, and the f's are the fractions of the income spent upon imports by each country.

It can easily be shown that if $f^{(1)}$ and $f^{(2)}$ are constants it is necessary for their sum to equal unity if the terms of trade are to remain unchanged.[7]

In this case the gain in money in the receiving country turns out to be:[8]

[7] The proof is simple.
From (8.25) and (8.18) we have

(a)
$$y_1 I_1^{(1)} = f^{(1)} P^{(1)} = f^{(1)} (\overline{X}_1^{(1)} y_1 + \overline{X}_2^{(1)} + Z),$$

$$I_2^{(2)} = f^{(2)} P^{(2)} = f^{(2)} (\overline{X}_1^{(2)} y_1 + \overline{X}_2^{(2)} - Z).$$

Equilibrium requires that for every given amount of reparations Z:

(1) the terms of trade y_1 shall be such that the imports of X_1 by the receiving country (1) shall equal the imports of X_2 by the receiving country (2) plus the amount of the reparations; and

(2) for terms of trade y_1 above the equilibrium level (less favorable to the receiving country) the import demand of country (1) shall be less than the sum of the import demand of country (2) and reparations.

This means that

(b)
$$y_1 I_1^{(1)} = I_2^{(2)} + Z,$$

and, on the assumption that $f^{(1)}$ and $f^{(2)}$ are constant, that

(c)
$$\frac{\partial [y_1 I_1^{(1)} - I_2^{(2)} - Z]}{\partial y_1} = f^{(1)} \overline{X}_1^{(1)} - f^{(2)} \overline{X}_1^{(2)} < 0.$$

Substituting from (a) into (b), transposing, and factoring out y_1, we obtain

(d)
$$y_1 = \frac{Z(1 - f^{(1)} - f^{(2)})}{f^{(1)} \overline{X}_1^{(1)} - f^{(2)} \overline{X}_1^{(2)}} + \frac{f^{(2)} \overline{X}_2^{(2)} - f^{(1)} \overline{X}_2^{(1)}}{f^{(1)} \overline{X}_1^{(1)} - f^{(2)} \overline{X}_1^{(2)}}.$$

The change in terms of trade as Z changes is given by the coefficient of Z in this equation. Since the denominator is negative from the stability conditions (c), it follows that

(e)
$$\frac{dy_1}{dZ} \begin{smallmatrix} < \\ = \\ > \end{smallmatrix} 0 \quad \text{according as} \quad 1 - f^{(1)} - f^{(2)} \begin{smallmatrix} > \\ = \\ < \end{smallmatrix} 0;$$

namely, the terms of trade will change favorably for the receiving country, remain unchanged, or change in favor of the paying country according as the sum of the fractions of each country's incomes devoted to imports is less than, equal to, or greater than unity.
See also Viner, *Studies*, pp. 329, 338 ff.

[8] The reader may check this formula against the cases given by Viner in his *Studies*, Table 5, p. 370. There $p_2^{(1)} dZ = 600$, $f^{(1)} = 1/3$, $f^{(2)} = 2/3$.
For case A, $V^{(1)} = 1$, $V^{(2)} = 1$, $dM^{(1)} = 600$;
For case B, $V^{(1)} = 2$, $V^{(2)} = 1$, $dM^{(1)} = 450$;
For case C, $V^{(1)} = 1/2$, $V^{(2)} = 1$, $dM^{(1)} = 720$.

In his discussion of the relationship between specie movements and velocity of money, Professor Viner makes the following statement with regard to the case considered in the text where $f^{(1)}$ and $f^{(2)}$ are constants and their sum is equal to unity:

" . . . assuming no change to occur in either country in the final purchases velocity of money, the greater is the weighted average final purchases velocity of

$$(8.29) \qquad dM^{(1)} = \frac{p^{(1)}_2 dZ}{f^{(1)} V^{(1)} + f^{(2)} V^{(2)}}.$$

If the terms of trade do change, then the relative change in the quantity of money in each country is given by equations (8.23). Professor Viner argues that if we adopt the assumption that the quantity

money in the two countries combined, the smaller will be the amount of money necessary to be transferred to restore a disturbed equilibrium, other things remaining the same." (P. 368.)

It can be seen from (8.29) that this conclusion is not universally valid. For the sake of illustration let us take the case where the exchange rate between the two currencies is unity. The weighted average final purchases velocity is then defined as

$$\bar{v} = \frac{M^{(1)} V^{(1)} + M^{(2)} V^{(2)}}{M^{(1)} + M^{(2)}}.$$

In Viner's illustration $M^{(1)} = 3000$ and $M^{(2)} = 1500$, so that the weighted average velocities are:

Case A, $\bar{v} = 1$,

Case B, $\bar{v} = 5/3$,

Case C, $\bar{v} = 2/3$.

For these cases Viner's generalization appears to be valid, since the money flow varies inversely with $\bar{v}$. If, however, we take the following case, the generalization breaks down:

Case D, $V^{(1)} = 3/5$, $V^{(2)} = 3/2$.

For then we have:

$$dM^{(1)} = 500 \quad \text{and} \quad \bar{v} = 9/10.$$

In fact the transfer of money will be less than 600 with a weighted average velocity *less* than unity for all $V^{(1)}$ and $V^{(2)}$ such that the following two inequalities hold simultaneously:

$$dM^{(1)} = \frac{600}{V^{(1)}/3 + 2V^{(2)}/3} < 600,$$

(a)

$$\bar{v} = \frac{3000\, V^{(1)} + 1500\, V^{(2)}}{4500} < 1.$$

This means that

$$V^{(1)} + 2V^{(2)} > 3,$$

(b)

$$2\, V^{(1)} + V^{(2)} < 3,$$

which includes the limitation that

$$1 < V^{(2)} < 3,$$

(c)

$$0 < V^{(1)} < 1.$$

Similarly the transfer of money will be greater than 600 with a weighted average velocity greater than unity for all $V^{(1)}$ and $V^{(2)}$ such that the inequalities in (a) are reversed. This means that the inequalities in (b) are also reversed and that

$$1 < V^{(1)} < 3,$$

(d)

$$0 < V^{(2)} < 1.$$

Since in all of his illustrations Professor Viner chose $V^{(2)} = 1$, he failed to observe that his generalization was not valid for all cases.

of money held in each country is proportional to the money value of income including reparations receipts and excluding reparations payments, the receiving country must always gain money from the paying country no matter how the terms of trade change.[9]

It can be shown that this conclusion is not universally valid. Indeed, the receiving country may conceivably lose money not only when the terms of trade turn against her, but even when the terms of trade change in her favor.

It is obvious from the equations for the amounts of money holdings in each country that the country which has the algebraically larger percentage change in real income (measured in terms of the *numéraire*) will gain money from the other. Normally the country receiving reparations will experience a rise in its real income (income being defined as including reparations receipts and excluding reparations payments), while the country paying reparations will experience a decline. The receiving country will, therefore, normally gain money from the paying country. If, however, the terms of trade change sufficiently in favor of the paying country its real income may rise in greater proportion than that of the receiving country, in which case the paying country will gain money. The larger the receiving country's propensity to import and the smaller the paying country's propensity to consume its own export commodity the greater will be the rise in the terms of trade in favor of the paying country. Likewise the less elastic the receiving country's import demand and the less elastic the paying country's export supply with respect to the terms of trade (i.e., the less elastic the reciprocal-demand curves of either country), the greater will be the rise in the terms of trade in favor of the paying country.

If the terms of trade change against the paying country its real income will, of course, decline. If, however, the receiving country's supply of the commodity which it imports is sufficiently large relative to that of the paying country, its real income may decline in even greater proportion than that of the paying country. In this case too, the receiving country will lose money to the paying country. It will be shown, however, that this is possible only under very restrictive conditions.

The proof of these statements is as follows:

From (8.23) the receiving country will lose money whenever the

[9] See Viner, *Studies*, p. 366: "In its most extreme application this erroneous doctrine has led to the conclusion that if unilateral payments should perchance result in a relative shift in price levels in favor of the *paying* country, the movement of specie will be from the receiving to the paying country!" See also Viner's reply to Robertson in the *Quarterly Journal of Economics*, Vol. 53, February, 1939, pp. 314–16.

proportionate change in its real income is algebraically smaller than that of the paying country:

(8.30a)
$$P^{(2)} \frac{dP^{(1)}}{dZ} - P^{(1)} \frac{dP^{(2)}}{dZ} < 0.$$

Substituting from equations (8.20) and (8.21) we have:

(8.30b)
$$\frac{dy_1}{dZ} (P^{(2)} \overline{X}_1^{(1)} - P^{(1)} \overline{X}_1^{(2)}) + P^{(1)} + P^{(2)} < 0.$$

Dividing through by $P^{(1)} + P^{(2)}$ and making use of (8.26) and (8.27), we obtain

(8.30c)
$$\frac{dy_1}{dZ} \left(\frac{f^{(1)} \overline{X}_1^{(1)} - f^{(2)} \overline{X}_{,1}^{(2)}}{f^{(1)} + f^{(2)}} \right) < -1.$$

Normally $f^{(1)} \overline{X}_1^{(1)} - f^{(2)} \overline{X}_1^{(2)}$ is negative. Indeed as we showed in footnote 7 this expression is necessarily negative if the fractions $f^{(1)}$ and $f^{(2)}$ are constants. Consequently if the rise in the terms of trade in favor of the paying country is sufficiently large (8.30c) will be satisfied and the receiving country will lose money. From equation (8.6) we obtain the factors affecting the magnitude of dy_1/dZ cited above.

If $f^{(1)}$ and $f^{(2)}$ are not constants but appropriate functions of the terms of trade y_1 then it is possible for $f^{(1)} \overline{X}_1^{(1)} - f^{(2)} \overline{X}_1^{(2)}$ to be positive.[10] In that case the receiving country would lose money if the terms of trade fell sufficiently, since its real income would decline in greater proportion than that of the receiving country.

B. Under Robertson's Assumption

Robertson assumes that the quantity of money held in each country is proportional to income excluding reparations receipts but in-

---

[10] As we saw in footnote 7 the stability conditions require that
$$\frac{\partial [y_1 I_1^{(1)} - I_2^{(2)} - Z]}{\partial y_1} < 0.$$
Substituting from equations (a) of footnote 7, we have
$$\frac{\partial [y_1 I_1^{(1)} - I_2^{(2)} - Z]}{\partial y_1} = f^{(1)} \overline{X}_1^{(1)} - f^{(2)} \overline{X}_1^{(2)} + \overline{X}_1^{(1)} y_1 \frac{\partial f^{(1)}}{\partial y_1} - \overline{X}_1^{(2)} y_1 \frac{\partial f^{(2)}}{\partial y_1} < 0.$$
If the difference between the last two terms is negative and sufficiently large numerically, then the difference between the first two terms may be positive.

cluding reparations payments. Instead of (8.23) we shall then have for the transfer of money:

$$(8.31) \quad \frac{dM^{(1)}}{M^{(1)}} = \frac{K^{(2)}[(P^{(2)} + Z)\bar{X}_1^{(1)}dy_1 - (P^{(1)} - Z)\bar{X}_1^{(2)}dy_1]}{(P^{(1)} - Z)[K^{(1)}(P^{(1)} - Z) + K^{(2)}(P^{(2)} + Z)]}.$$

In other words, the gain or loss of money by the receiving country will be directly proportional to the expression in brackets in the numerator of (8.31). It follows, therefore, as Robertson showed, that if the terms of trade y_1 remain unchanged there will be no transfer of money between the two countries. Robertson also states that under his assumption money will be lost by the country against whom the terms of trade change. This means that $dM^{(1)}/dy_1$ must be negative, or that

$$(8.32) \quad (P^{(2)} + Z)\bar{X}_1^{(1)} - (P^{(1)} - Z)\bar{X}_1^{(2)} < 0.$$

If we start with a situation in which the initial reparations payment (before the change) is zero, then condition (8.32) becomes:

$$(8.33a) \quad P^{(2)}\bar{X}_1^{(1)} - P^{(1)}\bar{X}_1^{(2)} < 0,$$

or, stated in terms of the fractions f,

$$(8.33b) \quad f^{(1)}\bar{X}_1^{(1)} - f^{(2)}\bar{X}_1^{(2)} < 0.$$

If, as Robertson assumed, the importing country has no initial supply of the commodity which it imports ($\bar{X}_1^{(1)} = 0$), then (8.33) must be satisfied, and Robertson's conclusions are valid. As we have already seen, however, it is quite consistent with the stability conditions that $\bar{X}_1^{(1)}$ shall be so large that condition (8.33) is reversed. In that case the country against which the terms of trade changed would gain money.

CHAPTER V

THE GENERAL EQUILIBRIUM OF PRODUCTION IN INTERNATIONAL TRADE

I. DESCRIPTION OF EQUILIBRIUM

Thus far we have been considering an economic world in which no production takes place, but in which the only economic activity is that of exchange. Individuals are assumed to come to the market with fixed supplies of goods and services which they exchange for other goods and services. The chief problem introduced by the theory of production is the fact that the supply of commodities available for exchange is not fixed but is itself a variable depending upon the price system.

Since the mathematical theory of production has already been treated at length by several writers including the present one,[1] and since it has so much in common with the theory of exchange, only a brief review is required here.

A. *The Entrepreneurial Supply Functions*

1. *The equilibrium of the firm*

It is assumed that each firm employs various quantities of productive services a_1, a_2, $\cdots$, a_m, to produce various quantities of products x_{m+1}, x_{m+2}, $\cdots$, x_n. The quantities of some of the services used as well as of some of the products produced may, of course, be zero. The transformation function of the firm showing the relationship between the quantities of the various products that can be produced with different quantities of the services is

---

[1] R. G. D. Allen, *Mathematical Analysis for Economists* (London: Macmillan Company, 1938), pp. 369–74 and 505–09; J. R. Hicks, *Value and Capital* (Oxford: Clarendon Press, 1939), Chaps. VI–VIII, and the Appendix, pp. 319–25; *Théorie mathématique de la valeur en régime de libre concurrence*, No. 580 of the *Actualités scientifiques et industrielles* (Paris: Hermann et Cie, 1937), pp. 33–49; Harold Hotelling, "Edgeworth's Taxation Paradox and the Nature of Demand and Supply Functions," *Journal of Political Economy*, Vol. 40 (1932), pp. 590–98; Jacob L. Mosak, "Interrelations of Production, Price, and Derived Demand," *ibid.*, Vol. 46 (December, 1938), pp. 761–87; Heinrich von Stackelberg, "Angebot und Nachfrage in der Produktionswirtschaft," *Archiv für Mathematische Wirtschafts- und Sozialforschung*, Band 4, Heft 2 (1938), pp. 73–99. The summary given here follows along the lines of Hicks's Appendix.

(9.1a) $f(a_1, a_2, \cdots, a_m, x_{m+1}, x_{m+2}, \cdots, x_n) = 0$.

When the quantities of all the factors and all but one of the products are given this equation shows the maximum amount that can be produced of the remaining product. When the quantities of all the products and all but one of the factors are given this equation shows the minimum amount required of the remaining factor. Corresponding to the marginal rate of substitution in the theory of exchange we have two distinct marginal rates of substitution and a marginal rate of transformation in the theory of production. The marginal rate of substitution of the factor a_i for the factor a_j is defined as the decrement in a_j which will just offset an addition of a marginal unit of a_i when the quantities of all other factors and the quantities of all products remain unchanged:

$$R_{a_i}^{a_j} = -\frac{\partial a_j}{\partial a_i} = \frac{f_{a_i}}{f_{a_j}}.$$

Similarly, the marginal rate of substitution of the product x_s for the product x_t is the decrement in x_t which results from producing an additional marginal unit of x_s when the quantities of all other products and the quantities of all factors remain unchanged:

$$R_{x_s}^{x_t} = -\frac{\partial x_t}{\partial x_s} = \frac{f_{x_s}}{f_{x_t}}.$$

We have, further, the marginal rate of transformation of the factor a_i into the product x_s which is defined as the increment in x_s which the firm obtains from the addition of a marginal unit of a_i when the quantities of all other products and all other factors remain unchanged:[2]

$$R_{a_i}^{x_s} = \frac{\partial x_s}{\partial a_i} = -\frac{f_{a_i}}{f_{x_s}}.$$

As was shown by Stackelberg and by Hicks, it is very convenient

---

[2] If but one product is produced with the aid of several factors, then equation (9.1a) reduces to
$$f(a_1, a_2, \cdots, a_m, x) = 0.$$
This may be rewritten in the ordinary form of a production function:
$$x = x(a_1, a_2, \cdots, a_m),$$
where $\partial x/\partial a_i = -f_{a_i}/f_x$ is the marginal productivity of a_i or the rate of transformation of a_i into x. It is with such a production function that I dealt in **my** article, "Interrelations of Production, Price, and Derived Demand," *op. cit.*

for purposes of analysis to treat factors as negative products, writing $x_s = -a_s (s \leq m)$. Equation (9.1a) then becomes:

(9.1b)
$$f(x_1, x_2, \cdots, x_n) = 0.$$

With this convention we may combine all three marginal rates discussed above into one broad category of the marginal rate of substitution of x_t for x_s, where x_t and x_s may each be either a product or a factor:

$$R_s^t = -\frac{\partial x_t}{\partial x_s} = \frac{f_s}{f_t}.$$

Let v denote the surplus of the firm, defined as the difference between the firm's total receipts and its total costs. Then we have:

(9.2a)
$$v = -\sum_{i=1}^{m} p_i a_i + \sum_{t=m+1}^{n} p_t x_t,$$

or, again letting $x_s = -a_s (s \leq m)$,

(9.2b)
$$v = p_1 x_1 + p_2 x_2 + \cdots + p_n x_n.$$

The aim of the firm is to maximize its surplus v subject to the transformation function f. This problem may be treated in a manner parallel to that of the individual consumer demand. Introducing a Lagrange multiplier μ we have:

(9.3)
$$\sum_{s=1}^{n} p_s x_s - \mu f(x_1, x_2, \cdots, x_n) = \max.$$

This implies that:

(9.4)
$$d(v - \mu f) = 0, \quad \text{and}$$
$$d^2(v - u f) < 0.$$

From the first of these equations we obtain the first-order equilibrium conditions for the firm:

(9.5a)
$$p_s - \mu f_s = 0,$$

where

$$\mu = \frac{v}{\sum f_s x_s}.$$

Eliminating μ, we have:

(9.5b)
$$\frac{f_1}{p_1} = \frac{f_2}{p_2} = \cdots = \frac{f_n}{p_n}, \text{ or}$$

$$(9.5c) \qquad \frac{f_1}{f_n} = \frac{p_1}{p_n}, \quad \frac{f_2}{f_n} = \frac{p_2}{p_n}, \quad \ldots, \quad \frac{f_{n-1}}{f_n} = \frac{p_{n-1}}{p_n}.$$

These correspond to equations (1.4) for the individual consumer demand. They state that in equilibrium the marginal rate of substitution between any two products or any two factors or between a product and a factor (namely, the marginal rate of transformation) must equal the ratio of their prices. The condition that the marginal rate of transformation between a product and a factor must equal the ratio of their prices is simply another way of stating the more familiar proposition that the value of the marginal product must equal the price of the factor or that the marginal cost of the factor must equal the price of the product.

In order that the equilibrium position should be stable, it is necessary that the surplus should be a maximum rather than a minimum. This means that the surplus must decline for small displacements from the equilibrium position in every direction. If we treat factors as negative products, then this will be true if the marginal rate of substitution between products *increases* for substitutions in every direction. If we separate factors from products, then this rule subdivides into three parts:

1.   The marginal rate of substitution between products must be increasing; namely, the decrement in x_t resulting from the production of a marginal unit of x_s must grow larger as we continue to substitute x_s for x_t.

2.   The marginal rate of substitution between factors must diminish; namely, the decrement in a_j which will just offset a marginal increase in a_i will diminish as more of a_i is substituted for a_j.

3.   The marginal rate of transformation of factor into product will diminish; namely, the increment in x_s resulting from a marginal increase in a_i will diminish as more of a_i is transformed into x_s.

These conditions must hold not only for substitutions between any two products, any two factors, or any one product and any one factor, but also between any two groups of products, any two groups of factors, or any one group of products and one group of factors.[3] Thus, if in our last rule we treat a_i as the entire group of factors and x_s as some one product, we obtain the familiar rule that the marginal productivity of expenditure must diminish as expenditure increases or that the marginal cost of producing any particular product must rise.

The condition that the marginal rate of transformation between

---

[3] As we have already seen in Chapter I, any group of commodities whose prices remain unchanged may be treated as a single commodity.

the entire group of factors and the entire group of products shall be diminishing explicitly rules out the case of a homogeneous production function. This means that we must assume that the entrepreneur possesses some fixed productive opportunity which prevents output from changing in the same proportion as input, and to which the surplus v may be imputed as earnings.

These conditions are all contained in the second part of (9.4). Since v is linear in x_s, $d^2v = 0$, and the second condition of (9.4) becomes $d^2f > 0$ subject to $df = 0$. This implies that the determinants

$$
\begin{vmatrix} 0 & f_1 & f_2 \\ f_1 & f_{11} & f_{12} \\ f_2 & f_{21} & f_{22} \end{vmatrix}, \quad
\begin{vmatrix} 0 & f_1 & f_2 & f_3 \\ f_1 & f_{11} & f_{12} & f_{13} \\ f_2 & f_{21} & f_{22} & f_{23} \\ f_3 & f_{31} & f_{32} & f_{33} \end{vmatrix}, \quad
\begin{vmatrix} 0 & f_1 & f_2 & \cdots & f_n \\ f_1 & f_{11} & f_{12} & \cdots & f_{1n} \\ f_2 & f_{21} & f_{22} & \cdots & f_{2n} \\ \cdot & \cdot & \cdot & \cdot & \cdot \\ f_n & f_{n1} & f_{n2} & \cdots & f_{nn} \end{vmatrix},
$$

must *all* be negative. Again we let F be the last of these determinants, F_{11} the cofactor of f_{11} in F, $F_{11,22}$ the cofactor of f_{22} in F_{11}, et cetera. Then these conditions state that

$$
\frac{F_{11}}{F}, \frac{F_{11,22}}{F}, \cdots, \frac{F_{11,22,\cdots,(n-1)(n-1)}}{F},
$$

must all be positive. These conditions are invariant against a substitution of $\phi(f)$ for f as a transformation function (provided $\phi = 0$ when $f = 0$). Since the first-order equilibrium conditions (9.5) are likewise invariant against such a substitution, it follows that the transformation function like the utility function is arbitrary.

The stability conditions simply insure that the surplus shall be a maximum, but not that it shall necessarily be positive. In order that anyone should permanently engage in the process of production the surplus must not only be a maximum but must also be positive. This implies that not only the marginal cost but also the average cost of producing each product and each group of products (including the whole group of all products) must be rising.

2.   The supply functions

The equilibrium equations for the firm are given by (9.5a) plus the transformation function $f(x_1, x_2, \cdots, x_n) = 0$. To determine the effects of a change in any one of the prices upon the equilibrium situation we need but differentiate these equations with respect to that price. We then have:

$$f_1 \frac{\partial x_1}{\partial p_t} + f_2 \frac{\partial x_2}{\partial p_t} + \cdots + f_n \frac{\partial x_n}{\partial p_t} = 0,$$

$$f_1 \frac{\partial \mu}{\partial p_t} + \mu f_{11} \frac{\partial x_1}{\partial p_t} + \mu f_{12} \frac{\partial x_2}{\partial p_t} + \cdots + \mu f_{1n} \frac{\partial x_n}{\partial p_t} = 0,$$

(9.6) $\cdot \quad \cdot \quad \cdot \quad \cdot \quad \cdot \quad \cdot \quad \cdot \quad \cdot \quad \cdot$

$$f_t \frac{\partial \mu}{\partial p_t} + \mu f_{t1} \frac{\partial x_1}{\partial p_t} + \mu f_{t2} \frac{\partial x_2}{\partial p_t} + \cdots + \mu f_{tn} \frac{\partial x_n}{\partial p_t} = 1,$$

$\cdot \quad \cdot \quad \cdot \quad \cdot \quad \cdot \quad \cdot \quad \cdot \quad \cdot \quad \cdot$

$$f_n \frac{\partial \mu}{\partial p_t} + \mu f_{n1} \frac{\partial x_1}{\partial p_t} + \mu f_{n2} \frac{\partial x_2}{\partial p_t} + \cdots + \mu f_{nn} \frac{\partial x_n}{\partial p_t} = 0.$$

The solution to this system of equations is given by:

(9.7)
$$\frac{\partial \bar{\bar{x}}_s}{\partial p_t} = \frac{F_{st}}{\mu F}.$$

(The double bar is used to indicate the entrepreneurial supply of products or the entrepreneurial demand for productive services, to distinguish it from the single bar which designates the initial fixed supplies of the goods and services and the unbarred variables which relate to the *consumer* demand for the commodities.) Comparing the stability determinants in the theory of production with those given in the theory of exchange, it is evident that the negative of the term $F_{st}/\mu F$ must obey the identical rules that are obeyed by the substitution terms $x_{st} = \lambda U_{st}/U$ in the theory of exchange. Let us therefore write:

$$\bar{\bar{x}}_{st} = - \frac{F_{st}}{\mu F}.$$

Then equation (9.7) becomes:

(9.8)
$$\frac{\partial \bar{\bar{x}}_s}{\partial p_t} = - \bar{\bar{x}}_{st},$$

where the same set of rules applies to $\bar{\bar{x}}_{st}$ in the theory of production as to x_{st} in the theory of exchange. In particular, we have:

(9.9)
$$\frac{\partial \bar{\bar{x}}_s}{\partial p_s} = - \bar{\bar{x}}_{ss} > 0.$$

This means that the entrepreneurial supply curve for any product is positively sloped with respect to its own price. Since $x_s = - a_s$ for $s \leq m$, it follows that:

$$(9.10) \qquad \frac{\partial \bar{a}_s}{\partial p_s} = \bar{x}_{ss} < 0,$$

or the entrepreneurial demand curve for any productive service is negatively sloped with respect to its own price. The other properties of the term $\bar{x}_{st}$ parallel those of the substitution terms x_{st} in the theory of exchange. Thus we have:

(1) $\quad \bar{x}_{st} = \bar{x}_{ts}$,

(2) $\quad \bar{x}_{ss} < 0$,

(3) $\quad \sum\limits_{s=1}^{n-1} \sum\limits_{t=1}^{n-1} p_s\, p_t\, \bar{x}_{st} < 0$,

(4) $\quad \sum\limits_{s=1}^{n} p_s\, \bar{x}_{st} = 0$,

(5) $\quad \sum\limits_{s \neq t} p_s\, \bar{x}_{st} > 0$,

(6) $\quad \sum\limits_{s=1}^{m} \sum\limits_{t=m+1}^{n} p_s\, p_t\, \bar{x}_{st} > 0 \qquad\qquad (m < n)$.

The sign of $\bar{x}_{st} = - \partial \bar{x}_s / \partial p_t$ provides us with a definition of substitution and complementarity in production. If $\bar{x}_{st} > 0$, then x_s and x_t are substitutes. If x_s and x_t are products, this means that an increase in the price of one leads to a decrease in the output of the other. If they are factors, it means that an increase in the price of one leads to an increase in the entrepreneurial demand (equals negative supply) for the other. If one is a product and the other a factor, it means that an increase in the price of the product leads to an increase in the demand for the factor, and that an increase in the price of the factor leads to a decrease in the supply of the product. Normally products and factors are substitutes.

If $\bar{x}_{st} < 0$, then x_s and x_t are complements. If they are products, an increase in the price of one leads to an increase in the supply of the other. If they are factors an increase in the price of one leads to a decrease in the demand for the other. If one is a product and the other is a factor, then an increase in the price of the product leads to a decrease in the demand for the factor, and an increase in the price of the factor leads to an increase in the supply of the product.

Hicks uses the term "regression" to denote complementarity between a factor and a product.[4]

It follows from this analysis that the entrepreneurial supply of any product and demand for any productive service are functions of the prices of all of the productive services and products the firm uses and sells. However, from the equilibrium conditions (9.5) we see immediately that these functions are homogeneous of degree zero, so that if all the prices were doubled the entrepreneurial supply of products (and demands for productive services) would remain unchanged. We may, therefore, write the firm's supply equations for products (and demands for factors) in the form:

$$(9.11) \qquad \vec{x}_s = \vec{x}_s(y_1, y_2, \cdots, y_{n-1}) \qquad s = 1, 2, \cdots, n,$$

where $y_s = p_s/p_n$ is the ratio of the price of X_s to the *numéraire* X_n.

Summing for all firms in the country, we obtain the entrepreneurial market supply (and demand) functions:

$$(9.12) \qquad \bar{X}_s = \bar{X}_s(y_1, y_2, \cdots, y_{n-1}),$$

where $\bar{X}_s = \sum \vec{x}_s$ for all firms. Since $\vec{x}_{st} = - \partial \vec{x}_s/\partial p_t$ obeys the same rules for all firms, it is clear that $\bar{X}_{st} = - \partial \bar{X}_s/\partial p_t = - \sum \partial \vec{x}_s/\partial p_t$ also obeys the same rules.

Parallel to our definitions of substitution and complementarity with respect to consumption we have similar definitions with respect to production. Two products (positive or negative) will be considered as substitutes in production if $\bar{X}_{st} > 0$ and as complements if $\bar{X}_{st} < 0$. It should be noted, however that whereas in the theory of consumption X_{st} relates only to a part rather than to the total effect of a price change, here $\bar{X}_{st}$ relates to the total effect.[5]

B. *The Consumer Demand Functions*

The theory of production also requires that some modifications be made in the theory of consumer demand. In the individual's utility function we must now include the quantities of the various produc-

---

[4] Hicks, *op. cit.*, p. 93. I observed but did not name the phenomenon of regression in my article, "Interrelations of Production," *op. cit.*, pp. 778–79.

[5] In my article, "Interrelations of Production," *op. cit.*, I subdivided the total production effect into two parts in two alternative ways:

1. A "substitution effect" which measures the change that would result if the total *expenditure on input* remained fixed, and a scale effect which measures the change due to the change in expenditure.

2. A "substitution effect" which measures the change that would result if the total *output* remained fixed, and a scale effect which measures the change due to the change in output.

tive services, in so far as the direct consumption of these services renders direct utility to their users. The budget equation must also be modified to include on the one hand the consumer demand and supply for productive services and on the other hand the entrepreneurial surplus which may accrue to the individual as owner of the firm. Instead of the budget equation of the theory of exchange, we have therefore:

$$(9.13) \qquad \sum_1^n p_s\, x_s = \sum_1^n p_s\, \bar{x}_s + v = r,$$

where $v = \sum_1^n p_s\, \bar{\bar{x}}_s$ is the individual's profits as owner of the firm. As before, the $\bar{x}_s$ includes both products and factors, the latter being treated as negative products. The fundamental equation of the market consumer demand both for products and for productive services now becomes:

$$(9.14) \qquad \frac{\partial X_s}{\partial p_t} = \sum \frac{\partial X_s}{\partial p_t} = \sum (\bar{x}_t + \bar{\bar{x}}_t - x_t)\, \frac{\partial x_s}{\partial r} + X_{st},$$

where the summation is taken over all individuals.[6] The demand functions are again homogeneous of zero degree, namely, if all prices (and reparations payments or receipts) change in the same proportion the demand for each commodity remains unchanged. It follows that we can again write the total-market consumer demand functions in country (i) in the same form as before. If there are reparations and the receipts or payments $Z^{(i)}$ remain unchanged when the price ratios change, then we have:

$$(9.15a) \qquad X_s^{(i)} = X_s^{(i)}\, (y_1, y_2, \cdots, y_{n-1}, Z^{(i)}).$$

If, however, $Z^{(i)}$ is a function of the $n-1$ price ratios and of a parameter of shift α, then we have:[7]

$$(9.15b) \qquad X_s^{(i)} = X_s^{(i)}\, (y_1, y_2, \cdots, y_{n-1}, \alpha).$$

It is understood that if X_r is a domestic commodity of a foreign country, then the demand for it in country i is identically zero, and the

---

[6] The reason for the additional term $\bar{\bar{x}}_t$ is that in differentiating the budget equation (9.13) we get instead of the first equation of (2.6):

$$\sum_{s=1}^n p_s\, \frac{\partial x_s}{\partial p_t} = \bar{x}_t - x_t + \bar{\bar{x}}_t + \sum_{s=1}^n p_s\, \frac{\partial \bar{\bar{x}}_s}{\partial p_t}.$$

But $\sum_{s=1}^n p_s\, \partial \bar{\bar{x}}_s / \partial p_t = 0$, from Rule (4) for $\bar{\bar{x}}_{st}$.

[7] See Chapter III, Sections II-A and II-B.

demand for any other commodity is completely unaffected by its price $(X'^{(i)}_r \equiv 0$ and $\partial X'^{(i)}_s / \partial y_r \equiv 0)$.

C. Market Equilibrium

Equations (9.15) give us the consumer demand functions for goods and services in each country (i). Equations (9.12) give us the entrepreneurial supply functions for products and demand functions for factors. Equilibrium requires that for each product and for each factor the total-world consumer plus entrepreneurial demand shall equal the total-world initial plus entrepreneurial supply. If, as before, we treat the entrepreneurial demand for factors as a negative supply, then we may write this condition in the form:

(9.16a)
$$X^{(1)}_s + X^{(2)}_s + \cdots + X^{(v)}_s = \overline{X}^{(1)}_s + \overline{\overline{X}}^{(1)}_s + \overline{X}^{(2)}_s + \overline{\overline{X}}^{(2)}_s + \cdots + \overline{X}^{(v)}_s + \overline{\overline{X}}^{(v)}_s$$
$$(s = 1, 2, \cdots, n-1).$$

If X_s is a product, this equation states that the consumer demand is equal to the initial plus the entrepreneurial supply. If it is a factor, then the equation states that the consumer demand is equal to the initial supply minus the entrepreneurial demand. If it is both a product and a factor, then the consumer demand is equal to the initial plus the entrepreneurial supply minus the entrepreneurial demand.

Let

(9.17)
$$I^{(i)}_s = X^{(i)}_s - \overline{X}^{(i)}_s - \overline{\overline{X}}^{(i)}_s$$

be the net import demand for X_s (if positive) or the net export supply of X_s (if negative) in country (i). Then equations (9.16a) may be written in the form:

(9.16b) $$I^{(1)}_s + I^{(2)}_s + \cdots + I^{(v)}_s = 0 \qquad (s = 1, 2, \cdots, n-1),$$

which states that in equilibrium the world import demand for each product and for each factor must equal zero.

As in the theory of exchange we have but $n-1$ rather than n independent equations since in determining $I^{(i)}_s$ we have made use of the budget equation which when summed for all individuals and for all countries becomes $\sum_{i=1}^{v} \sum_{s=1}^{n} I^{(i)}_s = 0$. Consequently, if (9.16) holds for $n-1$ equations, it must also hold for the nth.

The conditions of stability for the general equilibrium of production are strictly analogous to those in the general equilibrium of exchange. Let a_{st} be the rate of change in the world import demand for X_s with respect to y_t:

$$(9.18) \qquad a_{st} = \frac{\partial \sum\limits_{i=1}^{v} (I_{s}^{(i)})}{\partial y_t} = \frac{\partial \sum\limits_{i=1}^{v} (X_{s}^{(i)} - \overline{\overline{X}}_{s}^{(i)})}{\partial y_t}.$$

Perfect stability again requires that the principal minors of successive orders of the determinant $J = |a_{st}|$ shall be alternately negative and positive. Since a_{st} is the sum of a market consumer income effect, a market consumer substitution effect, and a market producer substitution effect, and since both the consumer and producer substitution effects satisfy the condition that the a_{st} terms should satisfy, it follows that the general equilibrium of production like the general equilibrium of exchange can be rendered unstable only through income effects. It should be noted, however, that the income effects are much more dangerous to stability in the equilibrium of production where consumers deal with firms than in the equilibrium of exchange, where there are only consumers. This is due to the fact that the entrepreneurial demand and supply are not subject to any income effect so that there is nothing to offset the income effect of the consumer demand and supply. This is particularly dangerous in the market for factors where the income effect of a price reduction might conceivably lead to a greater increase in the supply of the factor than in the entrepreneurial demand for it. We shall again assume that the income effect is never sufficiently large to offset the combined consumer and producer substitution effects, so that the system is always perfectly stable.

Analogous to our definitions of market complementarity in an exchange economy we have similar definitions for a production economy. We define X_s as a market substitute for X_t if a rise in the price of X_t leads to an increase in the world import demand for X_s $(a_{st} > 0)$, as a market complement if the world import demand for X_s decreases $(a_{st} < 0)$, and as independent if it remains unchanged $(a_{st} = 0)$. We are assuming that income effects are not sufficiently large to offset the substitution effects so that we need not distinguish between true and gross substitutes. The market substitution effect is the sum of the consumer and producer substitution effects. Consequently commodities which are substitutes (complements) in both consumption and production will be market substitutes (complements). Commodities that are complements in consumption and substitutes in production will be market complements or substitutes according as the consumption effect is greater or smaller than the production effect. In general we may assume products to be market substitutes for factors since the production substitution effect is ordinarily greater than any consumption complementarity which might exist. A limited degree of market complementarity may exist between products and more especially between factors. ·

II. THE LAWS OF THE WORKING OF THE
GENERAL EQUILIBRIUM OF PRODUCTION

It follows from the preceding analysis that the laws of the working of the general equilibrium of production are analogous to those deduced for an exchange economy. If there is an increase in the world import demand for only one commodity X_t in terms of the *numéraire*, then its price must rise in terms of the *numéraire*. For a product, such an increase in the world import demand may be due either to an increase in the consumer demand or to a decrease in the entrepreneurial supply. For a factor, it may be due either to a decrease in the consumer supply or to an increase in the entrepreneurial demand. The effects on other products and factors will depend upon the market substitution and complementarity relationships in the familiar way. Substitutes for X_t will tend to move in the same direction and complements in the opposite direction. Substitutes for substitutes and complements of complements will move in the same direction, while substitutes for complements and complements of substitutes will move in the opposite direction.

The effects of changes in unilateral payments in a production economy may again be analyzed just as in an exchange economy. The change in payments represents a redistribution of income which leads to changes in the import demands for various commodities. The solution to this problem is again given by system (7.4), the only change being that a_{st} is now defined by equation (9.18) rather than (7.1). It is instructive to summarize the results which can be obtained up to this point relating to the effects of unilateral payments. We may distinguish the following possibilities:

1. All $b_s = 0$.

It is conceivable that in the equations (7.4) all b_s should be zero. This could occur if there were no domestic commodities (or if the income elasticity for each domestic commodity were zero) and if for each internationally traded commodity the rate of change of demand with respect to income were exactly the same in the paying as in the receiving country. In this case all price ratios y_s between commodities would remain unchanged.

2. $b_s = 0$ for international commodities only.

This case can occur in one of two ways: (a) if the income elasticity for each internationally traded commodity is zero in every country,[8] or (b) if the rate of change of demand with respect to income for each internationally traded commodity is the same in every country. The effect of the unilateral payments is therefore to increase the demand for domestic commodities in the receiving country and to decrease the demand in the paying country.[9] Domestic prices in the receiving country will therefore have to rise relative to those in the paying country. The change in the prices of domestic factors will be in the same direction as products since the two are usually close substitutes.

The effect on the relative import and export prices will depend upon the relationships of substitution and complementarity between the commodities. We may briefly summarize the changes that are possible under varying assumptions:

(a) *In both countries export products are market substitutes for domestic products and factors, but import products are independent of both domestic and export goods.* In this case the prices of the receiving country's exports must rise, relative to those of the paying country. The commodity terms of trade therefore must change in favor of the receiving country. The rise in the export prices of the receiving country is, however, proportionately less than the rise in its domestic prices,[10] since the effect of the reparations has been to increase the demand for its domestic products (and indirectly for the factors used to produce those products) relative to the aggregate demand for the export goods. Consequently the output of export goods in the receiving country will decline. Likewise the demand for those factors used in producing exports but not domestic products will decline, and their prices will therefore fall relative to domestic products. Conversely, in the paying country the fall in export prices is proportionately less than the fall in its domestic prices so that the output of export goods increases.[11]

(b) *Import products are market substitutes for domestic products, but export products are entirely independent of both domestic and import products.* Import products may, of course, be substitutes

---

[8] This corresponds to the assumption made by Yntema, in all except Section 4 of Chapter V. of his book. See the Appendixes to this chapter and to Chapter I.

[9] In case (b) but not in case (a) of this paragraph it is possible that domestic commodities taken as a group should be inferior commodities in each country. In that case all of the conclusions of this section would be reversed.

[10] An exception to this rule should be noted in case there is but *one* domestic good (be it product or factor), and *one* export good. Under the assumptions of this paragraph the domestic and export good would then move in the same proportion.

[11] Some export products may be regressive against the factors used to produce domestic goods or complementary with domestic products. For them the conclusions in this paragraph must be reversed.

for domestic products, both on the demand and on the supply side since each country may (and generally does) produce many of the products which it imports. On the other hand, export products may be entirely independent on the demand side and conceivably on the supply side as well if they are produced by noncompeting factors of production. Under such circumstances the imports of the receiving country must rise in price relative to the imports of the paying country. The change in favor of the paying country will, of course, be reinforced if the export products are regressive against the domestic factors or complementary with the domestic products.

(c) *Both import and export products are market substitutes for domestic products (and factors) but are independent of each other.* Whether the export prices rise or fall relative to the import prices or remain constant now depends upon the relative degrees of substitution between (1) export and domestic goods in the two countries on the one hand and between (2) import and domestic goods in the two countries on the other. The greater the substitution within the former class the greater will be the change in favor of the receiving country, while the greater the substitution within the latter class the greater will be the change in favor of the paying country. The total effect on the commodity terms of trade is, of course, the algebraic sum of these two opposing forces.

(d) *Import and export products are market substitutes for domestic products (and factors), and they are not independent of each other.* If the imports are market substitutes for the exports the results are qualitatively the same as under assumptions (c) above. If, however, imports and exports are complementary then their prices may move in opposite directions even though they are each market substitutes for domestic goods.

3. $b_r = 0$ for domestic goods only.

Reversing now the assumptions of paragraph 2, suppose that the income elasticity of demand for domestic products is zero and that the direct result of the reparations is an increase in the aggregate consumer demand for some internationally traded commodities and a decrease in the demand for others. The interesting case for general analysis is, of course, that in which the increased demand is for the exports of one country while the decreased demand is for the exports of the other country. The export prices of the country for whose goods the demand has increased will then rise relative to the export prices of the other country. The relative changes in the other prices, however, cannot be analyzed without additional assumptions about the relationships of substitution and complementarity between the different commodities.

(a) *The domestic products and factors are market substitutes for each other and for the export products of the country but are independent of the import goods.* In this case the relative change in the domestic prices of the two countries is the same in direction as the relative change in the export prices. Let us assume that the reparations have resulted in an increased aggregate demand for the export goods of the receiving country and a decreased aggregate demand for the export goods of the paying country. [This assumption will be retained in paragraph (b).] Then the "commodity terms of trade" will change in favor of the receiving country and so will the "double factoral terms of trade." The domestic prices of the paying country will fall relative to the exports of the receiving country but will rise relative to its own exports.[12] The domestic prices of the receiving country will rise relative to the exports of the paying country, but will fall relative to its own exports.[13]

(b) *Domestic products and factors are substitutes for each other and for both export and import products.* In this case domestic prices of the receiving country will fall or rise relative to domestic prices of the paying country according as the substitution of domestic products and factors for import products is greater or smaller than the substitution for export products. There is thus no necessity that the "commodity terms of trade" shall move in the same direction as the "double factoral terms of trade." The former may move in favor of the receiving country and the latter in favor of the paying country. Conversely, if we assume that the direct effect of the reparations is an increase in the aggregate demand for the paying country's exports, the commodity terms of trade will move in favor of the paying country but the "double factoral terms of trade" may move in favor of the receiving country.

4. The more general case in which the reparations directly change the aggregate demand for every product may be analyzed in exactly the same manner as were the special cases. Little need therefore be added to the previous analysis. In the "normal case" when domestic products are noninferior, and they are closer substitutes for export than for import products, the domestic product prices of the receiving country will rise relative to those of the paying country unless the reparations lead to a sufficiently large direct increase in the

---

[12] An exception to this rule must be noted when there is but one domestic good and one export good in each country in which case the domestic and export prices move proportionately.

[13] Some domestic products may be net complements of, while some factors may be regressive against, export goods. The relative change in the prices of such domestic products and factors in the two countries will then be in the opposite direction from the relative change in the export prices.

aggregate demand for the paying country's exports relative to those of the receiving country. On the other hand, the commodity terms of trade may turn against the paying country even when the aggregate demand for its exports directly increases, if the demand for the receiving country's domestic products rises sufficiently in comparison with the paying country's demand for domestic goods, and the export products in each country are sufficiently closer substitutes for domestic goods than are import goods.

It should be noted that the present analysis is equally applicable to the case in which there is a consumer demand for factors of production so that the supply of nonproduced (original) factors to firms is a function of the prices rather than a constant. It may be worth mentioning that if factors of production are not inferior commodities in either country, the direct consumer demand for these factors will increase in the receiving country and decrease in the paying country. Unless offset by substitution effects through other markets this would mean that the volume of employment would decline in the receiving country and increase in the paying country.

In conclusion it may be noted that though we have treated here only the problem of reparations payments the techniques employed may be utilized to analyze the effects of any disturbance whatsoever to the general equilibrium of production under international trade.

APPENDIX TO CHAPTER V

YNTEMA'S GENERAL THEORY OF INTERNATIONAL TRADE

We may now compare our system of equations with those postulated by Yntema.[14]

1. As we noted in the Appendix to Chapter 1, Yntema writes the demand for each internationally traded commodity in each country as a function of the money price of that commodity deflated by the level of domestic prices. He further assumes that the income elasticity for each internationally traded commodity is zero in each country.

2. Yntema further assumes that the entrepreneurial supply of each internationally traded product is also a function of its money price deflated by the level of domestic prices. We should arrive at such a function by means of our analysis if we made the following threefold assumption: (a) that the prices of all domestic commodities and services changed in equal proportion, (b) that each internation-

---

[14] Op. cit.

ally traded product was made from domestic commodities and services only, and (c) that all internationally traded goods were produced independently of one another.

3. It follows that the net import demand, or export supply, is also a function of the same variable. Thus we may write for each internationally traded commodity t in country (j)

$$I^{(j)}_t = I^{(j)}_t (p^{(j)}_t / p^{(j)}_j) \ ,$$

where $p^{(j)}_j$ is the price of country j's domestic commodity in terms of its own currency.

4. The deflated price of every commodity in each country may be expressed in terms of the currency of the first country as follows:

$$\frac{p^{(j)}_t}{p^{(j)}_j} = \frac{p^{(1)}_1}{p^{(j)}_j} \frac{p^{(j)}_t}{p^{(1)}_1} = \left(\frac{p^{(1)}_1}{p^{(j)}_j} e_{1j} \right) \frac{p^{(1)}_t}{p^{(1)}_1}.$$

The expression in parentheses represents the ratio of the two domestic price levels multiplied by the exchange rates between the two currencies. Yntema names this expression the "net monetary factor" and represents it by the symbol $z_{1/j}$. We thus have for each internationally traded commodity in each country:

$$I^{(j)}_t = I^{(j)}_t \left(z_{1/j} \frac{p^{(1)}_t}{p^{(1)}_1} \right) .$$

5. In equilibrium the world net import demand (or export supply) for each internationally traded commodity must, of course, be equal to zero. This condition, however, is insufficient to establish equilibrium in Yntema's system since he does not explicitly introduce equations for domestic commodities. Yntema therefore uses an additional set of equations which states that the balance of payments is zero for each country in equilibrium. This implies, of course, the equality between the demand and supply in each country for its domestic commodities taken as a group. Thus Yntema's system of equilibrium equations is

$$\begin{cases} \sum_j I^{(j)}_t = 0 & \text{for each internationally traded commodity } t, \\ \sum_t p^{(j)}_t I^{(j)}_t = 0 & \text{for each country } j. \end{cases}$$

He therefore has two sets of equations to deal with instead of one, in analyzing the effects of disturbances to equilibrium.

6. The stability conditions postulated by Yntema differ from those given here, but these differences need not be discussed in this Appendix.

7. By virtue of the assumptions listed in the first two paragraphs above, it becomes necessary to rule out all of case 3 of Section II of the present chapter. Except for one section where Yntema relaxes these assumptions somewhat, he therefore confines himself to a discussion of our case 2.

PART II
INTERTEMPORAL-EQUILIBRIUM THEORY IN INTERNATIONAL TRADE

CHAPTER VI

INDIVIDUAL CONSUMER PLANNING

We have thus far viewed the economic system from the standpoint of the interrelationships between markets at a given point of time. We have now to consider the economy from the standpoint of the interrelationship between markets through time. The basic factor in dynamic theory is the fact that decisions of individuals and firms to buy and sell are part of a general plan which relates not only to the present but also to the future.

Dynamic theory, therefore, involves two separate types of problems: first, the determination of equilibrium for any given period of time, and second, the change of equilibrium through time. The first problem is similar to that which we encountered in static theory. Taking the sets of price expectations held by individuals at any one moment as given, we have to show how their decisions are determined at that moment (the equilibrium of the economic unit) and what the immediate consequences of these decisions will be (temporary market equilibrium). The properties of the temporary equilibrium must be examined and the laws of its working must be deduced. The second problem is to show how the decisions are modified in the next period as a result of the consequences of the previous decisions and how they thus lead to a new set of consequences (intertemporal equilibrium). The laws of the working of the intertemporal equilibrium must also be developed. This second problem is commonly referred to in the literature as process analysis. For this problem the formal logic of marginal economics is useless; what is needed is direct empirical investigation of the way in which past and present experiences determine estimates for the future. We shall find it worth while, however, to indicate the consequences for a given period of different sets of assumptions as to the way in which such estimates are formed.

I. PLANNING UNDER CERTAINTY

We shall first assume that all plans are made in a world of subjective certainty, i.e., that each individual and entrepreneur acts *as if* he knows for certain what future prices and interest rates will be.

We shall also assume that in each period loans can be made for only one period. Since we have ruled out risks by assumption, this means that all securities available in each period are homogeneous.

A. *Derivation of Individual Consumer Demand Functions*

If we treat the same commodity for different periods of time as different commodities, then we may reduce the problem of dynamic planning to the form of a static problem. If we let x_{rt} be the quantity of x_r planned to be consumed in period t, then we may write the individual's utility function as

(10.1)
$$u = u(x_{10}, x_{20}, \cdots, x_{n0}, x_{11}, x_{21}, \cdots, x_{n1}, \cdots, x_{1\tau}, x_{2\tau}, \cdots, x_{n\tau}).$$

Let e_t be the expected value of the individual's planned "consumption" (of both products and factors) in each period t:

(10.2) $e_t = p \; x_{1t} + p_{2t}x_{2t} + \cdots + p_{nt}x_{nt}$ $(t = 0, 1, 2, \cdots, \tau),$

where p_{rt} is the expected price of X_r in period t and x_{rt} is the quantity of X_r planned to be consumed in period t.[1] Let m_t be the expected value of his (expected) initial supplies of both products and factors, and let l_t be the volume of his expected lendings and b_t his expected borrowings. Renewals are included along with new loans both under lendings and under borrowings. We shall consider lendings as the purchase of securities and borrowings as the sale of (old) or issue of (new) securities. Let the rate of interest expected to be collected or paid in each period on loans made in the preceding period be i_t. No interest is paid in any period on loans made in the same period. For each period the expected value of his initial supplies plus the receipts of interest and principal previously lent plus borrowings must equal the expected value of his consumption plus payments of interest and principal previously borrowed plus lendings. (All expected values for the current period are assumed to be identical with the actual values.) Thus we have for each successive period from $t = 0$ to $t = \tau$:

(10.3a)
$$m_0 + (1 + i_0)l_{-1} + b_0 = e_0 + (1 + i_0)b_{-1} + l_0,$$
$$m_1 + (1 + i_1)l_0 + b_1 = e_1 + (1 + i_1)b_0 + l_1,$$
$$m_2 + (1 + i_2)l_1 + b_2 = e_2 + (1 + i_2)b_1 + l_2,$$
$$\cdots \cdots \cdots \cdots \cdots \cdots$$
$$m_\tau + (1 + i_\tau)l_{\tau-1} + b_\tau = e_\tau + (1 + i_\tau)b_{\tau-1} + l_\tau.$$

---

[1] The reader should note that the meaning of x_{rt} here is entirely different from its meaning in Part I.

Unless the lendings and borrowings involve different interest rates—a condition which we have here ruled out by assumption—it is convenient not to write lendings and borrowings separately in our budget equations, but to take the difference between lendings and borrowings only. Let $c_t = l_t - b_t$ be the net lendings or the difference between lendings and borrowings for the period t. We shall consider net lendings as the net purchase of securities. (Negative net lendings represent net borrowings.) The budget equations (10.3a) may now be rewritten in the form:

(10.3b)
$$m_0 + (1 + i_0)c_{-1} = e_0 + c_0,$$
$$m_1 + (1 + i_1)c_0 = e_1 + c_1,$$
$$m_2 + (1 + i_2)c_1 = e_2 + c_2,$$
$$. \quad . \quad . \quad . \quad . \quad . \quad .$$
$$m_\tau + (1 + i_\tau)c_{\tau-1} = e_\tau + c_\tau.$$

The $\tau + 1$ budget equations (10.3b) may be reduced to a single budget equation over the planning period as a whole by discounting the values in these equations to the current period and summing for all periods. If we let $\beta_0 \equiv 1$ then we shall have

(10.4a)

$$\sum_{t=0}^{\tau} \beta_0 \beta_1 \cdots \beta_t m_t = \sum_{t=0}^{\tau} \beta_0 \beta_1 \cdots \beta_t e_t + \beta_0 \beta_1 \cdots \beta_\tau c_\tau - (1 + i_0)c_{-1}.$$

This equation states that the present value of the individual's stream of current and expected initial supplies of commodities must equal the present value of his stream of current and expected consumption of commodities plus the present value of the sum of securities which he plans to hold at the end of the planning period minus the value of his initial security holdings.

Let $c = \beta_0 \beta_1 \cdots \beta_\tau c_\tau - (1 + i_0)c_{-1}$ be the present value of the sum of securities which he expects to have acquired or sold during the planning period. It is assumed that the individual's plan to acquire (or sell) securities is a function f of the present value of his stream of current and expected initial supplies of commodities. This function may be zero, positive, or negative. If we let $m = \sum_{t=0}^{\tau} \beta_0 \beta_1 \cdots \beta_t m_t$ and $e = \sum_{t=0}^{\tau} \beta_0 \beta_1 \cdots \beta_t e_t$, then the budget equation (10.4a) may be written in the form

(10.4b) $$m = e + c = e + f(m).$$

It is obvious that, given m and f (or c), the individual is definitely restricted with respect to his expected total value of consumption e for the planning period as a whole. For the more he consumes in any one period the less he will be able to consume in other periods if he is to acquire a fixed sum of securities c during the planning period. Let $a \equiv m - c$ be the difference between the value of his initial supplies of commodities and the value of the securities which he expects to acquire during the planning period. Then a represents the present value of his planned allotment for consumption on commodities for the whole planning period, or what we shall call the capital value of the individual's plan. It is clear that the capital value of the plan plays the same role in dynamic theory as does "income" in static theory.

The problem of the individual consumer is to choose his consumption in each period in such a manner as to maximize his utility function (10.1) subject to the budget equation (10.4). Introducing a Lagrange multiplier λ, we have

$$(10.5) \qquad u(x_{rt}) - \lambda \left[\sum_{t=0}^{\tau} \{\beta_0 \beta_1 \cdots \beta_t (e_t - m_t)\} + c \right] = \max.$$

$$(r = 1, 2, \cdots, n;$$
$$t = 0, 1, 2, \cdots, \tau).$$

As in static theory the individual consumer under pure competition is assumed to take the current prices p_{ro} (and the current discount ratio β_1) as fixed constants, which are independent of the total value and distribution of his consumption of commodities. Given his expectations as to future prices and discount ratios, we may therefore obtain his equilibrium selection of commodities just as in static theory by setting the partial derivative of (10.5) with respect to x_{rt} equal to zero. Analogous to the static individual equilibrium conditions we therefore obtain the $n(\tau + 1)$ dynamic conditions:

$$(10.6a) \qquad\qquad \frac{\partial u}{\partial x_{rt}} = \lambda \beta_0 \beta_1 \cdots \beta_t p_{rt},$$

or, upon eliminating λ,

$$(10.6b) \qquad \frac{\partial u}{\partial x_{sv}} \bigg/ \frac{\partial u}{\partial x_{rt}} = \frac{\beta_0 \beta_1 \cdots \beta_v \, p_{sv}}{\beta_0 \beta_1 \cdots \beta_t \, p_{rt}}.$$

Equations (10.6b) state that the marginal rate of substitution between any two commodities planned to be consumed at any two dates must equal the ratio of their expected discounted prices.

The stability conditions are strictly analogous to those in static theory. The marginal rate of substitution between any two commodities at any two dates must be diminishing for substitutions in every direction.

The $n(\tau + 1) - 1$ equations (10.6b) together with the budget equation (10.4) permit us to determine the $n(\tau + 1)$ quantities planned to be consumed in each period, once we are given the current and expected prices and interest rates. We may, therefore, write the expected consumption of each commodity in each period in the form:

(10.7)
$$x_{rt} = x_{rt}(p_{10}, p_{20}, \cdots, p_{n0}, \beta_1 p_{11}, \beta_1 p_{21}, \cdots, \beta_1 p_{n1}, \cdots, \beta_1 \beta_2 \cdots \beta_\tau p_{1\tau},$$
$$\beta_1 \beta_2 \cdots \beta_\tau p_{2\tau}, \cdots, \beta_1 \beta_2 \cdots \beta_\tau p_{n\tau}) \qquad (t = 0, 1, 2, \cdots, \tau).$$

Similarly, the current and planned value of consumption in each period e_t [as defined by equations (10.2)] is also a function of these same parameters.

It is important to note that the equilibrium conditions (10.6) imply that the marginal rate of substitution between the expected values of consumption of any two dates t and v must equal the discount factor used in discounting values of the latter date to values of the earlier date. In particular this means that the marginal rate of substitution between current consumption and the expected consumption for any future period must be equal to the discount factor used to discount values of that period to current values. Thus we have from equations (10.6)[2]

$$(10.8a) \qquad \frac{\partial u}{\partial e_t} = \frac{1}{p_{rt}} \frac{\partial u}{\partial x_{rt}} = \lambda \beta_0 \beta_1 \cdots \beta_t,$$

$$(10.8b) \qquad \frac{\partial u}{\partial e_v} \Big/ \frac{\partial u}{\partial e_t} = \frac{\beta_0 \beta_1 \cdots \beta_v}{\beta_0 \beta_1 \cdots \beta_t} = \beta_{t+1} \beta_{t+2} \cdots \beta_v.$$

It should be understood that equations (10.8) are defined for a given set of prices and price expectations.

The meaning of equations (10.8) may be clearer if we observe that the problem of maximization of utility over time may be subdivided into two parts: (1) the problem of choosing in each period the optimum bundle of commodities for any given total value of consumption, and (2) the problem of determining what the total value of consumption in each period shall be. Assuming that the individual always chooses the optimum bundle of goods for each given value of consumption, then his total utility through time may be written as a function of the value of his consumption in each period:

$$u = u(e_0, e_1, \cdots, e_\tau).$$

[2] This follows from the fact that
$$\frac{\partial u}{\partial x_{rt}} = \frac{\partial u}{\partial e_t} \frac{\partial e_t}{\partial x_{rt}} = \frac{\partial u}{\partial e_t} p_{rt} \qquad \text{[from equation (10.2)]}.$$

Maximizing this function subject to the property restriction (10.4) gives us the set of equations (10.8). Here we may consider the total consumption value in any given period t as a single commodity and the discount factor $\beta_0 \beta_1 \cdots \beta_t$ as its "price." The τ equations (10.8b) together with the budget restriction (10.4) determine the consumption for each period as functions of the current and expected discount ratios when the set of current and expected prices is given. Thus we may write:

$$(10.9) \qquad e_t = e_t(\beta_1, \beta_1 \beta_2, \cdots, \beta_1 \beta_2 \cdots \beta_\tau) \quad (t = 0, 1, 2 \cdots, \tau).$$

The stability conditions are exactly the same as in the static equilibrium of the individual consumer, except that ϵ_t is substituted for x_t and $(\tau + 1)$ for n. From the budget equations (10.3b) it follows that the volume of net lendings or net purchases of securities in each period is also a function of these same parameters.

It should be emphasized that the stability conditions imply that, for given current and expected prices and given expected discount rates, there will be a determinate value of current total consumption and, therefore, a determinate sum of net lendings corresponding to each value of the current discount ratio β_1. (Multiple equilibrium points are ruled out by assumption.) This means that for each given interest rate there will be a limited rather than an indefinitely large sum of net lendings for all lenders taken together. In an exchange economy, therefore, the equilibrium interest rate would be determined at a point where the sum of net lendings for all lenders taken together would be equal to the sum of net borrowings (= negative net lendings) for all borrowers taken together. It follows that even in an economy such as we have assumed, where all risk of default and of changes in capital values is ruled out, and where there is no cost or trouble in buying or selling securities, there would still generally be some rate of interest. The rate of interest would be the price necessary to induce lenders to forgo consumption to a sufficient extent to make their net lendings equal to the demand for loans by borrowers. The only point to remember here is that in such an economy no one would hold his surplus funds in the form of money, since everyone would invest them only in interest-earning bills. There would thus be no true demand function for money, and no true money would exist.

An interesting point which may be discussed here is the question of whether the rate of interest can possibly be zero in an exchange economy. The answer to this question depends upon the assumption we make concerning the marginal rate of substitution between the current and planned consumption of the same commodity. The stability conditions, as we have already noted, require that the marginal rate of substitution between x_{r0} and x_{r1} should diminish as more of x_{r0} is substituted for x_{r1}. Suppose, however, that though diminishing it is always greater than unity, namely, that no matter how much of x_{r0} and x_{r1} the individual plans to consume, the substitution of an additional unit of x_{r0} for an additional unit of x_{r1} would always increase the individual's utility. Then

$$\frac{-\partial x_{r1}}{\partial x_{r0}} \equiv \frac{\partial u}{\partial x_{r0}} \Big/ \frac{\partial u}{\partial x_{r1}} = \frac{p_{r0}}{\beta_1\, p_{r1}} > 1.$$

Suppose further that future prices are expected to be the same as current prices. Then we have

$$\frac{1}{\beta_1} \equiv 1 + i > 1, \text{ or } i > 0.$$

Thus if we adopt the assumption that the marginal rate of substitution between current and planned consumption of commodities is greater than unity, then the rate of interest must be greater than zero if future prices are expected to be the same as current prices. Only if we drop this assumption can the interest rate be zero in an exchange economy in which future prices are expected to be the same as current prices.

The objection is sometimes made that at a zero rate of interest each individual would borrow indefinitely large sums since he could pay off each loan by reborrowing. This argument is not valid, however. There is no more reason why he should borrow indefinitely at a zero rate of interest than at any other rate, for no matter what the rate of interest may be, he could under pure competition always repay an old loan together with the interest by reborrowing. We must therefore assume that there is some factor which prevents the individual from borrowing more than a fixed amount as shown by the budgetary restriction (10.4). In an economy in which we do not abstract from risk and uncertainty it is easy to see what that factor is. In a riskless economy, however, we must assume that there is some arbitrary psychological or institutional factor which limits the extent of an individual's borrowings.

B. Properties of the Dynamic Demand Functions

1. Variation of current and planned consumption with changes in the capital value of the plan

It should be obvious by comparing the dynamic-equilibrium conditions (10.6) and (10.4) for the planned consumption in each period

t with the static-equilibrium conditions for determining the consumption of individual commodities in a static economy, that the capital value of the plan plays exactly the same role in a dynamic economy as does "income" in a static economy. An increase in the capital value of the plan, all current and expected prices and interest rates being given, will, therefore, lead to an increase in the current and planned consumption of every commodity that is not an "inferior" good. It is just conceivable that all commodities in a given period should be inferior so that an increase in the capital value of the plan will lead to a decrease in the total value of consumption for that period. This case, however, may be ruled out as extremely unlikely, although not inconsistent with the stability conditions for equilibrium. An increase in the capital value of the plan for given current and expected prices and interest rates may occur in one of two ways: (1) an increase in the expected value of initial supplies of commodities m_t; and (2) a decrease in the sum of securities c which the individual plans to acquire during his planning period. Either of these changes will, therefore, ordinarily lead to an increase in consumption in every period.

2. Variation of consumption with changes in prices

The effect of any isolated change in the expected price of some commodity (all other prices and interest rates being given) may be analyzed into two parts, just as in static theory. There is first a substitution effect due to the relative changes in the discounted prices of the commodities planned to be bought at different dates. This substitution effect will tend to decrease the planned consumption of the commodity whose price has risen. It will also lead to an increase in the current and planned consumption of substitute commodities and to a decline in that of complements. It should be emphasized that the various commodities are interrelated both in a given period of time and over different periods of time. Thus a rise in the expected price of milk will tend to increase current consumption of milk. Milk today is a substitute for milk tomorrow. On the other hand, an expected increase in school tuition might deter a student from entering school in the current period, since he might not be able to complete his training. School training today would then be complementary to school training tomorrow.

In addition to the substitution effect of a price change there is in the dynamic system a "capital effect" which corresponds to the income effect in a static system. For apart from any substitution effect, a change in the expected price of any commodity will be equivalent to a change in the capital value of the plan. An increase in the expected price of any given commodity will be equivalent to a reduction in the capital value of the plan for a person who plans to buy that commodity, and to an increase in the capital value for one who plans to sell. The converse holds for a reduction in the expected price.

The total effect of a price change is the sum of its substitution and income effects. For noninferior commodities the capital effect works in the same direction as the substitution effect for buyers, but in the opposite direction for sellers. For sellers, therefore, an increase in the expected price of a given commodity might lead to a planned increase in its consumption (namely, to a planned decrease in its sales). This, as we have already seen in static analysis, is particularly applicable to the sale of labor services.

The effect of a single price change upon the current or planned total value of consumption in any period is made up of the weighted sum of the effects upon the consumption of the individual commodities in that period. It is clear, therefore, that such a price change may lead either to a decrease or to an increase in the value of consumption.

The effect of an isolated change in the *current* price of a commodity, on the assumption that all other current prices and all expected prices remain unchanged, may be analyzed in exactly the same manner as an isolated change in the expected price of a commodity. There will be a substitution effect away from the current consumption of the commodity whose price has risen. The current and planned consumption will rise for substitute commodities and decline for complements. In addition to the substitution effect, we must take into account the "capital effect" which works in the same direction as the substitution effect for buyers but in the opposite direction for sellers.

This analysis of the effects of a change in the current price, however, is not very satisfactory since it forces us to confine ourselves only to those cases in which the change in the current price has no effect upon the expected price of any commodity. We want a technique which will enable us to allow for the effects of current price changes upon future price expectations.

This is not very difficult, however. For if the expected price changes as a result of the current price then we are dealing with a case in which two prices change simultaneously, the price of the current commodity and that of the future commodity. And the effects of a simultaneous change in two or more prices may be determined simply by combining the individual effects. Thus if one price rises and another falls there will be a substitution effect away from the commodity whose price has risen in favor of the one whose price has fallen. If both prices rise or both fall there will be a substitution effect in favor of that commodity for which the proportional price rise is smaller, or the proportional price decline larger. If the proportional rise (or fall) in price is the same for both commodities then there will be no substitution effect between these two commodities, but there will be a substitution against (or in favor of) these two commodities taken together relative to other commodities. Indeed, as we have already seen, a group of goods whose prices change in the same proportion behaves just as if it were a single commodity.[3] This analysis of simultaneous price changes enables us to allow for possible resulting changes in price expectations when analyzing the effects of changes in current prices. Before going on to this analysis, however, we need to introduce the concept of elasticity of expectations.

3. Elasticity of expectation

Expectations of future prices may be assumed to depend upon two different sets of factors: (1) factors unrelated to the course of past and present prices such as crop reports, the weather, the political news, and the like, which induce autonomous changes in price expectations; and (2) the course of past and present prices. The first set of factors is outside the scope of our analysis; they may be considered as the "shocks" to which the economic system is constantly subjected. The second set of factors, past and present prices, may be further analyzed.

From the point of view of the current period, past prices are simply data. If their influence on price expectations were completely dominant we could take the latter as data too. We could then analyze the effects of changes in current prices upon the assumption that price expectations remain unaffected. This is the case which we considered in the previous section. In general, however, past prices are not the completely dominant influence upon price expectations, so that we must take into account the effect of current prices. For this purpose, Hicks has introduced the concept of elasticity of expectations.[4] He assumes that, given the set of past prices, the price of X that is expected to rule in any given future period is some function of the current price of that commodity. He then defines the elasticity of a particular person's expectation of the price of X as the ratio of the proportional rise in the expected future price of X to the proportional rise in its current price. Thus, given the set of past prices we have for each individual the expectation functions

$$p_{rt} = f_{rt}(p_{r0})$$

and the corresponding elasticities of expectation,

---

[3] See Chapter I, Section II, subheading 6.
[4] Hicks, *Value and Capital* (Oxford, 1939), p. 205.

$$e = \frac{dp_{rt}}{dp_{ro}} \frac{p_{ro}}{p_{rt}}.$$

If expectations are completely inelastic ($e = 0$) then we have the case in which the expectations are given data, unaffected by current prices. If the elasticity is unity then the expected price changes in the same proportion as the current price. This means that the ratio between the current and expected price remains constant.[5] Two extreme cases may also be mentioned. If the elasticity is greater than unity, then the proportional rise in the expected price is greater than the proportional rise in the current price. If the elasticity is negative a rise in the current price leads to a decline in the expected price.

We may now briefly consider the effects of a change in the current price of a commodity under varying assumptions as to the elasticity of expectations.

1. If the elasticity is less than unity, then a rise in the current price will be accompanied by a less than proportional change in the expected price. There will, therefore, be a substitution effect against present in favor of future consumption. The analysis here is qualitatively no different from that which we obtained in the case of zero elasticity of expectation.

2. In the case of unit elasticity of expectation, the proportional change in the expected price is equal to that of the current price. There is, therefore, no substitution effect between the current and the planned consumption of the commodity. Indeed we can treat the commodities of different dates as the same commodity, and say that there will be a decline in the planned consumption of X over the planning period as a whole. This does not mean, of course, that the decline will be evenly divided over all the periods. Indeed, we may expect current consumption in most cases to decline less than planned consumption, since it is generally rather difficult to change one's buying habits very rapidly. Likewise in case of a decline in price with unit elasticity of expectations we may generally expect current consumption to rise less than future consumption. In other words, the longer the lower price is in effect the greater will be the rise in consumption, other things being equal. This difference between short-run and long-run demand corresponds to the well-known difference between short-run and long-run supply.

3. The results under elastic price expectations are in striking

[5] This is not the same as saying that changes in current prices are expected to be permanent, unless the initial expected price is the same as the current price, namely, unless we are at that point of the expectations function which lies on the 45-degree line through the origin. Cf. Erik Lindahl, *Studies in the Theory of Money and Capital* (London, 1939), p. 49.

contrast to those given above. In this case a rise in the current price is accompanied by a more than proportional rise in the expected price. There is, therefore, a substitution effect away from future consumption in favor of current consumption. A rise in price leads to an increase and a fall in price to a decline in current consumption.

It is a simple matter to extend this analysis by assuming that the expected price of each commodity is a function of the current prices of all commodities:

$$p_{rt} = f_{rt}(p_{10}, p_{20}, \cdots, p_{no}).$$

We then have both partial and total elasticities of expectations, the partials relating to the effects of changes in single current prices and the totals relating to the effects of changes in all current prices. One total elasticity is of especial importance, that elasticity which relates to the effect of a proportional change in all current prices. If this elasticity is unity, then a proportional rise in all current prices will raise the expected price of X in the same proportion; if it is less than unity then the expected price will rise in lesser proportion, and if it is greater than unity, in greater proportion.

If all current prices rise in the same proportion then all current commodities may be treated as a single good. If all price expectations are inelastic, then there will be a substitution effect against current in favor of future consumption. If the individual is a current seller he will want to sell more; if he is a buyer, he will want to buy less. If all price expectations are elastic, then the substitution effect will work in the opposite direction. An interesting case to consider at this point is one in which all price expectations have unit elasticity. In this case all current and expected prices change in the same proportion. There is therefore no substitution between current and future consumption, and all commodities both current and future may be treated as a single commodity. Does this mean that the individual's planned consumption of every commodity both current and future will remain unchanged? In our static analysis we saw that if the prices of all commodities change in the same proportion the individual's demand for every commodity remains unchanged. Is the same thing true in our dynamic analysis?

To answer this question we should first recall the basis for our conclusion in static analysis. A change in price of a given commodity gives rise not only to a substitution effect but also to an income effect. If all prices change in the same proportion there can be no substitution effect between the commodities. Can there, however, be an income effect? In our static analysis we saw that there cannot be. A given proportionate change in the prices of all commodities changes the individual's income in the same proportion and leaves his budget equation completely unchanged. Both the income and the substitution effects are therefore absent and the demand for every commodity remains unchanged.

Will there be a capital effect in our dynamic analysis if all current and expected prices change in the same proportion? The answer to this question depends upon the elasticity of the capital value of the individual's plan with respect to a proportionate change in all prices. If the capital value of the individual's plan changes in the same proportion as the prices, then his budget equation remains absolutely unchanged. In that case his planned consumption of every commodity, current and future, will remain unchanged. If, however, the capital value of the individual's plan rises less than in proportion to the rise in prices, then the price rise is equivalent to a decline in the capital value of his plan under constant prices. His planned consumption over the period as a whole will therefore decline. Conversely if the capital value of his plan rises more than in proportion to the rise in prices, his planned consumption over the entire period will rise.

The capital value of the individual's plan has been defined as the difference between (1) the discounted value of his current and expected initial supplies of commodities and (2) the discounted value of the securities which he expects to acquire during the period. The discounted value of his initial supplies will, of course, change in the same proportion as the change in prices. Consequently if the discounted value of the securities which he plans to acquire is zero or if it changes in proportion to the price change, the capital value of the plan will also change in the same proportion as the price change. Otherwise the capital value of the plan will change in greater or lesser proportion than the change in prices according as the discounted value of the securities which he plans to acquire changes in lesser or greater proportion.

Hicks assumes throughout his analysis that a proportionate rise in all current and expected prices will leave the consumption of every commodity unchanged. He therefore assumes *implicitly*, not explicitly, that the discounted value of securities which a person plans to acquire or sell over the entire period of his plan will change in the same proportion as the change in prices. There appears to be no reason for confining the analysis to this case only. Indeed, as we have already seen, if all current prices rise in the same proportion the net volume of current lendings will ordinarily not change in the same proportion. By generalization from this result, it would appear that the net volume of lendings over the period as a whole will ordinarily also fail to move in the same proportion as a change in all current and expected prices.

4. *Variation of consumption with changes in interest rates*

As has been shown above, if current and expected prices are constant, then we may treat the total value of consumption in each period as a single commodity. The discount factor which we use to discount values of each period to current values may then be treated as the "price" of the consumption value for each period. It follows immediately, therefore, that we may analyze the effects of changes in interest rates in exactly the same manner as we have analyzed the effects of price changes.

Thus suppose that the discount factor β_1 rises but that the change in β_1 is accompanied by an inversely proportional change in the expected discount ratio β_2, so that all other discount factors $\beta_1 \beta_2$, $\beta_1 \beta_2 \beta_3$, $\cdots$, $\beta_1 \beta_2 \cdots \beta_\tau$ remain unchanged. Then the effect of the change may again be subdivided into a substitution effect and a capital effect. There will be a substitution effect against consumption in the period 1 in favor of consumption in other periods. Ordinarily this would mean that current consumption would tend to rise (unless, as is highly improbable, current consumption should be complementary to planned consumption for period 1). The rise in β_1 is, however, also equivalent to a change in the capital value of the plan, so that the capital effect must be added to the substitution effect in order to obtain the total effect.

A glance at equations (10.6) and (10.4) shows that the effect of a change in β_1 accompanied by an inversely proportional change in β_2 is exactly the same as the effect of an equal proportional change in the expected prices of all commodities for the period 1, all interest rates and all other prices remaining constant.

To study the effects of a change in β_1 unaccompanied by any other changes in expected discount ratios or prices, we must again make use of the familiar property which permits us to treat commodities whose prices change proportionately as a single commodity. If only β_1 changes, then the "prices" of all consumption values e from the periods $t = 1$ to τ will change proportionately. We may, therefore, group them together and treat them as a single commodity. Let us, therefore, define the "composite commodities"

(10.10) $$e_f = e_1 + \beta_2 e_2 + \beta_2\beta_3 e_3 + \cdots + \beta_2\beta_3 \cdots \beta_\tau e_\tau ,$$

(10.11) $$m_f = m_1 + \beta_2 m_2 + \beta_2\beta_3 m_3 + \cdots + \beta_2\beta_3 \cdots \beta_\tau m_\tau .$$

In equilibrium the marginal rate of substitution between future and current consumption must equal the current discount ratio:

(10.12) $$\frac{\partial u}{\partial e_t} \bigg/ \frac{\partial u}{\partial e_0} = \beta_1 .$$

A rise in β_1 (a decline in the current rate of interest) will therefore lead to a substitution effect against future in favor of current consumption. Conversely, a decline in β_1 will lead to a substitution effect against current in favor of future consumption.

If the elasticity of expectations of the discount ratios for each period is positive, then the proportional change in the "prices" β_1, $\beta_1 \beta_2$, $\cdots$, $\beta_1 \beta_2 \cdots \beta_\tau$ is greater for the later periods and smaller for the earlier periods. Thus if β_1 rises and the elasticity of expectations is positive there will be a substitution effect against later in favor of earlier consumption. The earlier the period, the greater the substitution effect in favor of consumption; the later the period, the greater the substitution effect against consumption.

II. PLANNING UNDER RISK

In the previous section we have assumed that the expectations of the individual as to future prices and interest rates are subjectively certain. We have now to drop this assumption and to consider the necessary modifications in our analysis which result from the fact that the individual does not generally have certain expectations concerning future prices and interest rates. Thus he will ordinarily have not a single-valued expectation as to what the price of X_r in period t may be but a whole probability distribution of possible prices. Among the various possible prices he may consider one to be the most probable price expectation or perhaps the mean price expectation. We cannot assume, however, that the individual will react in the same way to an uncertain as to a certain price expectation of a given magnitude. Obviously he will want to make some allowance for the fact that the future price is uncertain, the degree of allowance depending not only on the extent of the uncertainty but also on the degree of his aversion to risk. With respect to interest rates there is not only uncertainty as to what future interest rates may be but there is also risk of default on both present and future loans. Moreover securities issued by different persons may be subject to different degrees of risk so that we can no longer consider all securities as homogeneous. Our problem will therefore now contain many different kinds of securities rather than just one.

We shall assume that corresponding to each probability distribution of expected values or interest rates there is a certain unique price or interest-rate expectation, which we may call the representative expectation, such that the individual reacts in the same manner to the probability distribution as he would to the representative expectation. (The magnitude of the representative expectation will, of course, be different for different individuals.) With this assumption we may replace the probability distribution of prices or interest rates by its representative expectation. Formally therefore our analysis will involve only single-valued expectations just as in planning under certainty.

The analysis will differ according as we do or do not assume that the representative expectations are constants, unaffected by the amounts of each commodity purchased or the sums lent on each commodity.

A. Under Assumption that the Representative Expectations Are Fixed Constants for Each Individual

Under this assumption the individual's problem of planning under risk is formally the same as planning under certainty. It is true that there may now be many securities rather than just one. But each individual will invest all his surplus funds in only one kind of security, that security in which the representative interest rate is the greatest. He may, of course, invest in several securities if the representative interest rate is the same on all of them. But in that case he will be completely indifferent as to the relative proportions in which he holds these securities, and we may treat them all as the same security.

If the risk of default is the same on all securities, then all loans will have to be made at the same rate of interest. That rate of interest will have to be sufficiently high so that the volume of net lendings will equal the net borrowings. If, on the other hand, the risk of default is not the same for different securities, then the rate of interest will not be the same. In fact if there is one kind of security which is considered perfectly safe, there may be many individuals who will prefer to hold that security even though it earns no interest rate, rather than to hold a security which does earn interest but which is subject to risk of default. We may define such a security which is free from risk of default and which earns no interest as true money. We have here, therefore, one element in the explanation of why people may hold their surplus funds in the form of money. An individual will hold money if the representative interest rate on any other security is equal to or less than zero.

B. Under Assumption that the Representative Interest Expectations Are Functions of the Amounts Invested in Each Security

It has just been shown that if the representative interest expectations are constants, then each individual will invest in only one kind of security, that security in which the representative interest rate is the greatest. In order to obtain a situation in which the individual invests in many different securities we must assume that the representative interest rates are functions of the amounts invested in each security.

Let there be θ different securities in each period and let the sums invested in the different securities be $c_{1t}, c_{2t}, \cdots, c_{\theta t}$. The representative rates of interest expected in each period on the securities bought in the preceding period are $i_{1t}, i_{2t}, \cdots, i_{\theta t}$. Let $a_{jt} = 1 + i_{jt}$. Then $a_{jt}c_{j,t-1}$ is the representative expected value in the period t of the sum $c_{j,t-1}$ invested in the preceding period in the given security. For the sake of simplicity we shall assume that each representative interest rate and therefore each a_{jt} is a function only of the amount invested in that security:

$$(10.13) \qquad a_{jt} = a_{jt}(c_{j,t-1}) \qquad (j = 1, 2, \cdots, \theta; t = 1, 2, \cdots, \tau).$$

We may now rewrite the individual's budget equation (10.3b) as follows:

$$(10.14) \quad \begin{aligned}
m_0 + k & & & = e_0 + c_0, \\
m_1 + a_{11}c_{10} &+ a_{21}c_{20} &+ \cdots + a_{\theta 1}c_{\theta 0} &= e_1 + c_1, \\
m_2 + a_{12}c_{11} &+ a_{22}c_{21} &+ \cdots + a_{\theta 2}c_{\theta 1} &= e_2 + c_2, \\
& \cdots & & \\
m_\tau + a_{1\tau}c_{1,\tau-1} &+ a_{2\tau}c_{2,\tau-1} &+ \cdots + a_{\theta\tau}c_{\theta,\tau-1} &= e_\tau + c_\tau,
\end{aligned}$$

where

$$(10.15) \qquad c_{1t} + c_{2t} + \cdots + c_{\theta t} = c_t \qquad (t = 0, 1, 2, \cdots, \tau - 1).$$

The equations in (10.14) state that for each period the representative expected value of the initial supplies of commodities plus the total of the representative expected values of the securities must be equal to the planned value of consumption plus lendings (including renewals) in that period. We assume as before that the individual attempts to maximize his utility function subject to his set of budgetary restrictions.

Let us call the rate of change of the representative expected value of any security with respect to the amount invested in it the representative expected marginal value of the security. Then, given the current and representative expected prices of commodities, the equilibrium conditions for the total expenditures and for lendings on each kind of security are these:

1) The representative expected marginal value must be the same for every security in any given period.

2) The marginal rate of substitution between the values of con-

sumption of the periods t and $t + 1$ must be equal to the representative marginal value for each security bought in the period t. These conditions may be shown mathematically as follows:

Introducing the Lagrange multipliers λ_t and μ_t, we have

$$(10.16) \quad G = u(e_0, e_1, e_2, \cdots, e_\tau) - \lambda_0[e_0 + c_0 - m_0 - k]$$

$$- \sum_{t=1}^{\tau} \lambda_t[e_t + c_t - m_t - \sum_{j=1}^{\theta} \alpha_{jt}\, c_{j,t-1}]$$

$$- \sum_{t=0}^{\tau-1} \mu_t[c_{jt} - c_t] = \max.$$

Setting the partial derivatives with respect to each variable equal to zero we obtain the following equilibrium conditions:

$$\frac{\partial G}{\partial e_t} = \frac{\partial u}{\partial e_t} - \lambda_t = 0 \qquad\qquad (t = 0, 1, 2, \cdots, \tau),$$

$$(10.17) \quad \frac{\partial G}{\partial c_t} = -\lambda_t + \mu_t = 0 \qquad\qquad (t = 0, 1, 2, \cdots, \tau - 1),$$

$$\frac{\partial G}{\partial c_{jt}} = \lambda_{t+1} \frac{d(\alpha_{j,t+1}\, c_{jt})}{d\, c_{jt}} - \mu_t = 0$$

$$(j = 1, 2, \cdots \theta; t = 0, 1, 2, \cdots, \tau - 1).$$

Eliminating the Lagrange multipliers we obtain the set of equations:

$$(10.18) \quad \frac{\partial u}{\partial e_t} \Big/ \frac{\partial u}{\partial e_{t+1}} = \frac{d(\alpha_{j,t+1}\, c_{jt})}{d\, c_{jt}}$$

$$(t = 0, 1, 2, \cdots, \tau - 1; j = 1, 2, \cdots, \theta).$$

The $\theta\tau$ equations (10.18) together with the $2\tau + 1$ equations (10.14) and (10.15) are sufficient to determine the equal number of unknowns[6] e_t ($t = 0, 1, 2, \cdots, \tau$), c_t ($t = 0, 1, 2, \cdots, \tau - 1$), and c_{jt} ($j = 1, 2, \cdots, \theta; t = 0, 1, 2, \cdots, \tau - 1$) as functions of the $\theta\tau$ representative interest rates i_{jt} ($t = 1, 2, \cdots, \tau$).

---

[6] If we want to determine the consumption of each individual commodity rather than the total consumption value in each period, we make use of the following relation:

$$\frac{\partial u}{\partial x_{rt}} = \frac{\partial u}{\partial e_t} \frac{\partial e_t}{\partial x_{rt}} = \frac{\partial u}{\partial e_t} \frac{\partial(\sum_r p_{rt}\, x_{rt})}{\partial x_{rt}}.$$

If the representative price expectations are independent of the planned consumption, then the equation reduces to (10.8) above.

The right-hand side of (10.18) is the representative marginal value of the security c_{jt}. The equilibrium conditions (10.18) thus state that the representative marginal values must be the same on all securities bought by the individual in any given period and that the marginal rate of substitution between the values of consumption in the periods $(t + 1)$ and t must equal this marginal value.[7]

Now suppose that an individual holds some of his surplus funds in the form of money, a security which is completely free of risk of default and earns no interest. Then since the marginal value of money is unity, the representative marginal value for all other securities which he holds in that period must be unity by virtue of (10.18). It follows, therefore, that the marginal rate of substitution between his present and future consumption is also unity. His representative interest rate is therefore zero. In other words, for that individual interest is not a payment for refraining from consumption. The interest he receives on securities other than money is to him not a pure interest rate but simply a risk premium. If everyone held some of his surplus funds in the form of money then there would be no pure interest in such a community, all interest payments being simply risk premiums rather than payments for refraining from consumption. It should be noted, however, that it is only if surplus funds which are set aside for *future* purchases are held in the form of money that interest becomes only a risk premium. If money is held only temporarily in any given period for consumption in the same period, all other funds that are set aside for purchases in future periods being held in the form of interest-bearing securities, then the interest rate is not simply a risk premium but also includes pure interest in payment for forgoing present consumption. In other words, since funds that are invested in any given period do not draw any interest in that period but only in the next period, the temporary holding of money within any given period for consumption within that period does not at all imply that the individual is willing to forgo present consumption without receiving any interest.

---

[7] It will be observed that if all securities are free of all risk. conditions (10.18) reduce to (10.8) as they obviously should. In other words, if securities are free of risk, all securities in any given period are homogeneous and the equilibrium conditions are only that the marginal rate of substitution between expenditures for two periods shall be equal to the discount ratio.

The reader may readily extend the analysis of this entire section by assuming that each representative interest rate is a function of the amounts invested in every security, or that:

$$\alpha_{jt} = \alpha_{jt}(c_{1,t-1}, c_{2,t-1}, \cdots, c_{\theta,t-1}).$$

III. NONHOMOGENEITY OF SECURITIES FOR REASONS OTHER THAN RISK

A. *Differences in Cost of Making Transactions in Securities*

Securities may differ not only in the extent of risk but also in the cost and trouble involved in purchasing and selling them. It should be obvious that this cost may be treated in exactly the same way as risk. Thus suppose that all securities are free from risk, but that they are not all generally acceptable. Assume that only one security, money, is generally acceptable, so that in order to acquire securities individuals must make separate transactions (exchanging money for securities) which involves them in cost and trouble. Then the interest on securities must include an element as payment for the cost and trouble involved in buying and selling them. Here we have an additional explanation of why some individuals may hold their surplus funds in the form of money. They will do so if the interest payments on securities are only enough, when allowance is made for risk, to cover the cost and trouble of buying and selling securities.

The fact that only money is generally acceptable provides us also with an explanation of why people hold money temporarily within any given period for purchases within that period. Barter is more costly than exchange of goods for money. It should again be noted that if people hold money only for convenience in buying during the period but invest all of their surplus funds in interest-bearing securities, then the interest they receive is not only a payment for risk and the cost of buying and selling securities but also includes an element of pure interest in payment for forgoing present consumption.

B. *Differences in Length of Time for which Loans Run*

We have assumed throughout this chapter that loans in each period can be made for one period only and must be repaid with interest at the beginning of the next period. We shall now indicate very briefly the consequences of taking into account differences in length of time for which loans run.[8]

If all securities were completely free of risk of default and if future rates of interest on loans of one period were definitely known, then a very simple relationship would have to exist between short-

---

[8] For a more detailed discussion see J. R. Hicks, *Value and Capital*, Chaps. XI–XIII; F. A. Lutz, "The Structure of Interest Rates," *The Quarterly Journal of Economics*, Vol. 53, No. 1 (November, 1940), pp. 36–63; F. R. Macaulay, *Some Theoretical Problems Suggested by the Movement of Interest Rates, Bond Yields and Stock Prices in the United States since 1856*; T. de Scitovszky, "A Study of Interest and Capital," *Economica*, Vol. 7, (N.S.), No. 27 (August, 1940), pp. 303–08.

and long-term rates. The long-term yield ratio would have to be equal to the geometric mean of the short-term yield ratios.[9] Thus if we let R_n be the current long-term rate for loans of n weeks, then assuming that future short-term rates are definitely known we must have

$$(1 + R_n)^n = (1 + i_1)(1 + i_2) \cdots (1 + i_n).$$

For if these two were not equal it would pay to borrow long and lend short or vice versa, and thus arbitrage transactions would restore the equality.

If, however, the future short-term interest rates are not definitely known, then considerations of risk enter into the analysis. The risk is again of two kinds: (a) risk of default, and (b) risk of changes in yield (or risk of changes in prices of securities running for more than one period). Again we must distinguish between the cases where the risk allowance is a constant and those where it is a function of the amount invested. If the risk allowance is a constant, then the individual will hold only one kind of security in each period, that security in which the expected true yield from that period to the next (equals nominal rate of interest plus expected capital gain or minus expected capital loss), adjusted for risk, is the greatest. Those individuals for whom the expected true yield on every interest-earning security is less than unity will prefer to hold their surplus funds in money instead.

If, on the other hand, the risk allowance is a function of the amount invested in each security then we again have the condition that in each period the individual will distribute his lendings amongst the various securities in such a way as to equalize the representative marginal value of all securities when allowance is made for risk of default and risk of changes in capital value. Moreover, these representative marginal values must equal the marginal rate of substitution between expenditures in this and the next period. The marginal value of money is unity so that if part of an individual's surplus funds is held in the form of money the marginal rate of substitution between the values of his consumption in this and the next period is unity. This means that he carries his current consumption up to the point where his time preference rate is zero, so that no price is paid for inducing him to refrain from additional consumption. Consequently, to an individual who holds part of his surplus funds in the form of money the interest on securities is payment only for the following factors: (1) cost of purchasing the securities, (2) risk of default on interest and principal, and (3) risk of changes in capital value of the securities. To

[9] The formula assumes that interest is paid only when the loan is repaid.

those who hold all of their surplus funds in interest-bearing securities, however, there is also an element of pure interest as payment for forgoing consumption.

CHAPTER VII

ENTREPRENEURIAL PLANNING

I. UNDER CERTAINTY

A. *Derivation of the Demand and Supply Functions for the Firm*

After the rather lengthy treatment of the planning of the individual as a consumer, the theory of entrepreneurial planning may be summarized very briefly.[1] In this section we assume as before that loans in each period can be made only for one period, with a rate of interest to be collected in the next period equal to i_{t+1}, and a corresponding discount ratio equal to $\beta_{t+1} = 1/(1 + i_{t+1})$. Let the number of periods over which the firm makes its plan be $\tau + 1$. Let $a_{it} (i = 1, 2, \cdots, m; t = 0, 1, \cdots, \tau)$ denote the quantity of the ith factor in the period t and let $x_{jt} (j = m + 1, m + 2, \cdots, n; t = 0, 1, 2, \cdots, \tau)$ denote the quantity of the jth product in the period t.[2] It is assumed that each firm may be characterized by a dynamic transformation function indicating the relationship between current and expected inputs and outputs for the $\tau + 1$ periods. Again treating factors as negative products and writing $a_{it} = -x_{it} (i = 1, 2, \cdots, m)$ we have as our known transformation function:

$$(11.1) \qquad f(x_{10}, x_{20}, \cdots, x_{n0}, x_{11}, x_{21}, \cdots, x_{n1}, \\ \cdots, x_{1\tau}, x_{2\tau}, \cdots, x_{n\tau}) = 0.$$

Let $p_{rt} (r = 1, 2, \cdots, n)$ be the expected price of the commodity x_r (product or factor) in the period t. Let $k_t = \sum_{i=1}^{m} p_{it} a_{it}$ be the expected value of the inputs of the period t, $w_t = \sum_{j=m+1}^{n} p_{jt} x_{jt}$, the expected value of the outputs, and $v_t = w_t - k_t = \sum_{r=1}^{n} p_{rt} x_{rt}$ the excess of the expected value of the output over the expected value of the

---

[1] For supplementary material the reader is referred to Hicks, *Value and Capital*, Part IV, Chaps. XV–XVII. See also J. Marschak, "Money and the Theory of Assets," *Econometrica*, Vol. 6 (October, 1938), pp. 311–25; Sune Carlson, *A Study on the Pure Theory of Production* (London, 1939), Chap VI; Erik Lindahl, *Studies in the Theory of Money and Capital* (London, 1939), Part III; A. G. Hart, *Anticipations, Uncertainty and Dynamic Planning* (Studies in Business Administration, Vol. 11, No. 1 [Chicago: University of Chicago Press, 1940]).

[2] A word of warning with respect to notation may be in place here. The symbols a_{it} and x_{jt} each had different meanings in Part I. They will be used throughout Part II only in the sense given above.

input. We shall call v_t the expected surplus (positive or negative) of the period t. The present value of any surplus v_t is simply its discounted value. The aim of the firm is assumed to be to choose that stream of current and planned inputs and outputs which will have the maximum present value. We shall call the present value of any surplus its capital value, and the present value of the whole stream of surpluses we shall call the capital value of the plan, C. Again letting $\beta_0 \equiv 1$ we have

$$(11.2) \qquad C = \sum_{t=0}^{\tau} \beta_0 \beta_1 \cdots \beta_t v_t = \sum_{t=0}^{\tau} \sum_{r=1}^{n} \beta_0 \beta_1 \cdots \beta_t \, p_{rt} \, x_{rt}.$$

The aim of the firm is to maximize the capital value C subject to the transformation function f. Introducing a Lagrange multiplier λ, we have

$$(11.3) \qquad\qquad C - \lambda f = \max.$$

As in static theory, the firm under pure competition takes the current prices and current discount rates β_1 as fixed constants which are independent of its outputs and inputs. Given its expectations as to future prices and discount rates, we may, therefore, obtain the equilibrium current and planned outputs and inputs just as in static theory by setting the partial derivatives of (11.3) with respect to x_{rt} equal to zero. Analogous to the static conditions we, therefore, obtain the $n(\tau + 1)$ dynamic conditions:

$$(11.4a) \qquad\qquad \lambda \frac{\partial f}{\partial x_{rt}} = \beta_0 \beta_1 \cdots \beta_t \, p_{rt},$$

or, upon eliminating λ,

$$(11.4b) \qquad\qquad \frac{\partial f}{\partial x_{rt}} \bigg/ \frac{\partial f}{\partial x_{su}} = \frac{\beta_0 \beta_1 \cdots \beta_t \, p_{rt}}{\beta_0 \beta_1 \cdots \beta_s \, p_{su}}.$$

Equations (11.4b) provide us with equilibrium conditions that are strictly analogous to those given in static theory:

1a. The marginal rate of substitution between any two planned outputs for any two dates must equal the ratio of their discounted expected prices.

1b. The marginal rate of substitution between any two planned inputs of any two dates must equal the ratio of their discounted expected prices.

1c. The marginal rate of transformation of a planned input of any date into a planned output of any date must equal the ratio of their discounted expected prices.

Again making use of the familiar principle that a group of commodities whose prices remain unchanged may be treated as a single commodity, we may restate some aspects of the equilibrium conditions in several more familiar forms. Using the expected prices of inputs and outputs as weights, let us group together all inputs of a period into the single commodity k_t, all outputs of a period into the single commodity w_t, and all combined inputs (= negative outputs) and outputs of a period into the commodity v_t. The price of each such composite commodity is unity, and the discounted price is simply the discount factor $\beta_0 \beta_1 \cdots \beta_t$. We have therefore as special cases of the rules given above:

2a. The marginal rate of substitution between the values of output for any two periods must equal the ratio of the discount factors for the two periods.

2b. The marginal rate of substitution between the values of input for any two periods must equal the ratio of the discount factors over the two periods.

2c. The marginal rate of transformation of the value of input for any period into the value of output for any period must equal the ratio of the discount factors over the two periods. For inputs and outputs of the same period this reduces to the condition that the marginal rate of substitution must equal unity.

2d. The marginal rate of substitution between the surpluses of any two periods must equal the ratio of their discount factors.

Let us form new composite commodities by taking the capital values *as of the first future period* $t = 1$ of: (1) all future inputs, (2) all future outputs, and (3) all future surpluses. Thus let us define the composite commodities:

$$k_f = k_1 + \beta_2 k_2 + \cdots + \beta_2 \beta_3 \cdots \beta_\tau k_\tau,$$
$$w_f = w_1 + \beta_2 w_2 + \cdots + \beta_2 \beta_3 \cdots \beta_\tau w_\tau,$$
$$v_f = v_1 + \beta_2 v_2 + \cdots + \beta_2 \beta_3 \cdots \beta_\tau v_\tau.$$

The discounted price for each such commodity is simply the discount ratio, β_1. Consequently we have the following rules:

3a. The marginal rate of substitution between the value of current output w_0 and the value of future output w_f must equal the discount rate β_1.

3b. The marginal rate of substitution between the value of current input k_0 and the value of future input k_f must equal the discount rate β_1.

3c.   The marginal rate of transformation of the value of current input k_0 into the value of future output w_f must equal the discount rate β_1. This is a translation of Keynes's principle that the marginal efficiency of capital must equal the rate of interest.

3d.   The marginal rate of substitution between current and future surplus must equal the discount rate β_1.[3]

The stability conditions are also analogous to those in static theory except that our system now consists of $n(\tau + 1)$ commodities, n for each of $\tau + 1$ periods. The marginal rates of substitution must therefore satisfy the following conditions:

1a.   The marginal rate of substitution between any two planned outputs of any two dates must be increasing; namely, the decrement in output x_{rt} resulting from a planned increase of a marginal unit of output x_{su} must increase as additional x_{su} is substituted for x_{rt}.

1b.   The marginal rate of substitution between any two planned inputs of any two dates must be diminishing; namely, the decrement in the input a_{it} which just offsets an increase of a marginal unit of the input a_{ju} diminishes as additional a_{ju} is substituted for a_{it}.

1c.   The marginal rate of transformation of any planned input a_{ju} into any planned output x_{rt} must be diminishing; namely, the increment in x_{rt} resulting from an increase of a marginal unit of the input a_{ju} diminishes as additional a_{ju} is transformed into x_{rt}.

As in static equilibrium, these rules must hold not only for single commodities, but also for groups. In particular therefore similar rules must hold for the composite commodities k, w, and v. Thus the marginal rate of substitution of current surplus v_0 and future surplus v_f must satisfy these rules. It is these stability conditions which make it unprofitable for the firm, given the discount ratio β_1, to increase its current input (or decrease its current output) indefinitely in order to increase its future surplus. These stability conditions imply the existence of some fixed resources which give rise to diminishing returns to the variable factors included in the transformation function and thus prevent an indefinite increase in current input.

The same question about the possibility of a zero rate of interest arises in a production economy as well as in an exchange economy. Suppose that people expect future prices and interest rates to remain at current levels. Could the rate of interest then drop to zero in a production economy even if there were nothing to prevent it from

---

[3] For analogous conditions in the theory of consumption see Chap. VI, Sections IA and IB-4.

reaching zero so far as consumption is concerned? The answer to this question depends upon the assumption we make concerning the marginal rate of transformation of current value of input into future value of output. From the stability conditions this marginal rate must diminish with additions in current input. Suppose, however, that this marginal rate is greater than unity; namely, that an additional dollar of current input adds more than a dollar to the expected value of output. Then we have:

$$\frac{\partial w_f}{\partial k_0} = \frac{1}{\beta_1} \equiv 1 + i > 1, \quad \text{or} \quad i > 0.$$

In this case therefore the rate of interest would have to be greater than zero. This assumption appears to be the basis of Knight's argument concerning the impossibility of a zero rate of interest.[4]

The $n(\tau + 1) - 1$ equations (11.4b) together with the transformation function (11.1) permit us to determine the $n(\tau + 1)$ quantities of inputs and outputs planned for each period, once we are given the current and expected prices and interest rates. We may, therefore, write the planned supply function for each product and planned demand function for each factor (equals negative product) in the form

$$\bar{x}_{rt} = \bar{x}_{rt}(p_{10}, p_{20}, \cdots, p_{n0}, \beta_1 p_{11}, \beta_1 p_{21}, \cdots, \beta_1 p_{n1}, \cdots, \beta_1 \beta_2 \cdots \beta_\tau p_{1\tau}, \\ \beta_1 \beta_2 \cdots \beta_\tau p_{2\tau}, \cdots, \beta_1 \beta_2 \cdots \beta_\tau p_{n\tau}).$$

Given the volume of its interest and dividend receipts for the period, it follows that the firm's net purchase (equals purchase minus sales) of securities (or net loans) during each period is also a function of the same current and expected prices and interest rates.

---

[4] "In particular it is certain, a priori, that with other things held constant—meaning, especially, if there are no new inventions or other changes opening up new demand for capital—the rate [of interest] could *never* fall to zero. This is possible only if society as a whole approaches a state of complete satiation in which there would be no economic values and all economic categories would lose meaning. For it is certainly inadmissible to assume that society could reach a state in which no additional capital could be employed to any advantage whatever, before all other factors or their services became free goods." Frank H. Knight, "The Quantity of Capital and the Rate of Interest, II," *Journal of Political Economy*, Vol. 44 (October, 1936), pp. 623–24.

Professor Knight also contends that the marginal rate of transformation of current input into future output diminishes only at a very gradual rate, so that even a small rise in β_1 (a small decline in the interest rate) would lead to a very large increase in current input to be transformed into future output.

"The heart of a correct theory of interest is the fact, corresponding more or less to infinite 'elasticity of demand for capital,' that the investment market is capable of absorbing savings at the maximum rate at which they are forthcoming, with only a very gradual decline of the rate of return through time, other things equal. . . ." Frank H. Knight, "Capital, Time, and the Interest Rate," *Economica*, New Series, Vol. 1, (1934), p. 285.

B. *The Properties of the Dynamic Demand and Supply Functions for the Firms*

1. *Variation of demand and supply with changes in prices*

The properties of the dynamic functions for the firm are analogous to those of the static functions. A rise in the expected price of any product, all other current and expected prices and interest rates being given, will lead to an increase in the planned output for that date. It will also lead to an increase in the current and planned output of complementary products, to a decline in the current and planned output of substitutes, and to an increase in the current and planned input of factors of production, except those which may be regressive against the product whose price rose.

A rise in the expected price of any factor, all other current and expected prices and interest rates being given, will lead to a decline in the planned input of that factor for that date. It will also lead to a decline in the (current and planned) input of complementary factors and an increase in input of substitutes, and to a decline in outputs of products except those which may be regressive against the factor whose price rose.

To analyze the effect of a change in a current price we must again make some assumption as to the elasticity of price expectations. If the elasticity is zero, then expectations remain unaffected by current price changes and we may analyze the effects of the latter change in the same way as we analyzed the effects of changes in expected prices. If, however, the elasticity of expectations is unity then a change in the current price gives rise to a proportional change in the expected price so that we may lump together the outputs or the inputs of different dates and treat them as one commodity. Thus if there is a rise in the current price of a given commodity, its planned output over the period as a whole will rise. This does not mean, of course, that the increase in output will be spread evenly over all periods. For technical reasons the additional output which can be produced in the current period or planned for the near future is generally very small in comparison with that which can be produced in the distant future. This simply means that the short-run increase in output will generally be less than the long-run increase. Indeed it is even possible that the increase in the price of the product should lead to a decline in the current output (balanced by a greater increase in planned future output). Thus an increase in current prices accompanied by a proportional increase in expected prices may induce a firm even to shut down temporarily for alterations designed to increase its capacity.[5] If we take

[5] See also the example of South African gold mining cited by Hicks, p. 210.

a period of sufficient length, however, such cases would be extremely rare.

Similarly, if the current price of a factor changes and the elasticity of expectations is unity, we may treat the inputs of different periods as one commodity and thus conclude that there will be a change in the input of that factor over the planning period as a whole. Again the change will not be spread evenly over all periods; the effect will probably be much less for current inputs and inputs of the near future than for more distant inputs. The reason for this is again the technical difficulty of short-run adjustments.

The case of elastic price expectations gives us even more striking results. Since an increase in the current price is accompanied by a more than proportional increase in the expected prices, it follows that an increase in a product price will lead to a current decline in the output of that product, and an increase in a factor price will lead to an increase in the current input of that factor.

If all current and expected product prices rise in the same proportion there will be no substitution between any products of any date. Output as a whole will increase and so therefore will inputs. Similarly if all current and expected factor prices rise in the same proportion there will be no substitution between any factors of any dates. Input as a whole will decline and so therefore will outputs. If all current and expected product and factor-prices rise in the same proportion there will be no substitution anywhere for the firm. All outputs and inputs will therefore remain unchanged. This may readily be seen by multiplying the equilibrium conditions by a constant. Analogous to the conditions in static theory, therefore, the demand for each factor and the supply of each product is a homogeneous function of zero degree of the entire set of prices.

2. Variations of demand and supply with changes in interest rates

It has been shown that, if current and expected prices are given, we may treat the surplus in each period as a single "commodity" v_t with a "price" equal to the discount factor $\beta_0\,\beta_1\cdots\beta_t$. Consequently we may analyze the effects of changes in interest rates in exactly the same manner as changes in prices.

If there is a rise in the current discount ratio β_1, accompanied by an inversely proportional change in β_2, so that the discount factors for all other periods $\beta_1\,\beta_2\cdots\beta_t$ remain constant, then the planned surplus for the next period v_1 will rise. There will also be a decline in the planned surpluses for periods which may be considered as substitutes for that period, and an increase in the planned surpluses for complementary periods. Thus a decline in the current rate of interest that is accompanied by a corresponding increase in the expected interest rate for the next period will normally lead to an increase in input and a decrease in output of the current period and to a decrease in input and an increase in output in the next period. The effect is exactly the same as for a proportionate rise in all expected prices for the given period, all other expectations remaining unchanged.

If the change in β_1 is unaccompanied by any changes in the expected interest rates or commodity prices, then the "prices" $\beta_1 \beta_2 \cdots \beta_t$ of all future surpluses v_t will change proportionately. We may therefore combine these into a single composite commodity, future surplus v_f, which represents the sum of the planned future surpluses discounted up to the first future period $t = 1$. From the stability conditions it then follows that a rise in β_1 will increase the planned future surplus v_f and decrease the current surplus. Thus a decline in the current rate of interest (a rise in β_1), all interest-rate expectations and all current and expected prices being given, will normally lead to an increase in input and a decrease in output of the current period and to a decrease in planned input and an increase in planned output of future periods. The effect is identical with that of a proportionate decline in all current prices under zero elasticity of price expectation.

It is again of interest to consider the effects of a change in the current discount ratio upon the assumption that the expected discount ratio for each future period changes proportionately. In that case the proportional rise in the "prices" of the surpluses β_1, $\beta_1 \beta_2$, $\cdots$, $\beta_1 \beta_2 \cdots \beta_\tau$ is greatest for the later periods and smallest for the earlier periods. Such a rise in β_1 will, therefore, lead to a substitution effect in favor of the later against the earlier surpluses.

It should be noted that a change in β_1 is unlikely to have a very large effect upon the current surplus because of the difficulty of making large adjustments in the short run.

II. UNDER RISK

The modification of the theory of production to take account of risk follows along the same lines as in the theory of exchange. Instead of the single definite price or interest rate the individual firm has a whole probability distribution of expectations. As before we take one price or interest-rate expectation as representative of the whole probability distribution in the sense that the firm reacts in the same way to the probability distribution as it would to the representative expectation if it were certain. If this representative expectation is independent of the amounts bought and sold, borrowed or lent, then the formal analysis is exactly the same as in planning under certainty. The firm behaves just as if it had but one definite price expectation for each commodity in each period, and but one definite expectation as to the prevailing interest rate in each period. Although there may be many different securities with different interest rates in each period, the firm concerns itself with only one security, that security for which its representative interest-rate expectation is the highest. Formally therefore the analysis is identical with that of planning under certainty.

If, however, the representative price expectations are functions of the amounts bought and sold or if the representative interest-rate expectations are functions of the amounts borrowed or lent, the analysis must be modified considerably. Indeed in the latter case we must drop the entire assumption that the firm can be treated as a separate entity apart from its owners. This assumption was, of course, not essential to our analysis. Exactly the same results would have been obtained if we had merged the activities of the firm with those of the individual. We could then have assumed that each individual attempts to maximize his utility subject not only to his budgetary restrictions but also to the given technological conditions of production (i.e., his production function) by means of which he obtains a portion of his income. It was, however, a useful simplification since it permitted us to treat the consumption and production aspects separately. Thus we could assume that the individual as owner of the firm always maximizes his surplus or his discounted stream of expected surpluses, (i.e., the capital value of his plan). This increases his income and therefore makes it possible for him to increase his utility.

Under the present assumption, however, this separation of firm and individual is no longer possible. For as we have already seen in our consumption analysis, if the representative interest-rate expectation is a function of the amount invested in each security then the individual will invest in every security up to the point where the representative marginal value is the same for all securities.[6] These different securities will ordinarily have different interest rates. Only the marginal return is equalized. It is only this marginal rate, therefore, which is relevant in discounting future values to present values. But this marginal rate exists only in equilibrium. Consequently the capital value of the production plan or the discounted stream of surpluses can be determined only in equilibrium. We cannot therefore speak of the firm's maximizing the capital value of its plan, since this capital value cannot be defined except in equilibrium. The way out of this difficulty has already been indicated in the preceding paragraph.

[6] See Chapter VI, Sec. II B.

We assume that the individual attempts to maximize his utility subject not only to his budgetary restriction but also to his known production or transformation function. Let

$$u = u(x_{10}, x_{20}, \cdots, x_{n0}, \cdots, x_{1\tau}, x_{2\tau}, \cdots, x_{n\tau})$$

be the individual's utility function. Let his budgetary restrictions be

$$
\begin{aligned}
m_0 + v_0 + k &= e_0 + c_0, \\
m_1 + v_1 + \sum a_{j1}\, c_{j0} &= e_1 + c_1, \\
m_2 + v_2 + \sum a_{j2}\, c_{j1} &= e_2 + c_2, \\
\cdots \cdots \cdots \\
m_\tau + v_\tau + \sum a_{j\tau}\, c_{j,\tau-1} &= e_\tau + c_\tau,
\end{aligned}
$$

where, as before,

$m_t = \sum_r p_{rt}\bar{x}_{rt}$ is the value of the individual's initial supply of goods in the period t;

$v_t = \sum_r p_{rt}\bar{\bar{x}}_{rt}$ is the surplus earned through production in the period t;

$e_t = \sum_r p_{rt} x_{rt}$ is the planned value of consumption in the period t;

$c_t = \sum_j c_{jt}$ is the total amount invested in various securities in the period t;

$a_{jt} = 1 + i_{jt}$, where i_{jt} is the representative interest rate expected on the security j in the period t.

Finally, let the transformation function be as before

$$f(\bar{\bar{x}}_{10}, \bar{\bar{x}}_{20}, \cdots, \bar{\bar{x}}_{n0}, \cdots, \bar{\bar{x}}_{1\tau}, \bar{\bar{x}}_{2\tau}, \cdots, \bar{\bar{x}}_{n\tau}) = 0.$$

We assume for the sake of simplification that the representative interest-rate expectation is a function of the amount invested in the one security alone.

Introducing the Lagrange multipliers κ, λ, μ, we have

$$G = u - \kappa_0(e_0 + c_0 - m_0 - v_0 - k) - \sum_{t=1}^{\tau} \kappa_t\left[e_t + c_t - m_t - v_t - \sum_{j=1}^{o} a_{jt}\, c_{j,t-1} \right]$$

$$- \sum_{t=0}^{\tau-1} \lambda_t\left[\sum_{j=1}^{o} c_{jt} - c_t \right] - \mu f = \text{max.}$$

Setting the partial derivatives with respect to each variable equal to zero, we obtain as our first-order conditions:

$$\frac{\partial G}{\partial x_{rt}} = \frac{\partial u}{\partial x_{rt}} - \kappa_t p_{rt} = 0 \qquad (r = 1, 2, \cdots, n; t = 0, 1, 2, \cdots, \tau),$$

$$\frac{\partial G}{\partial c_t} = -\kappa_t + \lambda_t = 0 \qquad\qquad (t = 0, 1, 2, \cdots, \tau - 1),$$

$$\frac{\partial G}{\partial c_{jt}} = \kappa_{t+1} \frac{d(a_{j,t+1} c_{jt})}{d c_{jt}} - \lambda_t = 0 \qquad \begin{array}{l}(t = 0, 1, 2, \cdots, \tau - 1; \\ \quad j = 1, 2, \cdots, \theta),\end{array}$$

$$\frac{\partial G}{\partial x_{rt}} = \kappa_t p_{rt} - \mu \frac{\partial f}{\partial x_{rt}} = 0 \qquad (r = 1, 2, \cdots, n; t = 0, 1, 2, \cdots, \tau).$$

Eliminating the Lagrange multipliers, we have

$$\frac{\dfrac{\partial u}{\partial x_{rt}}}{\dfrac{\partial u}{\partial x_{s,t+1}}} = \frac{\dfrac{\partial f}{\partial x_{rt}}}{\dfrac{\partial f}{\partial x_{s,t+1}}} = \frac{p_{rt}}{p_{s,t+1}} \frac{d(a_{j,t+1} c_{jt})}{d c_{jt}}.$$

This set of equations states that:

1.   The marginal rate of substitution between any two commodities of any two periods must be the same with respect to both consumption and production.

2.   The representative marginal value of any security in any given period must be the same for all securities held by the individual.

3.   The marginal rate of substitution between any two commodities of successive periods must be equal to the ratio of their representative expected prices, multiplied by the marginal value of securities.

These equations, together with the budgetary and production restrictions, determine the amount of each commodity the individual plans to produce and consume in each period, and the amount he plans to invest in each security.

If the producer holds none of his surplus funds in the form of money, then it is evidence that his representative marginal value of securities is greater than unity and that therefore his marginal rate of current and expected transformation of current input value into future output value is greater than unity. This is so even though he holds money within any given period for purchases of inputs within the same period, since no return can be obtained in any period for funds invested within the period. In normal times people generally do not hold investible funds in the form of money, so that the interest on securities does include an element as payment for the "marginal productivity of investment." In periods of stagnation, however, people do hold investible funds in the form of money. This is evidence that their marginal rate of transformation of current input value into future output value is unity. The interest which they then receive on securities is simply a risk-premium and a payment for the cost and trouble of buying and selling securities.

The existence of risk has a very important bearing upon the plans of the producer. The greater the risk the lower is the effective "expected price" which the producer uses in his plans for future output. Since the more distant future is generally more uncertain than the near future, the allowance for risk for the more distant periods will be very great and the effective expected price will, therefore, be correspondingly low. It follows, therefore, that a decline in the interest rate may have very little effect even upon plans for future input and output. That it will have little effect upon current inputs and outputs we have already seen.

CHAPTER VIII

MARKET EQUILIBRIUM IN A CLOSED ECONOMY

I. EQUILIBRIUM AND STABILITY CONDITIONS

Having determined the demand and supply functions for each economic unit, we now proceed to determine the temporary market equilibrium for the current period. Given all of the price and interest-rate expectation functions, the excess demand for each individual and therefore the excess demand for the market as a whole for each commodity may be written as a function of the current prices and interest rates:

$$I_{r0} \equiv X_{r0} - \bar{X}_{r0} - \bar{\bar{X}}_{r0} = I_{r0}(p_{10}, p_{20}, \cdots, p_{n0}, i_{11}, i_{21}, \cdots, i_{\theta 1}),$$
$$(r = 1, 2, \cdots, n).$$

Similarly the net market demand C_{j0} for each security and the net market demand for money M_0 are also functions of the current prices and interest rates:

$$C_{j0} = C_{j0}(p_{10}, p_{20}, \cdots, p_{n0}, i_{11}, i_{21}, \cdots, i_{\theta 1}), \qquad (j = 1, 2, \cdots, \theta);$$
$$M_0 = M_0(p_{10}, p_{20}, \cdots, p_{n0}, i_{11}, i_{21}, \cdots, i_{\theta 1}).$$

The first-order conditions for temporary market equilibrium for the current period parallel those under a static system, except that in addition to products and factors we now have securities and money in our equilibrium system. These conditions are as follows:

(1) The excess market demand for each commodity (product or factor) must equal zero (n equations, $I_{r0} = 0$).

(2) The excess market demand for each security must equal zero (θ equations, $C_{j0} = 0$).

(3) The excess market demand for money must equal zero (1 equation, $M_0 = 0$).

As before, one equation follows from the rest, so that we have but $n + \theta$ independent equations to determine the n current prices p_{r0} and the θ current interest rates in terms of money. Analytically it is a matter of indifference as to which equation we omit from our system.

One important distinction between our dynamic and our static systems must be noted at once. In our static system we had no true money other than the *numéraire*. The system contained only n commodities for which there were excess-market-demand functions. One of the n functions followed from the rest, so that there were but $n - 1$ independent demand functions for commodities. Fortunately the excess demands were functions of the $n - 1$ price ratios in terms of the *numéraire* rather than of the n prices in terms of some token or counter money. The number of independent demand functions was therefore sufficient to determine the $n - 1$ price ratios.

In our dynamic system, however, we have a true money for which there exists a market demand function. Consequently the n excess-demand functions for the n commodities are all independent of one another. These are, in general, functions of the absolute levels of the n prices in terms of the true money rather than of the $n - 1$ price ratios in terms of the *numéraire*. In this system, therefore, it is the n prices in terms of money rather than the $n - 1$ price ratios in terms of the *numéraire* that are determined by the equilibrium equations.

The stability conditions are also similar to those in static theory, except for the addition of securities and money to our equilibrium system. In order for the dynamic system of multiple exchange to be perfectly stable, a rise in the price of any commodity must lead to a reduction in the excess demand for that commodity under all of the following conditions:

(a)   when all other prices are given,

(b)   when only one other price is adjusted so as to preserve equality between demand and supply in that market,

(c)   when only two other prices are so adjusted,

and so on until all other prices and all interest rates are so adjusted. The system will be imperfectly stable if a rise in the price of a commodity leads to a reduction in the excess demand for it only when all other prices and all current interest rates are adjusted so as to maintain equilibrium in those markets.[1]

A. *The Stability of the Partial System of Exchange for Commodities*

Let us first consider the partial stability of the system with respect to commodities for fixed values of the interest rates. This corresponds to testing the stability of the n independent equations for commodities, $I_{ro} = 0$, for given values of the interest rates.

1. *Inelastic price expectations*

We have previously shown that if the elasticities of all price and interest-rate expectations are zero, the stability properties of the individual demand functions for current products and factors are ana-

---

[1] See the discussion of the stability of exchange in Chapter II.

logous to those in static analysis. Except for the capital (income) effect a rise in the current price of any commodity (given the level of interest rates) would lead to a decrease in its current demand and an increase in its current supply, whether or not the prices of any other commodities were adjusted to maintain equilibrium in those markets. Even if the current prices of all n commodities changed in equal proportion, there would still be a decrease in the current demand for all goods taken together and an increase in the current supply as a result of the substitution over time. Thus, so far as the substitution effect is concerned, the system is completely stable with respect to commodities, under inelastic expectations. Unfortunately this stability may be upset by the capital effect, if the capital value of the individual's plan (i.e., the value of his planned allotment for consumption over time)[2] moves in the same direction as the price change. This corresponds to the instability which may arise in a static economy because the sellers' incomes change in the same direction as the change in the price. In a dynamic economy this may happen for two reasons. The first is identical with that in a static economy; namely the income effect of the sellers may outweigh that of the buyers to such an extent as to more than offset the market substitution effect. In this case a rise in price which made the individual sellers richer and the buyers poorer would lead to a net rise in the excess demand for the commodity. As we pointed out in our static analysis, however, this result is rather unlikely. This is particularly true in the case of products, since individuals—the only economic units for which there is an income effect—as distinguished from firms, are on the whole buyers rather than sellers of any given product. In the case of factors which are not at the same time products, i.e., labor services, the net income effect is likely to work in the opposite direction from the substitution effect, since individuals are on the whole sellers rather than buyers of any given type of labor service. Nevertheless it is rather unlikely that the consumer income effect should be sufficiently large to offset not only the consumer substitution effect but also the producer substitution effect as well.

The second possible basis for instability in our dynamic system arises from the fact that individuals may decide to acquire a smaller sum of securities and money over the planning period as a whole when prices rise. If the resulting increases in the capital values of the separate expenditure plans were sufficiently large, they would then lead to an increase in current consumption. It may readily be seen, however, that the increase in the capital values of the expendi-

[2] See Chapter VI, Sec. 1A.

ture plans would have to be more than in proportion to the rise in current prices in order to have this effect. For if the increase were only in proportion to the rise in current prices the effect would be the same as if both current prices and the capital value had remained unchanged but expected prices had all fallen. Current consumption would therefore decline. Since such a radical alteration in plans is extremely unlikely to accompany a change in prices which is expected to be only temporary, we may safely conclude that the exchange system will be stable if interest rates are fixed and price expectations are inelastic.

2.   Unit elasticity of price expectations

As long as the elasticity of price expectations is less than unity there remains some scope for substitution over time. So far as the substitution effect is concerned, therefore, the system remains stable. When, however, the elasticity of price expectations is unity, a rise in the current price of a given commodity leads to an equal proportionate increase in the expected prices of the commodity and there is no scope for substitution over time. If the current prices of some goods remain unchanged there is, of course, scope for substitution between commodities in the current period. But if all current prices change in the same proportion and the elasticities of expectation are all equal to unity there is no scope for substitution between commodities at all.[3] The stability of the system therefore depends on the extent to which the decision to acquire securities (and money) over the planning period as a whole is affected. If this sum (positive or negative) changes in less than proportion to the change in prices, then the rise in prices is equivalent to a reduction in the capital values of the expenditure plans under unchanged prices, and current consumption will decline. The system will therefore be rendered stable through the income effect. If, however, the sum changes in more than proportion to the change in prices, then the rise in prices is equivalent to an increase in the capital values of the expenditure plans under unchanged prices, and current consumption will rise. The system will therefore be rendered unstable through the income effect.

The most interesting case for discussion is that in which the sum of securities and money which individuals decide to acquire or sell over the planning period as a whole changes in exactly the same proportion as the change in prices. Here the capital values of the expenditure plans rise in the same proportion as the rise in prices. In this case therefore there is scope for neither a substitution effect nor an

[3] The same thing will be true if the expected price for each commodity is a homogeneous function in the first degree of all the current prices.

income effect. The excess demand for every commodity will remain unchanged. In other words, if the elasticities of expectation are all unity, and if the capital values of the expenditure plans all change in the same proportion as the change in current prices, then the excess-demand function for each current commodity is a homogeneous function of the current prices of degree zero. This means that the excess demand for each current commodity is a function of the $n - 1$ independent price ratios between the commodities rather than of the n money prices. Only the $n - 1$ price ratios can therefore be determined in equilibrium; the level of money prices is completely indeterminate.[4] If none of the money prices are controlled then a change in the money price of any one commodity (product or factor) will under these conditions lead to an equal proportionate change in the prices of all commodities and will leave the demand and supply for every commodity unchanged.[5]

In itself this conclusion does not appear too disturbing. For while the individual money prices are left indeterminate the price ratios are seen to be uniquely determined by the equilibrium system. This result therefore appears to be identical with that which we found in our static system. Unfortunately this is not so. For in our static system we had only $n - 1$ independent equations for commodities to determine the $n - 1$ price ratios, since the excess-demand function for one commodity followed from the rest. In our dynamic system, however, we have already seen that all of the n excess-demand functions for commodities are independent of one another. Consequently if we were to require as our equilibrium conditions that the excess demand for each commodity be zero we should have n independent equations to determine $n - 1$ unknowns. What this means therefore is that the excess demand for one of the commodities (product or factor) will not ordinarily be equal to zero. Thus in a dynamic economy with fixed interest rates and unit-elastic expectations, the demand need not equal the supply for some one commodity even in equilibrium.[6] The $n - 1$ price ratios are determined by the condition that the excess demand for each of $n - 1$ commodities shall be zero. These price ratios then determine the level of excess demand (positive, zero, or negative) of the nth commodity.

[4] Hicks apparently assumes implicitly that the capital values of the expenditure plans *must* change in the same proportion as the change in prices under unit-elastic expectations. He therefore concludes that under unit-elastic expectations the level of the money prices themselves *cannot* be determined by the equilibrium system if the interest rates are fixed.

[5] For proof see the Appendix to this chapter.

[6] See the Appendix to this chapter.

There is, of course, nothing in the model to indicate the specific commodity (product or factor) for which the demand will not ordinarily equal the supply in equilibrium. This is determined institutionally. In practice it has been labor, of course, for which the supply has exceeded the demand even in equilibrium.

It is important to emphasize that this equilibrium unemployment is *not* the result of any wage rigidities. For under the conditions postulated in this section the excess-demand functions for the n commodities are functions of the $n - 1$ price ratios rather than of the absolute money levels of the n prices themselves. Consequently only the price ratios and not the money prices can be determined in equilibrium. A change in the money wage rates would therefore change all money prices in the same proportion and leave the supply and demand for every product and factor unchanged. Unemployment could not therefore be affected by a change in money wage rates under these conditions. It is true, of course, that a reduction in real wage rates would reduce unemployment since the excess demand for labor services is a function of the price ratios between commodities. But a change in money wage rates could not change the real wage rates under the conditions assumed here. A mathematical demonstration of this point is presented in the Appendix to this chapter.

The conclusion of this section is essentially a modification of the Keynesian theory of employment in terms of what is basically a Walrasian system of equations.[7]

3. Elastic price expectations

It should be clear from the previous discussion that the system will tend to be unstable if the price expectations are elastic. For in this case a rise in price is accompanied by a more than proportionate rise in expected prices and, therefore, leads to an increased excess demand, so far as the substitution effect is concerned. The system can be rendered stable therefore only if the income effect works in the opposite direction from the substitution effect. This would be at all probable only if the capital values of the expenditure plans fell markedly when prices rose and expectations were elastic.

---

[7] One basic difference between our analysis and that of Lord Keynes is that in our analysis there is an excess supply of labor in equilibrium, so that the level of employment is not determined at the point where the supply of labor is equal to the demand. In Keynes's analysis the level of employment is determined at the point where the demand for labor crosses the supply curve. The involuntary unemployment in his system is simply the result of the fact that he assumes the supply of labor to be infinitely elastic with respect to money wage rates in the relevant range. It is this infinitely elastic supply curve which determines the level of money wages and therefore the level of money prices in Keynes's system.

B.   The Stability of the Total System

Thus far we have considered simply the stability of the partial-equilibrium system with respect to commodities only, assuming the interest rates to be fixed. We have now to consider the stability of the total system taking into account the effects on and through the rate of interest.

We have already seen that, if the rate of interest is given, a rise in current prices under inelastic expectations will ordinarily lead to a decrease in the current excess demand for commodities and thus tend to restore the prices to the equilibrium level. If the rate of interest is left free to vary, the decrease in the excess demand for commodities will be accompanied by an increase in the excess demand for securities. The rate of interest will therefore tend to fall, and the discounted expected prices will rise. This latter rise, of course, tends to offset to some extent the original substitution away from current expenditures resulting from the rise in current prices. Thus the effect of permitting the interest rate to fall is the same as that of a rise in expected prices under fixed interest rates. Indeed if the discount factor rises in the same proportion as the rise in all current prices when price expectations have zero elasticity, the result is the same as under unit-elastic price expectations with fixed interest rates. There is then no scope for substitution between commodities at all.[8]

The question naturally arises as to whether the discount factor will increase in equal proportion if all current commodity prices rise in the same proportion and price expectations have zero elasticity. Or more generally, will the discounted expected prices rise in equal proportion if all current commodity prices rise in the same proportion, and interest rates are free to vary. The answer to this question has already been given in the discussion of unit-elastic price expectations with fixed interest rates. It was there shown that the effect of a rise in one price upon the level of the other prices and upon the excess demand for every commodity depends upon the elasticity of the capital values of the expenditure plans with respect to an equal proportionate change in all of the current and discounted expected prices. If this elasticity is less than unity, then a rise in the price of one commodity would lead to a less than proportionate rise in the prices of other commodities and would thus reduce the excess demand for that commodity. If the elasticity were greater than unity then a rise in the price of one commodity would lead to a more than proportionate rise in the prices of other commodities and the excess demand for the com-

---

[8] This assumes that interest-rate expectations have zero elasticity with respect to current rates.

modity would rise. The system would then be unstable. If, however, the elasticity is equal to unity, then the excess demand for every commodity is a homogeneous function of degree zero in all the current and discounted expected prices. In that case a rise in the price of one commodity would lead to an equal proportionate rise in all of the current and discounted expected prices if the discount factors were permitted to move freely.

It follows immediately from this analysis that, if the elasticity of the capital value of the expenditure plan is unity and if the discount factors are permitted to move freely, then all of the excess-demand functions are homogeneous functions of degree zero in the current and discounted expected prices, no matter what the elasticity of price expectations may be. This, as we have already seen, means that only the ratios between the system of prices (current and discounted expected prices) can be determined by the set of equilibrium equations. It means further that there can be an excess supply of labor in equilibrium regardless of the elasticity of price expectations. Specifically it implies that in the case of zero elasticity of price expectations the current discount factors would, if permitted to move freely, change in the same proportion as the change in the current prices of commodities;[9] that in the case of unit elasticity of price expectations, the discount factors and therefore the interest rates would remain unchanged;[10] and that in the case of elastic price expectations the discount factors would change in the opposite direction from the change in the current prices, or that interest rates would move in the same direction as the current prices.

The conclusions of this section are valid only if the discount factors are permitted to move freely. Since the interest rates, however, can never fall below zero, the discount factors can never be greater

---

[9] This assumes zero elasticity of interest-rate expectations. The reader may readily modify the conclusion to take into account nonzero elasticities.

[10] Hicks (pp. 258–259) assumes in the case of unit-elastic price expectations that a rise in current prices would lead to an increased excess demand for money and thus raise interest rates if the latter were permitted to move freely. This would make the discounted expected prices rise less than in proportion to the rise in current prices and would thus reduce current demand. Similarly a decline in price would reduce interest rates and increase excess demand. He thus concludes that if the interest rate were permitted to move freely it would serve as a stabilizer. This is, of course, the Keynesian theory. But while the theory is appropriate to the Keynesian model, it is incorrect in Hicks's model. For this argument is valid only if the excess-demand function for money is not a homogeneous function of the first degree in all the current and expected discounted prices. Under Hicks's assumption in which all of the excess-demand functions for commodities are homogeneous functions of degree zero, the excess-demand functions for securities and money must be homogeneous of the first degree. In Keynes the supply function for labor is not a homogeneous function of degree zero, and therefore the excess-demand function for money need not be a homogeneous function of the first degree in price and wages.

than one. Indeed in an industrial economy the range of variation of interest rates is so limited as to make the proportionate changes in the discount factor negligibly small.[11] It is clear therefore that we cannot ordinarily expect our equilibrium system to be affected very significantly by changes in interest rates. However, the more elastic are the interest-rate expectations the more significant will be the effect of changes in the current interest rate.

II. THE WORKING OF THE TEMPORARY-EQUILIBRIUM SYSTEM

As we have just shown, the behavior of a dynamic economy depends in large part upon the elasticity of the capital values of the expenditure plans with respect to a proportionate change in all current and discounted expected prices. If this elasticity is less than unity, then every excess demand function is a function of the absolute level of all of the current and discounted expected prices. The equilibrium conditions then determine the absolute level of the current prices and discount factors or interest rates. These conditions are that the excess demand for each commodity and each security shall be equal to zero. If all prices and wages are left free to vary, there can be no unemployment under these conditions. The system will be stable so long as the elasticity of discounted price expectations is not greater than unity.

If the elasticity of the expenditure plans is equal to unity, then every excess-demand function is a homogeneous function of the current and discounted expected prices. The behavior of the economy then depends upon the elasticity of price expectations and the behavior of the interest rates. If the interest rates were perfectly free to move, then the equilibrium conditions would determine only the ratios between the current and discounted price expectations, no matter what the elasticity of price expectations might be. Furthermore, as we have already noted, unemployment might very well exist in such an equilibrium system. If, however, the interest rates are fixed, then these conclusions are valid only under unit-elastic expectations. Otherwise the results are the same as under inelastic expenditure plans.

If the elasticity of the expenditure plans is greater than unity, then the system will be unstable for elastic and for unit-elastic price expectations and it might possibly be unstable even for inelastic price expectations. On the other hand if the elasticity of the expenditure plans is negative the system will be stable for inelastic and for unit-

[11] A 50-per cent rise in the rate of interest from 2 per cent to 3 per cent would change the discount factor from 1/(1.02) to 1/(1.03).

elastic price expectations and might possibly be stable even for elastic price expectations.

We turn now to a brief summary of the laws of the working of the equilibrium system under these various conditions. To determine these laws we again suppose some small change in the initial data, such as a change in the preference functions of a few individuals, or a change in the production functions for a few firms, or a change in some expectation functions which change the current supply and demand functions. The changes in price, and in the quantities bought and sold that are necessary in order to restore equilibrium, are then obtained from the stability conditions, which give us the effects of a small change in the price of any item upon the demand and supply for every item in the economy.

It is convenient in this analysis to group all of the items in the economy into four categories, products, factors, securities, and money. For many purposes both products and factors will be grouped together as commodities.

A.   *Inelastic Expenditure Plans*

1.   Suppose that the current excess demand for commodities rises in terms of money, but that the current demand for securities in terms of money remains unchanged. This means that at the same prices and interest rates people now want to buy more commodities but that they do not want to lend less or borrow more than before. The shift is thus only from cash holdings to products and not from securities to commodities. In practice this is likely to represent an increase in the consumer demand for nondurable goods only, unaccompanied by a rise in the producer demand function for factors. For when the producer demand function for factors rises, the rise is generally at the expense of security holdings rather than of money; i.e., the producer's excess-demand function for securities declines. This case, however, is here ruled out by assumption since it is assumed that none of the increased demand will be financed by increased borrowings.

It is evident from the stability conditions in the case of inelastic expenditure plans that the increase in the demand for products must raise their current prices. For, in order to make supply again equal to demand, prices must change in such a way as to produce an excess supply of these products in other sectors of the economy which can be used to satisfy those whose excess demand has risen. This excess supply can be brought about only by an increase in the prices of these products. By virtue of the substitution effect the prices of the factors employed in producing these products as well as the prices of other substitute commodities generally are likely to rise. The price rise for these commodities, however, will be proportionately smaller than that for the products whose demand functions have increased.

Assuming that future commodities are also substitutes for current commodities, the rise in current prices will lead to an induced increase in the planned demand for future commodities. So far as current behavior is concerned, this will translate itself into an increase in the current excess demand for securities; i.e., there will be an induced rise in net lendings. Current security prices will therefore rise or interest rates will fall.

It may appear strange that a fall in interest rates should result from an increase in the demand function for commodities, since it is counter to the usual experience in a business upswing. This paradox disappears, however, when it is recalled that we are supposing here that there is an autonomous increase in the demand for products only, the demand function for securities remaining unchanged. The case under discussion is, therefore, approximately that of a temporary spurt in demand supported by inventory depletion rather than that of a general business upswing. In the latter case there would be an autonomous increase in the demand for factors to be financed out of securities. It is to this second case that we now turn.

2. We suppose now that there is an increase in the excess-demand function for commodities in terms of securities, i.e., that the demand function for commodities in terms of money rises and the demand function for securities in terms of money declines. This is the case when the demand for consumers' durable products rises, the new demand being financed out of a rise in consumer credit, or when the producers' demand function for factors rises as a result, say, of increased price expectations, the increased demand being financed, out of the sale of securities held or increased borrowings. In this case, the usual case of a general business upswing, there is a rise in the prices of commodities generally and a decline in security prices or a rise in interest rates.

3. If the current excess-demand function for securities rises in terms of money and the excess-demand function for commodities remains unchanged, then the price of securities will rise and interest rates will fall. The associated rise in the discount factor represents a rise in the discounted expected prices of future commodities. It will therefore induce an increase in the excess demand for current commodities, and current commodity prices will rise.

We have assumed thus far that all commodity prices were flexible and perfectly free to move in response to changes in demand and supply. Under this assumption the demand and supply for each product and factor must be equal in equilibrium when inelastic expenditure plans are assumed. If, however, the price of some commodity—

product or factor—is fixed rigidly at a level different from its equilibrium level, then the demand and supply for that commodity will not be equal. Thus, if under inelastic expenditure plans, product prices are fixed rigidly above or below their equilibrium level, the prices will not equate the demand and supply functions for these commodities. If the prices are fixed rigidly above the equilibrium level, consumption of these products will decline, and it will therefore be necessary to curtail output up to the point where it is equal to the quantity demanded at the fixed price. The producers will therefore behave as they would if the price were in fact lower than the equilibrium price. Thus, as Hicks points out, we may treat this problem as if there were in fact two prices for the given commodity—a rigid market price for the consumers and a lower "shadow price" for the producers, the difference between the two prices being given as a bonus to those who make the sales. The reverse of this argument holds if prices are fixed below the equilibrium level. Here the low market price will curtail production and it will be necessary to ration consumption in some form in order to enforce the lower price. Consumers will therefore be forced to behave as they would if prices were in fact higher than the equilibrium level. Here it is the market price which determines the producers' behavior and the shadow price which determines the consumers' behavior.[12]

[12] We may illustrate this mathematically in a two-product system. Ordinarily our equilibrium conditions are:

$$I_1 = X_1(p_1, p_2) - \overline{\overline{X}}_1(p_1, p_2) = 0,$$

$$I_2 = X_2(p_1, p_2) - \overline{\overline{X}}_2(p_1, p_2) = 0,$$

where X is the net consumer demand function and $\overline{\overline{X}}$ is the producer supply function. (The initial supply $\overline{X}$ is assumed to be zero.) Suppose however that p_1 is fixed at a higher level than that which would result from this system of equations. Then we should have instead:

$$p_1 = k,$$
$$X_1 = X_1(k, p_2) = \overline{\overline{X}}_1$$
$$p'_1 = p'_1(\overline{X}_1, p_2),$$

$$X_2(k, p_2) - \overline{\overline{X}}_2(p'_1, p_2) = 0,$$

where k is the fixed market price which is relevant for the consumer demand functions and p'_1 is the shadow price which is relevant for the producer supply functions.

It may be worth noting here that Hicks's diagrammatic solution of this problem (pp. 110–111) is faulty, since in a multi-commodity system the two-dimensional demand and supply curves for a commodity have no validity except at one point. Thus the curves can be drawn at all only on the assumption that the prices of all other commodities are fixed. But any change in price for the given commodity will change all other prices, so that the two-dimensional demand and supply curves for the given commodity will change.

The identical argument holds for rigid wage rates. If wages are fixed below the equilibrium level the demand for labor will have to be rationed in some form. If on the other hand wages are fixed above the equilibrium level there will be some unemployment. This unemployment, however, must be clearly distinguished from the unemployment which, we found, may exist under unit-elastic expenditure plans without any wage rigidities at all. The former can, whereas the latter cannot, be eliminated by lowering the money wage rates.

The effect on other products and factors of the imposition of rigid prices and wage rates cannot be so readily determined. If a product price is fixed above the equilibrium level it will give rise to a consumer substitution effect in favor of other commodities which will tend to raise other prices. On the other hand, since the shadow price which affects the producer behavior is lower than the equilibrium level, there will also be a producer substitution effect in favor of other commodities. The net effect on the other prices therefore depends on which substitution effect is dominant. The same thing is true in the case of rigid wage rates. If the wage rates are fixed above the equilibrium level there will be a producer substitution effect in favor of other factors which will tend to raise their prices. On the other hand the unemployed will tend to shift into other occupations and this will tend to lower the wage rates there.

In an economy with rigid wage rates and unemployment, the effects of shifts in demand and supply will be reflected not only in the movement of prices but also in changes in employment. Thus if the demand for commodities should rise in terms of money, not only would the prices of these commodities rise, but the demand for labor would also rise. Wage rates would remain unchanged but the volume of unemployment would decline. With wage rates unchanged there would be no producer substitution effect away from other factors and from products. The rise in prices of substitute factors and in prices of products would thus be smaller than in a system with flexible wage rates.

B.   Unit-elastic Expenditure Plans

We have already seen that under this assumption the excess-demand function for every commodity becomes a homogeneous function of the current and discounted expected prices. If the interest rates were perfectly flexible, then the equilibrium conditions would determine only the ratios between the current and discounted expected prices, no matter what the elasticity of price expectations might be. Since the interest rates are not perfectly flexible, this is true only if the price expectations have unit elasticity. Under this assumption only the price ratios are determined in equilibrium and there is generally some unemployment even in equilibrium. This unemployment, as we have emphasized, cannot be eliminated by reducing money wage rates since the effect of such a reduction is only to change all other money prices in proportion, and the demand and supply of every commodity will remain unchanged. The effect of rigid wage rates in such an economy is simply to determine the level of all prices; it is not to determine the level of employment.

The level of employment can change in such a system only if there is a change in the excess-demand functions. This will change the price ratios, the quantities bought and sold of every commodity, and the level of employment. Thus if there is an increase in the demand for products, the ratios of product to factor prices will rise This change in the price ratios will then lead to an increase in employment. Similarly if there is an increase in the excess demand for securities in terms of money, the prices of securities will rise and interest rates will fall. This will lead to an induced increase in the excess demand for both products and factors, and employment will increase.

APPENDIX TO CHAPTER VIII

EQUILIBRIUM CONDITIONS UNDER HOMOGENEOUS EXCESS-DEMAND FUNCTIONS

Let the n excess-demand functions

$$I_s = I_s(p_1, p_2, \cdots, p_n)$$

be homogeneous of degree zero with respect to the n prices. Assume that there is a change in p_1 and that the prices of all other commodities adjust themselves so as to maintain equilibrium in those markets. Then it can readily be shown that there will be no change in the excess demand for X_1 and all other prices will change proportionately. Thus, differentiating the functions with respect to p_1 and setting $dI_r/dp_1 = 0 \ (r \neq 1)$, we have

$$\frac{dI_1}{dp_1} = \frac{\partial I_1}{\partial p_1} + \frac{\partial I_1}{\partial p_2}\frac{dp_2}{dp_1} + \cdots + \frac{\partial I_1}{\partial p_n}\frac{dp_n}{dp_1},$$

$$0 = \frac{\partial I_2}{\partial p_1} + \frac{\partial I_2}{\partial p_2}\frac{dp_2}{dp_1} + \cdots + \frac{\partial I_2}{\partial p_n}\frac{dp_n}{dp_1},$$

(1)

$$\cdot \quad \cdot \quad \cdot \quad \cdot \quad \cdot \quad \cdot \quad \cdot \quad \cdot \quad \cdot \quad \cdot \quad \cdot$$

$$0 = \frac{\partial I_n}{\partial p_1} + \frac{\partial I_n}{\partial p_2}\frac{dp_2}{dp_1} + \cdots + \frac{\partial I_n}{\partial p_n}\frac{dp_n}{dp_1}.$$

Solving for dI_1/dp_1 we obtain

(2)
$$\frac{dI_1}{dp_1} = - \begin{vmatrix} \dfrac{\partial I_1}{\partial p_1} & \dfrac{\partial I_1}{\partial p_2} & \cdots & \dfrac{\partial I_1}{\partial p_n} \\ \dfrac{\partial I_2}{\partial p_1} & \dfrac{\partial I_2}{\partial p_2} & \cdots & \dfrac{\partial I_2}{\partial p_n} \\ \cdot & \cdot & \cdot & \cdot \\ \dfrac{\partial I_n}{\partial p_1} & \dfrac{\partial I_n}{\partial p_2} & \cdots & \dfrac{\partial I_n}{\partial p_n} \end{vmatrix} \div \begin{vmatrix} \dfrac{\partial I_2}{\partial p_2} & \dfrac{\partial I_2}{\partial p_3} & \cdots & \dfrac{\partial I_2}{\partial p_n} \\ \dfrac{\partial I_3}{\partial p_2} & \dfrac{\partial I_3}{\partial p_3} & \cdots & \dfrac{\partial I_3}{\partial p_n} \\ \cdot & \cdot & \cdot & \cdot \\ \dfrac{\partial I_n}{\partial p_2} & \dfrac{\partial I_n}{\partial p_3} & \cdots & \dfrac{\partial I_n}{\partial p_n} \end{vmatrix}.$$

Since the functions I_s are homogeneous of degree zero we have

(3)
$$p_1\frac{\partial I_s}{\partial p_1} + p_2\frac{\partial I_s}{\partial p_2} + \cdots + p_n\frac{\partial I_s}{\partial p_n} = 0.$$

The value of a determinant remains unchanged if we add to any row or column a multiple of any other row or column. Let us, therefore, multiply the first column of the numerator in equation (2) by p_1 (introducing a factor $1/p_1$ on the outside) and add to it the elements in each column i multiplied by the corresponding price p_i. We then obtain

(4)
$$\frac{dI_1}{dp_1} = -\frac{1}{p_1} \begin{vmatrix} \sum p_i\dfrac{\partial I_1}{\partial p_i} & \dfrac{\partial I_1}{\partial p_2} & \cdots & \dfrac{\partial I_1}{\partial p_n} \\ \sum p_i\dfrac{\partial I_2}{\partial p_i} & \dfrac{\partial I_2}{\partial p_2} & \cdots & \dfrac{\partial I_2}{\partial p_n} \\ \cdot & \cdot & \cdot & \cdot \\ \sum p_i\dfrac{\partial I_n}{\partial p_i} & \dfrac{\partial I_n}{\partial p_2} & \cdots & \dfrac{\partial I_n}{\partial p_n} \end{vmatrix} \div \varDelta,$$

where $\varDelta$ is the denominator of equation (2).

By virtue of (3) the first column in (4) consists of zeros, so that $dI_1/dp_1 = 0$.

Similarly it can be shown that $dp_2/dp_1 = p_2/p_1$.

For we have

$$(5) \quad \frac{dp_2}{dp_1} = - \begin{vmatrix} \dfrac{\partial I_2}{\partial p_1} & \dfrac{\partial I_2}{\partial p_3} & \cdots & \dfrac{\partial I_2}{\partial p_n} \\[2ex] \dfrac{\partial I_3}{\partial p_1} & \dfrac{\partial I_3}{\partial p_3} & \cdots & \dfrac{\partial I_3}{\partial p_n} \\[2ex] \cdot & \cdot & \cdot & \cdot \\[1ex] \dfrac{\partial I_n}{\partial p_1} & \dfrac{\partial I_n}{\partial p_3} & \cdots & \dfrac{\partial I_n}{\partial p_n} \end{vmatrix} \div \begin{vmatrix} \dfrac{\partial I_2}{\partial p_2} & \dfrac{\partial I_2}{\partial p_3} & \cdots & \dfrac{\partial I_2}{\partial p_n} \\[2ex] \dfrac{\partial I_3}{\partial p_2} & \dfrac{\partial I_3}{\partial p_3} & \cdots & \dfrac{\partial I_3}{\partial p_n} \\[2ex] \cdot & \cdot & \cdot & \cdot \\[1ex] \dfrac{\partial I_n}{\partial p_2} & \dfrac{\partial I_n}{\partial p_3} & \cdots & \dfrac{\partial I_n}{\partial p_n} \end{vmatrix}$$

Multiplying each column in the numerator by the corresponding price, adding to the first column, and making use of equation (3), we find that the determinant in the numerator becomes the same as that in the denominator except for a factor $- p_2/p_1$. Consequently $dp_2/dp_1 = p_2/p_1$.

This proof is sufficiently general since the order of the commodities is completely arbitrary.

Since the excess-demand functions are functions only of the $n - 1$ price ratios, these may be determined by the condition that $n - 1$ excess-demand functions shall equal zero. These ratios then determine the level of the excess demand for the remaining commodity. Thus we have as our equilibrium system to determine the $n - 1$ price ratios:

$$I_2 = I_2\left(\frac{p_2}{p_1}, \frac{p_3}{p_1}, \cdots, \frac{p_n}{p_1}\right) = 0,$$

$$I_3 = I_3\left(\frac{p_2}{p_1}, \frac{p_3}{p_1}, \cdots, \frac{p_n}{p_1}\right) = 0,$$

$$\cdot \quad \cdot \quad \cdot \quad \cdot \quad \cdot \quad \cdot \quad \cdot \quad \cdot \quad \cdot$$

$$I_n = I_n\left(\frac{p_2}{p_1}, \frac{p_3}{p_1}, \cdots, \frac{p_n}{p_1}\right) = 0.$$

When the $n - 1$ price ratios are determined, I_1 is given by

$$I_1 = I_1\left(\frac{p_2}{p_1}, \frac{p_3}{p_1}, \cdots, \frac{p_n}{p_1}\right).$$

CHAPTER IX

Market Equilibrium in an International Economy

I. DESCRIPTION OF EQUILIBRIUM

The market equilibrium in an international economy may be analyzed in essentially the same manner as the equilibrium in a closed economy. In each country there are market demand and supply functions for commodities, securities, and money, the arguments of these functions being the whole set of interest rates and prices in all countries. For each country the prices are expressed in terms of its own currency, but each such price may be expressed in terms of the currency of some one country and the exchange rates between the currencies of the two countries, both current and expected. (The expected exchange rate may, of course, differ from individual to individual just as the expected prices do.) This is the basic relationship which we have already considered in our static analysis of international trade. Thus we have:

$$p_{rt}^{(1)} = e_{1i,t} p_{rt}^{(i)} ,$$

where, as before, the superscript indicates the country, and where $e_{1i,t}$ is the expected (or current) number of units of currency i which one must give for one unit of currency 1 in period t.

If the exchange rates are fixed, it follows immediately that given the expectation functions of future prices and interest rates, the current demand and supply functions for every country may be written as functions of the current prices expressed in terms of the currency of country 1. We may, therefore, sum up the total world demand and supply for each commodity and for each security and for money as functions of the same variables.

The general market equilibrium conditions depend again on whether the excess-demand functions are homogeneous of degree zero. If they are not homogeneous then the equilibrium conditions require that the total world demand for each commodity and for each security (and consequently for money) shall equal the total world supply, or that the total world import demand for each of these shall equal zero. These conditions determine the current prices and interest rates in terms of the currency of country 1. The prices in terms of each country's own currency are then given by the exchange rates.

If the excess-demand functions are homogeneous of degree zero, then, as we have already seen, only the price ratios between commodities will be determined in equilibrium, and there will generally be some unemployment even in equilibrium.

Some commodities and securities may be "domestic" in each country—i.e., their exports may be identically equal to zero—but this does not require any alteration in our statement of the equilibrium conditions.

It is important to emphasize the differences between the dynamic equilibrium conditions that we have just presented and the static equilibrium conditions that we gave earlier. In a static economy the conditions of equilibrium required that for each country the value of exports of goods and services excluding "money" shall be equal to the value of imports. No money was supposed to move in equilibrium. These conditions were valid in our static economy because we had no true money in our system for which a demand function existed. There was no question for any individual as to how much of his income he should hold in the form of money and how much he should spend. Every individual was assumed always to spend all of his income. No substitution was possible between commodities and money. Money was simply a counter which was used to measure values but was not a store of value. It was, therefore, not a part of the equilibrium system at all. All of the equilibrium values of production and consumption were first determined in terms of price ratios between commodities without any reference to money at all. Money was then introduced simply to determine an absolute level for prices upon the arbitrary assumption that there was a fixed relationship between the quantity of money held and the value of one's income. In such an economy, it is perfectly clear that in equilibrium there will be no transfers of money between individuals and, *a fortiori*, no exports of money between countries. The value of exports of goods and services must then be equal to the value of imports for each country in the absence of reparations.

In our dynamic economy, however, we have introduced a true money for which demand and supply functions exist just as for any other security. Here money is no longer a counter which bears a fixed relationship to the value of one's "income" but a store of value very much like a security for which the demand and supply vary according as prices and interest rates vary. It is obvious, therefore, that the equilibrium conditions for any given period do not require that no transfers of money shall take place. The volume of exports or imports of money for each country may very well differ from zero in the equilibrium for any given period. As a corollary, the value of exports of goods and services (volume of money) may very well differ from the value of imports for each country even in the absence of reparations payments or international borrowings. This is an essential departure from the classical concept of international equilibrium which is based upon the assumption of neutral money.

If the exchange rates are not fixed but are left free to vary, then we have $v - 1$ additional variables to determine, one exchange rate for each but the first country. Free exchange rates, however, imply that each country determines for itself what quantity of money it shall hold. In this case we have $v - 1$ additional independent equations which must be satisfied in equilibrium. The demand for money in each of the $v - 1$ countries must be equal to the supply of money in that country. The equation for the first country follows from the rest. Our system, therefore, remains determinate. It may be worth noting that the exchange rates need not be free for every country; there may be a bloc of countries between which the exchange rate is fixed.

II. THE LAWS OF THE WORKING OF THE INTERNATIONAL EQUILIBRIUM

A.   Under Fixed Exchange Rates

The laws of the working of a general-equilibrium system have already been indicated for a closed economy. In this section, therefore, there remain to be treated only those problems which are especially related to international movements.[1] It is necessary, first of all, to distinguish between a world in which exchange rates are fixed and one in which they are variable. The analysis is simpler in the former than in the latter case by virtue of the rule which states that a group of commodities between whose prices fixed ratios are maintained may be treated as one commodity. Thus, when exchange rates are fixed, there are no separate demand and supply functions for individual currencies; there is but one demand and supply function for all currencies taken together. In this section we shall confine ourselves to the assumption of fixed exchange rates; in the next we shall treat variable exchange rates.

1.   Increase in demand for domestic commodities in terms of securities

This case represents a rise in the propensity to consume or to

---

[1] An excellent treatment of the theory of international-trade equilibrium along Keynesian lines is to be found in an article by Lloyd A. Metzler, "Underemployment Equilibrium in International Trade," *Econometrica*, Vol. 10, April, 1942, pp. 97–112. See also his article, "The Transfer Problem Reconsidered," *Journal of Political Economy*, Vol. 50, June, 1942, pp. 397–414. Professor Machlup's book, *International Trade and the National Income Multiplier*, appeared while this book was in press.

invest. Under full employment it will result in a rise in the prices of domestic goods and a shift in production from foreign-trade goods to domestic products. Export and import prices generally will also rise to some extent by virtue of the substitution effect. The quantities of exports will tend to decline while the quantities of imports will tend to rise. Although the value of exports may either rise or fall, the commodity balance of trade, i.e., the value of the country's exports minus the value of its imports, will almost certainly decline. In the rest of the world, prices generally will also tend to rise, and there will be a shift in production from domestic to foreign-trade goods.

If unemployment exists, the increase in demand for domestic commodities will lead not only to an increase in prices but also to an increase in total employment, output, and income. The increase in income as well as the increase in domestic prices will lead to a rise in imports also. This in itself serves as a damper on the expansion in the given country, but it raises employment, output, and income abroad. In turn the foreign countries affected will increase their imports from other countries (including the given country). Thus both exports and imports will rise for the country initiating the expansion as well as for the rest of the world. The commodity balance of trade for the initiating country will ordinarily decline, however, since the increase in the foreign demand for the country's exports is only the result of the increase in the country's demand for imports from abroad.

If the country is a net importer of capital, its net capital imports will tend to rise. The greater the elasticity of the foreign demand for securities, the greater will be the given country's capital imports. If the country is a net exporter of capital, its net capital exports will tend to decline. The greater the elasticity of the foreign supply of securities the greater will be the decline in its capital exports.

2.   *Increase in demand for import commodities in terms of securities*

This case represents a rise in the propensity to import without any offset in the propensity to spend at home. In the first instance it will result in a rise in the prices and output of export goods abroad. If there is unemployment abroad, total employment and output will increase in the foreign countries. Otherwise there will simply be a shift in employment and output from their domestic commodities to their export goods. The increase in prices or employment (or both) abroad will, in turn, lead to some increase in prices or employment (or both) in the given country. The balance of trade of the given country will again almost certainly decline.

3. Shift in demand from domestic to import commodities

In a system of fully flexible prices this shift will result in a decline in domestic prices, and, by virtue of the substitution effect, probably in export prices as well. Import prices, however, will rise. These price changes will be associated with a shift in production from domestic to foreign-trade goods. In the rest of the world the effect will be qualitatively the same as that discussed in the previous paragraph. Quantitatively, however, the effects on the rest of the world of a given autonomous increase in a country's demand for import goods will be different according as the given country's demand for domestic goods does or does not change. For, as we saw in the first case, an autonomous change in the demand for domestic goods gives rise to an induced change in the demand for import goods. In this case therefore the autonomous increase in the demand for import goods will be dampened to some extent by the reduction resulting from the autonomous decline in the demand for domestic goods.

If wage rates are rigid the shift from domestic to import goods will result at first in a decline in employment in the given country and a rise in employment in the rest of the world. Each of these changes in employment will, of course, tend to spread to the rest of the world. It is possible therefore, but not likely, that the shift should finally result in an increase or in a decrease of employment in both places.

4. Rise in demand for commodities generally in terms of securities

This case is characteristic of a general business upswing. Under a system of flexible prices, domestic, export, and import prices generally will rise. Domestic prices may be expected to rise most, and import prices least.[2] This implies a shift in employment and output from foreign-trade goods to domestic goods. It further implies a rise in the quantities of goods imported and a decline in those exported. Although the value of the country's exports may rise or fall, its commodity balance of trade will almost certainly decline.

If unemployment exists, the rise in demand will lead not only to an increase in prices but also to a rise in total employment and output. Since the increase in demand is also directed at foreign goods, it will increase employment and output in the rest of the world as well.

---

[2] The percentage increase in the price of any commodity will tend to be the greater:
    (a) the greater is the percentage rise in the aggregate world demand for the commodity;
    (b) the lower is the elasticity of demand for that commodity with respect to its own price;
    (c) the lower is the elasticity of supply for that commodity with respect to its own price.

In turn this will lead to an increase of exports and therefore a further rise in output and employment in the given country.

5. Effects of reparations payments

In our static analysis the payment of reparations implied a decrease in the paying country's demand function for commodities by the full amount of the reparations and a corresponding increase for the receiving country. The reason for this correspondence lay in the fact that our system really contained only commodities; there were no securities or real money in the system. Our dynamic system, however, contains commodities, securities, and money. It is conceivable therefore that the payment of reparations should leave the demand functions for commodities in one or both countries unaltered. Thus in the paying country the Government may finance its payment of reparations through the flotation of a loan. The reparations payments would therefore be offset by an increased demand function for securities rather than by a decreased demand function for commodities. Similarly in the receiving country the Government may use the reparations to repay a part of the public debt, rather than to increase the demand for commodities. We may consider a number of possibilities at this point:

(a)   If the reparations payments are made through the flotation of a loan and the receipts are used to repay the debt, then the primary effect of the reparations will be reflected in movements of the interest rates in the two countries. Prices and output of products will be affected only through the changes in interest rates. And these effects, as we have already noted in the previous chapters, are likely to be small.

(b)   If the reparations payments are financed through taxes and the receipts are used to repay the debt, then the reparations will have a seriously deflationary effect on the world as a whole. For they will lead to a significant decrease in the demand for goods in the paying country (the magnitude depending on the income elasticity of demand) which will not be offset by an increase in the demand in the receiving country. Prices or output or both will therefore decline in the paying country and the decline will spread to the rest of the world through the fall in the country's demand for imports (both primary and induced).

(c)   If the reparations payments are financed through borrowing and the receipts are used to reduce taxes or to increase Government expenditures directly, then the effect is likely to be inflationary on the world as a whole. The reasoning here is parallel to that of the preceding paragraph. Lest the point be misinterpreted it might be well to emphasize the fact that the expansionary effect here is the direct result of the primary increase in expenditures in the receiving country. The reparations receipts simply make it possible for the Government to increase expenditures or to reduce taxes without increasing the national debt.

(d)   The case in which the reparations payments are financed through taxes and the receipts are used to reduce taxes or to increase Government expenditures is a combination of the preceding two cases. The direct effect of the reparations will be deflationary for the paying country and inflationary for the receiving country. The indirect effects through foreign trade, however, will work in the opposite direction in each case. If the direct effects are of equal magnitude, the indirect effects will generally not suffice to counteract them in either country, since the propensity to import is usually smaller than the propensity to spend at home. If, however, the direct effects are of unequal magnitudes, then the indirect effect of the country exercising the greater direct influence may be sufficient to counteract the direct effect of the other country. Thus if the direct contraction in demand in the paying country is greater than the direct expansion in the receiving country, the reparations may prove to be deflationary for the world as a whole. This result is extremely likely in a period of general depression.

6.   Effects of capital movements

The effects of capital movements may be analyzed in much the same way as those of reparations payments. In the classical theory of international trade it was usually assumed that capital movements implied a reduction in the lending country's demand for goods by the amount of the money lent, and an equivalent increase in the borrowing country's demand. The conclusion was therefore that capital movements were likely to be deflationary on the lending country and inflationary on the borrowing country. It should be quite evident at this stage that such an analysis is extremely oversimplified. An autonomous increase in capital exports is likely to represent an increase in the demand for foreign securities in terms of money rather than in terms of commodities.[3] The direct effect of the capital exports is therefore likely to be limited to the markets for securities—i.e., domestic interest rates are likely to rise. This will tend to depress the demand for durable goods in the lending country, but, as we have already noted, the effect of a rise in interest rates on the demand for

---

[3] A decline in the demand for commodities which lasts for any length of time is not likely to be accompanied by an increase in the supply function for foreign loans.

goods is likely to be small. On the other hand in the borrowing country the capital imports are likely to represent a primary shift from securities to commodities. If, as is frequently the case, a substantial fraction of the increased demand for commodities is directed at the capital-lending country, the effect of the capital movements will be inflationary on both the lending and the borrowing country.[4]

7. The imposition of foreign-trade restrictions

It is clear that an increase in imports is directly deflationary whereas an increase in exports is directly inflationary. It is this fact, of course, that lies behind the almost stifling trade restrictions which developed in the twenties. Economists have usually argued that trade barriers are harmful to all countries, including the one that imposes them. Even in the pure theory of international trade, however, it was shown that, although the world as a whole would lose, an individual country could gain by imposing a tariff, provided that the tariff was not too large. (The gain is essentially the same as that enjoyed by a monopolist seller as compared with a seller under pure competition.) This theory, however, did not take into account the possibility of the existence of unemployment. Furthermore it assumed that (in the absence of continuing capital movements) the value of exports must be equal to the value of imports. Consequently any reduction in the value of a country's imports would necessarily lead to an equivalent decrease in the value of its exports. It could not, therefore, result in an expansion of total output and employment.

This analysis now appears oversimplified. Import restrictions do have a direct inflationary effect on the country that imposes them even though they have a deflationary effect on the rest of the world. This statement, of course, does not imply that the imposition of such restrictions is wise even when unemployment exists. In the first place such actions generally lead to retaliatory measures which curtail exports. The net result is therefore likely to be a general decline in the demand for goods, in which all countries lose. A very strong argument against import restrictions may be made, however, even in the case where the foreign governments do not retaliate. It has already been pointed out that the direct effect of the import restrictions on the rest of the world is deflationary. If their exports constitute an important fraction of their income, the secondary repercussions may aggravate the contraction to such an extent as to lead

[4] Cf. Jacob Viner, *Studies in the Theory of International Trade*, (New York, 1936), p. 434.
"Paradoxical though it may seem at first glance, the increased export of capital may be the cause, and may in fact constitute the bulk, of the internal expansion of business activity."

to a general world depression which spreads to the first country as well. This is particularly likely under elastic price expectations.

B.   Under Free Exchange Rates[5]

The previous analysis was based on the simplifying assumption of fixed exchange rates. Under this assumption all currencies may be treated analytically as one commodity (namely, money) for which there exists a world demand and supply. Money then flows freely from one country to another in accordance with the conditions of world demand and supply for commodities, securities, and money. Under the inverse assumption of free exchange rates money cannot flow at all between countries. The volume of currency in each country is then determined by the demand and supply conditions for the currency in each country separately, rather than by the world demand and supply conditions for currency as a whole. Instead of the free flow of currency between countries, however, we have the free variation of exchange rates between currencies in accordance with the equilibrium conditions of demand and supply.

It may be worth while to consider in somewhat greater detail the nature of the general-equilibrium determination under a system of free exchange rates. In each country there are demand and supply functions for commodities, for securities, and for money, each expressed as functions of the commodity prices and interest rates (or security prices) in terms of the currency of that country. (Given expectation functions are assumed.) These may be expressed as functions of the commodity prices and interest rates in terms of the currency of some base country and the exchange rates between the two currencies. Our unknowns are, therefore, reduced to the following: the commodity prices and interest rates in terms of some one currency and the exchange rates between every currency and that of the base country. To determine these unknowns we proceed as follows: For each commodity and for each security we may add the demand and supply function for all countries to obtain the total world demand and supply functions. In equilibrium the total world demand for each commodity and for each security must equal the total world supply. These equations are insufficient to determine all the unknowns, since the number of unknowns exceeds the number of these equations by the number of exchange rates (one less than the number of countries) between the currencies of each country and the currency of

[5] For a more extended treatment of international trade under free exchanges which differs in several respects from our analysis, see G. Haberler, *Prosperity and Depression.*

country 1. However, we have an equal number of additional independent equations which must be satisfied in equilibrium. The demand for money in each of the $v - 1$ countries (v equals the total number of countries) must be equal to the supply of money in that country. (The equation for the first country follows from the rest.)

In this analysis we have omitted the equation of demand and supply for foreign exchange from our general-equilibrium system. The demand for foreign exchange in any country is, of course, equivalent to the sum of the value of the country's imports of commodities and securities, while its supply of foreign exchange is equivalent to the sum of its exports of commodities and securities. Since our equilibrium system states that the total world demand for commodities and for securities must equal the total world supply, and that the demand for money in each country must equal the supply of money in that country, it follows immediately that the total world demand for bills of foreign exchange must equal the total world supply.

Instead of retaining in our equilibrium system the equation for money in each country and eliminating the equation for foreign exchange, we may reverse our procedure. We may eliminate the equation for money and instead introduce the equations for foreign exchange. We should thus have $v - 1$ independent equations specifying that the total world demand for foreign exchange of each of the $v - 1$ countries in terms of one currency must be equal to the total world supply. This corresponds more closely to the usual procedure of determining the exchange rates by the demand for and supply of foreign exchange. It should be noted, however, that in our system, the exchange rates are determined simultaneously with the other unknowns (the prices and interest rates) by the equation of the demand and supply in all markets, including the commodity and security markets.

Under a system of free exchanges, money does not move between boundaries, so that the value of a country's imports of commodities and securities must equal the value of its exports. The implications of this statement should be clearly understood. It means for instance that where there are no international transactions in securities, any increase in the value of the commodity imports of country X must of necessity lead to an equivalent increase in the value of the commodity imports of country Y. (Country Y represents the rest of the world.) It does not mean, however, that this shift is neutral in its effect upon the total volume of expenditures on goods produced in Y. This would be true only if the increase in the value of Y's imports (resulting from the increase in the value of its exports) were exactly offset by an equal decrease in its expenditures on its own goods. This, however, is not a necessary result. The assumption of free exchange rates implies that the increase in the value of X's imports is exactly offset by an increase in the value of Y's imports. It does not imply that the latter is also exactly offset by an equal reduction in Y's expenditures on its own goods.

With these preliminary statements in mind we may now proceed to analyze in somewhat greater detail the effects of shifts in demand in a system of free exchanges. Before doing so, however, we must consider the effects of changes in exchange rates. We define X's exchange rate on Y as the number of units of X's currency which must be paid for a unit of Y's currency. A rise in X's exchange rate, therefore, makes its imports from Y more expensive in terms of its own (X's) currency and its exports to Y cheaper in terms of Y's currency. Conversely, a fall in X's exchange rate makes its imports from Y cheaper in terms of its own currency and its exports to Y more expensive in terms of Y's currency. What is the effect of a rise in X's exchange rates upon the demand for commodities? On the assumption that the elasticity of exchange-rate expectations is not greater than unity, country X's demand for foreign exchange will decline, namely, its demand for imports will go down. On the further assumption that all goods are substitutes, its demand for its own goods will increase. Its expenditures on its own goods will, therefore, definitely increase, but its expenditures (in terms of its own currency) on imports may either rise or decline. Its total expenditures on all goods (native and imports combined) may, therefore, either rise, or decline, or remain unchanged. On the other hand, country Y's demand for imports from X will increase while its demand for its own goods will decline. Here there is a definite decline in its expenditures on its own goods, but its expenditures (in terms of its own currency) on imports from X may either rise or fall. Thus country Y's expenditures on all goods may also rise or decline or remain unchanged.

We may now consider several illustrations of shifts in demand. It will be convenient to abstract from international transactions in securities in the first stage of our analysis.

1. Suppose that in country X there is a shift in demand from money to Y's export goods, the demand for its own goods remaining unaffected. Then X's demand for foreign exchange increases and its exchange rate rises. For X this is equivalent to a rise in the price of its imports, but for Y it is equivalent not to a rise in the price of Y's exports but to a decline in the price of X's exports. In X the rise in the demand for Y's goods normally leads to an increase in X's expenditures (in terms of its own currency) on Y's goods. Since the

value of Y's imports must equal the value of its exports, Y's expenditures (in terms of X's currency) on X's goods will also increase.[6] The rise in the foreign-exchange rate also leads to an increase in X's expenditures on its own goods (assuming all goods to be substitutes). The shift in demand from money to import goods thus leads to a secondary increase in the total demand for its own goods. This is essentially the same result as under a fixed exchange system.

In country Y, however, the results are quite different from what one would expect under a fixed exchange system. The change in the exchange rate leads to an increase in Y's demand for imports and to some decrease in its demand for its own goods. If the increase in Y's demand for imports is not sufficiently great to lead to a rise in its expenditures (in terms of its own currency) on these goods, then the total expenditures for its own goods will decline. On the other hand, its expenditures for imports may rise to such an extent as to more than offset the decrease in its expenditures on its own goods. Since its expenditures on X's goods must equal X's expenditures on its goods the total expenditures on its goods will rise. So far as country Y is concerned, therefore, the shift in X's demand *from money to goods of country Y* has essentially the same effects as X's *shift from its own goods to money* would have in a system of fixed exchanges.

2. If there is a shift in demand in country X from money to its own commodities (its demand functions for Y's goods remaining unchanged), then the prices of its own goods will rise. In country X this will lead to an increase in the demand for Y's goods; in country Y it will lead to a decrease in demand for X's goods and to an increase in demand for its own goods. The shifts in demand for imports in the two countries are tantamount to a rise in the demand curve and a decrease in the supply curve for foreign exchange. Country X's exchange rate on Y will, therefore, rise until the quantity of foreign exchange (Y's currency) supplied is again equal to the quantity demanded. If the new quantity of foreign exchange supplied is equal to or greater than the old, this means that the value of Y's imports and, therefore, the value of its exports in terms of its own currency has remained unchanged or has risen. In that event the total expenditure in terms of Y's currency on the goods produced in Y will definitely have risen, since Y's demand for its own goods has

---

[6] It should be noted that since X's exchange rate on Y rises, the expenditures on import goods in terms of X's currency can rise even though the expenditures in terms of Y's currency may fall. Thus when X's demand for foreign exchange rises, the equilibrium quantity of foreign exchange (Y's currency) bought will fall if the supply curve for foreign exchange is negatively sloped. However, the total expenditure (in X's currency) on foreign exchange will rise unless the negative elasticity of supply is sufficiently small algebraically.

risen as a result of the increase in X's prices. This would seem to be the normal result. It is quite possible, however, that the supply of foreign exchange and, therefore, the value of Y's exports should decline to such an extent as to more than offset the rise in Y's demand for its own goods. Under these circumstances, the total expenditures in terms of Y's currency on the goods produced in Y would decline.

3.   The effects on Y of an expansion in X's demand for all goods (both its own and Y's) may be obtained by combining the results obtained in the preceding two paragraphs. It is assumed that normally the supply curve for foreign exchange is positively sloped. We may also assume that in the case of an expansion of demand in X, the demand for foreign exchange will normally rise more than the supply curve will decline.[7] Consequently, the new equilibrium quantity of foreign exchange will normally be higher than the old, namely, the value of Y's exports in terms of its own currency will normally rise. Since the rise in the prices of goods produced in X leads to an increase in Y's demand curve for its own goods, Y's expenditures on its own goods will normally also increase despite the rise in the exchange rate. Consequently, it appears that normally an expansion in one country will tend to overflow into the rest of the world. It is possible, however, that it should have no effect or that it should even lead to a contraction in the rest of the world.

4.   Thus far we have neglected capital movements or international transactions in securities. It should be clear from the whole analysis that we cannot analyze the effects of capital movements without clearly specifying the nature of the initial shift in demand which has produced these movements. The results in the case of an increased import demand for capital may be different from those of an increased export supply of capital. Within each of these two categories the results may further be different according as the shift in the demand or supply for capital takes place in terms of the demand or supply for commodities or in terms of the demand for or supply of money.

(a)   Suppose that in country X there is an increase in the demand for Y's securities in terms of money (namely, a shift from money to foreign securities). Then X's demand for foreign exchange rises and its exchange rate on Y rises. This rise leads to an induced decline in the quantities of imports demanded and to an induced increase in the demand for domestic goods. The rise in demand for

---

[7] The demand curve for foreign exchange rises both directly as a result of the rise in X's demand for Y's goods and indirectly as a result of the rise in X's prices, whereas the supply curve declines only indirectly as a result of the rise in X's prices.

foreign exchange means that X will spend more in its own currency on Y's commodities and securities. Since the combined value of its imports of commodities and its net purchases of securities must equal the value of its commodity exports, this means that the value of its commodity exports in terms of its own currency will also rise. The increase in capital exports thus has a stimulating effect on the exporting country.

For country Y the change in the exchange rates is equivalent to a fall in the prices of its import goods, which leads to a reduction in its demand for its own goods and to a rise in the quantities of imports demanded. Since the rise in the exchange rate also leads to a reduction in the quantities of imports demanded by X, it appears that the shift is likely to have a deflationary effect on the capital importing country.

(b)   The results we obtain under paragraph (a) are based on the assumption that the shift in X is from money to securities. If, however, the shift is from X's goods to foreign securities then the stimulating effect of the capital exports on X will be approximately cancelled by the initial decline in its demand for its own goods. Its capital exports will, therefore, tend to be neutral on country X. The depressing effect on the importing country Y, however, remains essentially unchanged.

(c)   We have seen that a contraction is not very likely to start in a capital-exporting country X as a result of an increase in its demand for foreign securities. Suppose, however, that there is a shift in demand in country Y from its securities to its commodities. Then the prices of its commodities rise and those of its securities fall. This may lead to a decline in X's total demand for foreign exchange, particularly if the demand for import goods is sensitive to price changes. Its combined expenditures (in terms of its own currency) on commodities and on the net purchase of foreign securities will then decline. The value of its commodity exports will, therefore, decline. Unless the increase in Y's commodity prices leads to a sufficiently large increase in X's demand for its own goods there will be a contraction in the total expenditure on goods produced in the capital exporting country.

It has sometimes been argued that a system of free exchanges prevents the spreading of expansions and contractions from one country to another. The examples cited, though merely illustrations, are sufficient to indicate, however, that countries cannot immunize themselves by adopting a system of free exchange rates.

CHAPTER X

CONCLUSION

The classical theory of international trade has suffered from the basic defect of not being integrated into the general body of economic thought. Traditionally, one approach has been employed in the theory of a closed economy, and another in the theory of international trade. The reason for this difference has been well analyzed by Viner in his *Studies in the Theory of International Trade*. The classical theory of international trade was developed with a view to solving macrocosmic problems; the effects of trade between two countries, the effects of unilateral payments, the effects of tariffs, bounties, etc. For such problems the partial-equilibrium approach developed by the classical writers for dealing with a domestic economy was totally inadequate. Such an approach is satisfactory only if all other determining conditions do in fact remain substantially equal when there is a change in any one of them. By assumption, however, the problems in the field of international trade were such that all other determining conditions did not remain equal. Resort was therefore had to a form of general-equilibrium analysis in this field.

This form, however, differed markedly from the general-equilibrium analysis of a closed economy which was developed by the Lausanne school. It was, on the one hand, far less general than the Lausanne theory, but on the other, considerably more fruitful. The Lausanne theory was sufficiently general in that it could include any number of individuals, firms, and commodities. But the system which it developed was so complex that, on the whole, the Lausanne theory satisfied itself with a demonstration of the possibility of equilibrium without analyzing the laws of its working. The classical theory of international trade, however, was basically concerned with the laws of change of the international equilibrium system. It therefore resorted to extreme oversimplification. Most of its analysis was developed in terms of two representative individuals within two countries trading in two representative commodities. That such an analytical system is insufficient to lay bare the complexities of an economic system in which there are millions of different individuals, firms, products, and factors in hundreds of countries requires no emphasis. The classical theory simply assumed this whole problem away. This is clearly shown by the quotation from Edgeworth cited at the beginning of this book:

A movement along a supply-and-demand curve of international trade should be considered as attended with rearrangements of internal trade; as the movement of the hand of a clock corresponds to considerable unseen movements of the machinery.

This book is essentially a study designed to lay bare these unseen movements of the machinery. It is thus designed to close the gap between the theory of international value and the theory of value in a closed economy. It is possible to do this, now that the laws of the working of a general-equilibrium system have been developed. We are thus able to discard the restrictive assumptions of two individuals trading in two commodities, and to consider the perfectly general case in which there are any number of individuals, countries, firms, products, and factors. The whole study resolves itself into two parts: (1) an analysis of the characteristics of the equilibrium position under given conditions, and (2) an analysis of how the equilibrium values differ for different values of the determining parameters. The theory is applied in successive stages, first to the static equilibrium of an exchange economy, then to the static equilibrium of a production economy, and finally to a dynamic temporary equilibrium. In each case the equilibrium of the economic unit is first considered and the laws of its working analyzed. The equilibrium of the whole economy is then arrived at by determining the conditions under which the equilibria of all economic units become mutually consistent. Once the properties of the general equilibrium of the entire economy are determined, it is possible to determine the laws of its working. By this means we may trace through the effects of a change in any of the determining conditions on the economic position of every unit in the world economy.

BIBLIOGRAPHY

ALLEN, R. G. D. *Mathematical Analysis for Economists* London: Macmillan and Company, 1938. 548 pp.

——. "A Note on the Determinateness of the Utility Function," *Review of Economic Studies*, Vol. 2, February, 1935, pp. 155–158.

——. "On the Marginal Utility of Money and Its Application," *Economica*, Vol. 13, May, 1933, pp. 186–209.

——. "Professor Slutsky's Theory of Consumers' Choice," *Review of Economic Studies*, Vol. 3, February, 1936, pp. 120–129.

BÔCHER, MAXIME. *Introduction to Higher Algebra.* New York: Macmillan Company, 1938. 321 pp.

BROWN, E. H. PHELPS, BERNARDELLI, H., and LANGE, O. "Notes on the Determinateness of the Utility Function," *Review of Economic Studies*, Vol. 2, October, 1934, pp. 66–77.

CARLSON, SUNE. *A Study on the Pure Theory of Production.* London: P. S. King, 1939. 128 pp.

COURT, L. M. "A Theorem on Maxima and Minima with an Application to Differential Equations," *Journal of Mathematics and Physics*, Vol. 20, January, 1941, pp. 99–106.

EDGEWORTH, F. Y. *Papers Relating to Political Economy.* Vol. II. London: Macmillan and Company, 1925, 491 pp.

GEORGESCU-ROEGEN, N. "The Pure Theory of Consumer's Behavior," *Quarterly Journal of Economics*, Vol. 50, August, 1936, pp. 545–593.

HABERLER, GOTTFRIED. *Prosperity and Depression.* Third edition, Geneva: League of Nations, 1941. 532 pp.

——. *The Theory of International Trade.* Translated from the original German edition. London: William Hodge & Co., 1936. 408 pp.

HART, A. G. *Anticipations, Uncertainty, and Dynamic Planning.* Studies in Business Administration, Vol. 11, No. 1. Chicago: The University of Chicago Press, 1940. 98 pp.

HICKS, J. R. "A Comment," *Review of Economic Studies*, Vol. 8, October, 1940, pp. 64–65.

——. "Théorie mathématique de la valeur en régime de libre concurrence. No. 580 of the *Actualités scientifiques et industrielles*. Paris: Herman et Cie, 1937. 55 pp.

——. *Value and Capital.* Oxford: Clarendon Press, 1939. 331 pp.

HICKS, J. R. and ALLEN, R. G. D. "A Reconsideration of the Theory of Value," *Economica.* New series, Vol. 1, February and May, 1934, pp. 52–76, 196–219.

HOTELLING, HAROLD. "Edgeworth's Taxation Paradox and the Nature of Demand and Supply Functions," *Journal of Political Economy*, Vol. 40, October, 1932, pp. 577–616.

JOHNSON, W. E. "The Pure Theory of Utility Curves," *Economic Journal*, 1913, pp. 483–513.

KEYNES, J. M. *The General Theory of Employment, Interest, and Money.* New York: Harcourt, Brace and Company, 1936. 403 pp.

KNIGHT, FRANK H. "Capital, Time, and the Interest Rate," *Economica*, New series, Vol. 1, August, 1934, pp. 257–286.
——. "The Quantity of Capital and the Rate of Interest," *Journal of Political Economy*, Vol. 44, August and October, 1936, pp. 433–463, 612–642.

LANGE, OSCAR. "Complementarity and Interrelations of Shifts in Demand," *Review of Economic Studies*, Vol. 8, October, 1940, pp. 58–63.
——. "The Determinateness of the Utility Function," *Review of Economic Studies*, Vol. 1, June, 1934, pp. 218–225.
——. "Say's Law," *Studies in Mathematical Economics and Econometrics*, pp. 49–68. Edited by O. Lange, T. O. Yntema, and F. McIntyre. Chicago: The University of Chicago Press, 1942. 292 pp.
——. "The Stability of Equilibrium," abstract in *Econometrica*, Vol. 10, April, 1942, pp. 176–177.

LINDAHL, ERIK. *Studies in the Theory of Money and Capital.* London: George Allen & Unwin, 1939. 391 pp.

LUTZ, F. A. "The Structure of Interest Rates," *Quarterly Journal of Economics*, Vol. 55, November, 1940, pp. 36–63.

MACAULAY, F. R. *Some Theoretical Problems Suggested by the Movement of Interest Rates, Bond Yields, and Stock Prices in the United States since 1856.* New York: National Bureau of Economic Research, 1938. 240 + 351 pp.

MACHLUP, FRITZ. *International Trade and the National Income Multiplier.* Philadelphia: The Blakiston Company, 1943. 237 pp.

MARSCHAK, J. "Money and the Theory of Assets," *Econometrica*, Vol. 6, October, 1938, pp. 311–325.

MARSHALL, ALFRED. *Money, Credit, and Commerce.* London: Macmillan and Company, 1923. 369 pp.

METZLER, LLOYD A. "Underemployment Equilibrium in International Trade," *Econometrica*, Vol. 10, April, 1942, pp. 97–112.
——. "The Transfer Problem Reconsidered," *The Journal of Political Economy*, Vol. 50, June, 1942, pp. 397–414.

MOSAK, JACOB L. "Interrelations of Production, Price, and Derived Demand," *Journal of Political Economy*, Vol. 46, December, 1938, pp. 761–787.
——. "On the Interpretation of the Fundamental Equation of Value Theory," *Studies in Mathematical Economics and Econometrics*, pp. 69–74. Edited by O. Lange, T. O. Yntema, and F. McIntyre. Chicago: The University of Chicago Press, 1942. 292 pp.

OHLIN, BERTIL. *Interregional and International Trade.* Cambridge: Harvard University Press, 1933. 617 pp.

PARETO, VILFREDO. *Cours d'économie politique.* Lausanne: F. Rouge, 1896. 426 pp.
——. "Economie mathématique," *Encyclopédie des sciences mathématiques*, Vol. IV, 1911.

————. *Manuel d'économie politique.* 2nd edition. Paris: Marcel Giard, 1927. 695 pp.

ROBERTSON, D. H. "Changes in International Demand and the Terms of Trade," *Quarterly Journal of Economics,* Vol. 52, May, 1938, pp. 539–540.
————. "Indemnity Payments and Gold Movements," *Quarterly Journal of Economics,* Vol. 53, February, 1939, pp. 312–314.
————. "Rejoinder," *Quarterly Journal of Economics,* Vol. 53, February, 1939, p. 317.
————. "The Transfer Problem," *Economic Essays and Addresses,* by A. C. Pigou and D. H. Robertson. London, 1931.

SAMUELSON, PAUL A. "The Numerical Representation of Ordered Classifications and the Concept of Utility," *Review of Economic Studies,* Vol. 6, October, 1938, pp. 65–70.
————. "Constancy of the Marginal Utility of Income," *Studies in Mathematical Economics and Econometrics,* pp. 75–91. Edited by O. Lange, T. O. Yntema, and F. McIntyre. Chicago: The University of Chicago Press, 1942, 292 pp.
————. "The Stability of Equilibrium: Comparative Statics and Dynamics," *Econometrica,* Vol. 9, April, 1941, pp. 97–120.
————. "The Stability of Equilibrium: Linear and Nonlinear Systems," *Econometrica,* Vol. 10, January, 1942, pp. 1-25.

SCHULTZ, HENRY. *The Theory and Measurement of Demand.* Chicago: The University of Chicago Press, 1938. 817 pp.

SCITOVSZKY, T. DE. "A Study of Interest and Capital," *Economica,* New series, Vol. 7, August, 1940, pp. 293–317.

SLUTSKY, E. "Sulla teoria del bilancio del consumatore," *Giornale degli economisti,* Vol. 51, 1915.

STACKELBERG, HEINRICH VON. "Angebot und Nachfrage in der Produktionswirtschaft," *Archiv für Mathematische Wirtschafts- und Sozialforschung,* Vol. 4, Heft 2, 1938, pp. 73–99.

VINER, JACOB. "A Reply," *Quarterly Journal of Economics,* Vol. 53, February, 1939, pp. 314-317.
————. *Studies in the Theory of International Trade.* New York: Harper and Brothers, 1937. 650 pp.

YNTEMA, T. O. *A Mathematical Reformulation of the General Theory of International Trade.* Chicago: The University of Chicago Press, 1932. 120 pp.

INDEX OF NAMES

(n signifies that name appears only in footnote on the page concerned)

INDEX OF SUBJECTS